# SHATTERED DREAMS, SLIDING DOORS

# SHATTERED DREAMS, SLIDING DOORS

## The Republic of Ireland's
## 1982 World Cup Qualifying Campaign

### PAUL LITTLE

pitch

First published by Pitch Publishing, 2025

1

**pitch**

Pitch Publishing
9 Donnington Park,
85 Birdham Road,
Chichester, West Sussex,
PO20 7AJ
www.pitchpublishing.co.uk
info@pitchpublishing.co.uk

A CIP catalogue record is available for this book
from the British Library.

ISBN 978 1 83680 183 2

Typesetting and origination by Pitch Publishing

MIX
Paper | Supporting
responsible forestry
FSC
www.fsc.org  FSC® C010615

Printed and bound on FSC® certified paper in line with
our continuing commitment to ethical business practices,
sustainability and the environment.

Printed and bound in India by Thomson Press

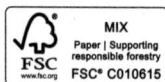

# Contents

*Love and thanks to Mam and Dad for the daily papers and the whole world on a wall.*

*To Eoin Hand and the team that beat France at Lansdowne Road in 1981 – thanks for that most enduring of football memories.*

# 1.

# Gary's Dad

GARY'S DAD *was having a hard time at work. Things weren't going his way. In fact, they were spiralling out of his control, no matter how hard he tried. This was bad enough for Gary but what made it worse was that just about everyone knew. And indeed, unfortunately, many were more than happy to talk about it and let him know what they thought about the situation and his dad. 'He's a fucking fool,' they would say. 'He should be gone. He's a shambles.'*

*Eoin was Gary's dad. He was having a very bad time at work. No matter how hard he tried, things were spiralling out of his control. He tried to hide his worries from his family. Tried to appear as if he was taking it all in his stride. But it was hard. Things just weren't going his way and they hadn't been for a while. That was bad enough for Eoin. But worse was that everyone could see it. And many people were only too happy to share their thoughts on the matter with him, whenever it suited them. 'You're a fucking fool,' they'd say. 'Why don't you just go? You're a shambles.'*

*They would walk into his shop and, while buying an item, would remark casually about just what an awful job he was doing. They would walk over to his table if he was out having a meal with his wife or his family and let them all know just what a fucking fool he was, what an embarrassment, what a shambles.*

*Eoin was getting used to it and never getting used to it. Eoin would often muse that in this world, you're either a hero or a bollocks. There is no inbetween. Currently, he was the latter.*

*In school, Gary would pay for his father's work troubles. Some lads felt that verbal abuse wasn't really enough of a humiliation. So, they would let the air out of the tyres on his bike – because his dad was an embarrassment. Or 'accidentally' bend a wheel because Gary's dad was an embarrassment. And even some teachers felt they could air their views freely and critically on Gary's father and Gary's father's work. Gary was getting used to it and never getting used to it.*

*Gary's dad was Eoin Hand, the manager of the Republic of Ireland football team. Gary's dad was really struggling in his job. And everyone knew about it. Everyone felt they could let Gary and Eoin know about it at every turn. It was 1985. Eoin Hand's Republic of Ireland were not going to the World Cup in Mexico. Just as they hadn't gone to the European Championships in France the previous year. Just as they had never qualified for anything.*

*Even if people had no reason to be surprised, people were nevertheless disappointed. Some loved having someone to point the finger at, someone to blame. Gary's dad was the fall guy. The patsy. Even if it wasn't all his fault, it was all his fault. Of course, he wasn't blameless. Eoin Hand was, after all, the Republic of Ireland football team's manager. But if it hurt the fans, then it hurt Eoin so much more. It stung. The barbs stung. They still sting, 39 years later.*

*Paul is in school with Gary. He's been in school with him since their first year of secondary school. September 1983. They've been in the same class for much of that time. They aren't best friends forever but they get on. They play in kickabouts after school. They love football. They share friends.*

*For the first few years, it never occurred to Paul just who Gary's dad was. But when it did occur, Paul struggled to understand why many in school weren't in awe. Not in awe of the fact that Gary's dad had been a professional footballer. That he had won the League of Ireland and the FAI Cup as player-manager with Limerick United. That he had played in the green of Ireland with distinction. That he was the Republic of Ireland manager. That he knew Liam Brady. That he knew Frank Stapleton and Mark Lawrenson and Ronnie Whelan. Paul struggled to understand why everyone focused just on Eoin's hard times at work. The more so when they were, in the main, the only kind of times any Ireland manager had ever experienced.*

*Paul always struggled to understand why so many people saw football as a vehicle for them to say whatever they wanted, to chant whatever they wanted. To let air from tyres, to verbally abuse, to utter and perform varying levels of horribleness. Paul still struggles to understand 39 years later.*

*But things could have been different for Eoin and Gary. They were so close to being so, so different. So cruelly close.*

*If only. If only four years earlier, a Portuguese man in black wielding the power of a whistle had looked and seen what everyone else saw. And made the correct decision. The only decision. If only Eoin and his team had got that little bit of luck that others sometimes got. If only they'd got that little bit of justice on a miserable, rain-sodden night in Brussels. Ah, if only. If only. And, indeed, what might have been …*

# 2.

# John Giles Has Had Enough

PERSONAL REASONS are the primary factors involved in my decision to resign, John Giles tells a packed press conference convened on Tuesday, 15 April 1980 at the headquarters of the Football Association of Ireland (FAI). Those assembled are there to hear more about his surprise decision to quit as manager of the Republic of Ireland football team. Flanked by FAI president Charlie Cahill and secretary Peadar O'Driscoll, Giles tells those in attendance that he wants to spend more time with his young family. His wife and six kids. He needs to spend more time on his full-time job with Shamrock Rovers. There are just too many commitments now. John Giles has too many commitments.

He can't give the Ireland job – which has grown and changed over his six-and-a-half-year tenure – the attention it deserves. He can't give the Under-21s and youth sides, recent additions to his role, the attention they deserve. He can't give his job as manager of Shamrock Rovers the attention it deserves. He doesn't just manage Shamrock Rovers. He owns 50 per cent of the club and is also its executive director. He can't give that work the attention it deserves. He can't give his wife and kids the attention they deserve. He can't give the twins born last year the attention they deserve. So, something has to give. At 39 years old, Johnny Giles decides it'll have to be the Ireland job and, so, he is stepping away from managing the Republic of Ireland football team.

FAI president Charlie Cahill says it came as a shock. But, that said, there is no animosity. They'll part on the best of terms.

It's a personal decision of John's, says Charlie Cahill, and there's certainly no friction between him and John, between the FAI and John.

There had been friction before, of course. This wasn't the first time John Giles resigned from the Republic of Ireland job. Two years before, John Giles resigned because the FAI wouldn't let him pick his own assistants. John Giles had fought to be allowed to select his own squads and pick his own players. He was the first Ireland manager to do so. He was the first Ireland manager with a standing in the game powerful enough to make the FAI suits back down. So, he was the first Ireland manager to select his own squad and his own team. His were the first Irish teams not to be selected by the blazers and their selection committee. But for a while, John Giles wasn't going to be the first manager to handpick his own assistants and coaches, not until John Giles resigned. And then John Giles's squad of international players, his players, stepped in. They wanted him to stay. They put it up to the FAI. Giles put it up to the FAI. To the men in blazers and the committees – and they backed down. And John Giles became the Ireland manager again.

But this time, there'd be no coming back. Giles wasn't coming back. He'd gone as far as he could. John Giles had managed the Irish team through qualifying campaigns for two European Championships and a World Cup. The Republic of Ireland hadn't qualified for any of these tournaments but John Giles was still proud of what he had achieved. Proud that, under his guidance, Ireland had grown in stature as a football nation. Proud that under John Giles, the Republic of Ireland had played 37 games, won 13, drawn 11 and lost 13. We're now respected by everyone, he tells the assembled media. And we've some very good young players who can only get better.

John Giles is a serious football man. A legendary figure in the game; not just in Ireland but on a European and world stage. And he is proud that the Republic of Ireland are now also being taken seriously. Or at least more seriously. The Irish international side is competitive. There is quality. Opponents recognise it. The Republic of Ireland under John Giles may not have qualified for a major tournament but the Republic of Ireland hadn't qualified for a major tournament under anyone. But before John Giles, few people took the Republic of Ireland seriously. Opponents might have dismissed the Irish on the pitch. But that wasn't the worst of it.

The worst of it was that the men in the blazers, the men on the committees, the men running Irish football didn't really take the senior international side seriously either. They didn't see the potential of the Irish football team, the potential of the game here. They couldn't see it because their minds were elsewhere. For many of these men, far too many of these men, running Irish football was less about improving the game and its structures than about using it as a vehicle for their own ends, their own betterment.

But John Giles is proud – and not just because in six and a half years in charge, no team has beaten his team in Ireland in a competitive fixture. John Giles is proud because he has helped shift the balance of power in the Irish set-up, helped tilt it, even if only a little, toward those who believe it can succeed. Those who know its potential. Those who believe that international football could be about more than a series of jollies for committee members and a chance to take the wife abroad.

John Giles tells the press that he's gone now, after one game of the 1982 World Cup qualifying campaign, to give his successor time to prepare for the important qualifiers later in the year. It hasn't been an easy decision and it isn't an overnight decision but it is the right decision for him.

John Giles is asked whether public and media criticism of his handling of the Irish team have played a part. He shrugs and shrugs it off. Anyone in the public eye expects that, he says. He adds, waspishly, that he's always welcomed constructive criticism. Hinting, perhaps, that not all the criticism he'd received was constructive.

John Giles is a respected and revered man in Irish football but there has, indeed, been criticism. Criticism of the style of play. Criticism of the fact that in his time in charge of the side, the Republic of Ireland have only won three times on their travels. And a team that is weak on its travels is not likely to qualify for anything.

Con Houlihan of the *Evening Press* is one such critic. And while he's not unhappy to see John Giles leave the managerial role, he'd like to see him retained in some way within the FAI. Houlihan hadn't been a fan of how Giles's Republic of Ireland went about their business on the pitch. And Con Houlihan was particularly scathing on such matters after February's defeat at Wembley against England in a European Championship qualifier.

Houlihan is one of the most esteemed of Irish sports columnists. His pieces appear three times a week in the *Evening Press* newspaper. Con Houlihan is given almost half of the back page on such days, half of a broadsheet back page. Houlihan writes about all sports and he has free rein. His pieces are known for their wit, often apparently meandering off course, down rabbit holes and away on flights of fancy, before making points with rapier-like precision.

Con Houlihan had often voiced concern that John Giles was being paid a full-time wage for what was essentially a part-time job. The columnist was of a like mind with Giles, in fact, believing the Irish supremo had too much on his plate. Trying to grow Shamrock Rovers on and off the pitch and engaging in several other business interests while managing the international side was too much for one man. And, for Con Houlihan, the international side was suffering.

He was particularly concerned that while John Giles was based in Ireland, most of his charges and potential charges lived and played across the water.

Houlihan also decried the many members of the Irish football press who seemed in thrall of Giles. Writing in the days after the manager's resignation, Con Houlihan said he found it very sad that so many of his colleagues in the journalism profession should have put their critical faculties in cold storage in the context of Johnny Giles and his Republic of Ireland team.

The general reaction of the football press to his abdication, wrote Houlihan, was as pathetic as it was predictable. Indeed, a few who were normally rational men, he said, had abandoned the ship of reason entirely.

The abject defeat in London that irked Con Houlihan so much had left the Republic of Ireland third in their qualification group, eight points behind England. More concerning, perhaps, were the facts that John Giles's Ireland had finished two points behind Northern Ireland and had only picked up one point on the road, away to the struggling Danes.

Houlihan was tired, not just of John Giles's managerial approach to the game but also of the relentlessly optimistic statements about progress being made when, in fact, in the last campaign, the opposite, for Con Houlihan, was clearly the case. Honest self-appraisal, he wrote, is good for us all.

According to Con Houlihan, the 2-0 defeat at Wembley was the nadir. To be Irish that night was intensely depressing, he wrote, not because the Republic of Ireland lost but because they lost so faint-heartedly. And yet, complained Con Houlihan of the *Evening Press*, the future is always bright, according to John Giles and most of the press. You may not be able to fool all the people all the time, he concluded, but possibly you can fool enough to get by.

Houlihan was critical of Giles's conservative approach, the percentage game often employed by Don Revie at Leeds, where the Irish manager had played out so many successful years. But for Con Houlihan, that approach got England under Revie nowhere and had got the Republic to much the same place.

For this revered journalist, an international game, be it a friendly or a competitive fixture, should be a showpiece. Not an exhibition of pretty football, he explained, but football infused with the philosophy of wisely organised adventure. The best way to get a result, an away draw, for example, is to play for a win, argued Con Houlihan. The percentage game is not only unattractive but it simply doesn't pay. If you must battle against opponents blessed with greater resources, then you must be bold, he contended.

Con Houlihan believed that in the aftermath of that sad occasion at Wembley – the most depressing he'd ever suffered in sport – that John Giles knew it was all over, that his moral credit had run out. You cannot go on indefinitely playing with the faith of the public, said Houlihan. And while it was unfortunate that he came home to a bitter climate in the immediate aftermath, that bitterness did not spring from the defeat itself, which was not unexpected, but from the manner of that defeat, as John Giles and his Republic of Ireland were ultimately guilty of simply not having a go.

Eamon Dunphy, who had played with Giles at international level and worked with him at Shamrock Rovers in recent years, is pursuing a career in journalism. Over successive Sundays after John Giles's departure, Dunphy gives readers of the *Sunday Independent* the inside story on his decision to quit.

John Giles's departure reproaches us all, he writes. For the past two years, he explains, John Giles has been the most abused man in Irish sport.

Few close to Giles would disagree with his decision, says his friend and colleague. When he resigned previously, those close to him urged him to reconsider. This time, they merely nodded their heads in approval, he reports.

The decision to go may only have been announced recently – but Giles had decided well before he told his employers in Merrion Square.

To discover why the job he held for nearly seven years had become an intolerable burden, it is necessary to go back to the start of February, Eamon Dunphy informs his readers. For, over a period of about ten days at that time, all the pressures – personal and professional – that combined to make his departure inevitable were at play.

John Giles was looking after three different teams – the international side, Shamrock Rovers and the Irish youths – in three different countries – England, Ireland and France. He barely got to see his family. All three games were lost. And after the defeat at Wembley, he returned home to take his regular dose of abuse.

Eamon Dunphy tells of a well-established pattern of criticism levelled by certain members of the Irish football press at John Giles and his Republic of Ireland players – although it was mostly aimed at Giles. Although the majority of the media pack did take each game on its merits and dispensed criticism based on an objective view of Ireland's place in the international game, there was a significant and noisy minority who were much more personal in their reproach, Eamon Dunphy explains.

For them, Dunphy writes, Giles was doing to Irish football what Richard Nixon did to US politics – he was *screwing it.*

There is no *dirty trick* to which his critics would not stoop, Dunphy tells his readers. Their *alternative analysis* of the England defeat and performance suggested, simplistically for Eamon Dunphy, that, had John Giles been more positive, the Irish team could have wiped the floor with the English.

But that was a relatively predictable and mild line of criticism, he believes. There has also been, writes Eamon Dunphy, a nasty strain of personal abuse in what was written about Giles in certain quarters. The aim was to undermine his integrity, undermine his work in Irish soccer. Ugly, gutter journalism, Eamon Dunphy calls it, and all the more disturbing because it seemed to be effective.

By way of example, a disbelieving Dunphy used the booing of John Giles's name by a section of the Lansdowne Road crowd when it was read out over the public address at matches in the last year. Booing that Giles's young sons, sat beside Dunphy, had to endure.

What part of the Irish psyche this reflected, Eamon Dunphy dreaded to think. Ultimately, to witness a great athlete, a man of immense natural dignity treated like that was, for this budding football journalist, nothing short of disgusting.

Eamon Dunphy was at pains to underline the progress made under John Giles's direction. The departing manager had built on the advancements of predecessors Mick Meagan and Liam Tuohy, imposing for the first time the discipline and organisation required of any international team. The flippant and almost apologetic approach to international football had ended under John Giles. For far too long it had been a shambles, a joke.

But crucially and most tangibly, John Giles's team had got results. The players had responded to his guiding hand, his standing in the game. Eamon Dunphy writes that John Giles's tenure was a draught of professional air all the more welcome and stimulating coming from a man respected and revered by all the players and the game in general.

Playing for Ireland, for those who took their football seriously, was no longer to be avoided. Indeed, John Giles had made it professionally respectable. Succumbing to pressure from clubs across the water not to travel – as the likes of Giles, Tony Dunne, Shay Brennan and Noel Cantwell had often done in the dark ages – had become less palatable, explains Dunphy. And this is why, he writes, players like Liam Brady, David O'Leary, Frank Stapleton and Mark Lawrenson go out of their way to play for their country.

Dunphy believes results improved dramatically during the John Giles reign. For him, the Republic of Ireland were now formidable opponents in the international game.

Eamon Dunphy admits, however, that the question of John Giles's style of football with the Republic of Ireland is a prickly one. The former Leeds midfielder's belief that possession should be retained, that the team that has the ball controls the game, was quite radical in an Irish context. Indeed, it is alien, says Eamon Dunphy, to our Celtic nature and our traditional way of playing. However, that the Giles approach was too conservative is incorrect in Eamon Dunphy's mind. Although this may all be in the eye of the beholder. But criticism of style is more acceptable than criticism of person, he insists. After all, writes Dunphy, the cut and thrust of argument is what sport is all about and whether route one or route four is the best route to goal is a legitimate topic for debate.

All that said, Eamon Dunphy insists that, ultimately, when assessing the outgoing manager's legacy, the question of style is beside the point. What's most important is that John Giles is leaving the Irish international team in much better shape than he found it. The side is being taken seriously in the FAI. The side is now taken seriously by opponents. And, crucially, the introduction to international football for players coming through the youth system like Ronnie Whelan, Gary Waddock and Kevin O'Callaghan has been educational and professional and vastly different to the shambles Eamon Dunphy experienced when he came into the international reckoning in 1965.

Writing in the week after Eamon Dunphy's *Sunday Independent* piece, Con Houlihan disagrees about John Giles's tenure as Ireland manager. And he disagrees with Eamon Dunphy about John Giles's treatment in the Irish media. And Con Houlihan hopes that Eamon Dunphy keeps a copy of his *Sunday Independent* article so that he may review it in a few years' time and know what it is to break out in a cold sweat!

Con Houlihan likes Eamon Dunphy and he hopes his ambition to be a full-time journalist is realised. But Con Houlihan thinks that Eamon Dunphy will need to be careful or he'll end up with the Catholic Truth Society writing pamphlets about the lives of the saints!

In his column, Con Houlihan takes umbrage at Eamon Dunphy's 'gutter press' jibe for those in the Irish football press pack who were less than effusive in their praise for Giles. Con Houlihan suggests Eamon Dunphy should read the English and Italian football press to educate himself on how mild the climate in Ireland is.

For Con Houlihan, it's ridiculous to contend that John Giles has been the most abused man in Irish sport. The truth being nearer the opposite, he says.

For Con Houlihan, John Giles was on borrowed time. John Giles's race was run. The hope and light of the early years, the crushing of the Soviet Union at Dalymount in 1974 and the thrilling defeat of the French at Lansdowne Road in 1977 had long faded. More and more, argues Con Houlihan, fear of defeat had come to dominate both John Giles's thinking and that of his team, as illustrated so painfully with their feeble Wembley showing.

\* \* \*

John Giles doesn't go after the Republic of Ireland's sorry defeat to England in February as Con Houlihan may have liked. In fact, John Giles leads the Republic of Ireland into the World

Cup qualifying campaign for Spain 82. But then he goes after the first game.

The draw for the qualifiers is less than kind to the Republic of Ireland. The balls in the UEFA group pots cared little for Irish dreams of qualifying for a first major tournament and joining its firmament of stars.

The Republic of Ireland are grouped with three heavyweights of the European game. First, there is Belgium, obdurate, tough, disciplined and talented. The Belgians have qualified for the 1980 European Championships in the summer in Italy. Only eight teams qualify. The best eight teams in Europe and the Belgians are amongst them. A squad of serious quality, a squad boasting Eric Gerets, Jan Ceulemans, Jean-Marie Pfaff, Rene Vandereycken and François Van der Elst under the wily, experienced Guy Thys.

And then there are the Dutch, who will also play in the European Championships in Italy in June. The Dutch have featured in the last two World Cup Finals. The Dutch are heading into a transitionary period but they are still good enough to be among the top eight sides in Europe.

But that is not all. Fortune must not consider Ireland to be brave. Because if fortune did so, then fortune wouldn't have added France to the Republic of Ireland's qualification group. France aren't going to the European Championships in Italy. They missed out on qualification by a point to reigning champions Czechoslovakia. But everyone knows the flamboyant French are the coming team of European football. Michel Hidalgo's team has Michel Platini. It has Jean Tigana. It has Larios, Bossis, Rocheteau and Lacombe. It has class all over the park, all over the bench.

But first, on Wednesday, 26 March 1980, there is Cyprus. John Giles's last game in charge of the Republic of Ireland will be in Nicosia against the Mediterranean minnows. John Giles knows this is the end, even if no one else knows. Perhaps the daunting make-up of UEFA World Cup qualification Group Two has played a part in his decision. Indeed, it's a group that would give any football manager pause for thought.

# 3

# Get Some Points on the Board

IN A sprawling Dublin suburb, nine-year-old Paul is tuning the radio, looking for RTÉ Radio 1. It's just after 7pm on Wednesday, 26 March 1980.

Paul remembers the 1978 World Cup – or at least the bits he was allowed to stay up and see. He remembers Archie Gemmill and Kenny Dalglish beating the Dutch but the Scots just not doing enough to progress. He recalls the players because he knew many of them from *Match of the Day* and the *Big Match*. From *Sportsnight*, *Midweek Sports Special* and BBC Radio 2. They weren't Ireland but he knew Souness, Robertson, Hartford and Co. and he wanted them to do well.

Paul remembers Gemmill's wonder goal and David Coleman's iconic commentary – etched in his memory but ultimately all in vain. World Cup magic. He remembers the River Plate on the evening of the final. World Cup romance and wonder. He remembers the ticker tape and the goals. Feeling sorry for the Dutch.

And he remembers the kids out on the green pretending to be Kempes, Luque, Ardiles, Krol, the Van der Kerkhof twins and Rep for days and weeks after. And he's hungry for more. Hungry for more memories.

This evening, the qualification campaign for the 1982 World Cup kicks off for John Giles's Republic of Ireland. This early spring evening, there is hope – hope just ahead of trepidation. For the Republic of Ireland's is a nightmare qualification group. European football powerhouses Belgium, France and the Netherlands await. Only two will go to Spain.

But first things first. First, it's Cyprus. The whipping boys, everyone says. Time to get some points on the board.

Paul leaves the Sony radio on as he goes about nothing much at all. Leaving it on RTÉ Radio 1. The Sony radio-cassette player is a source of news and music. Regularly used by his older brother to try to catch and record favourite songs off the pirate radio stations. A Beatles greatest hits tape is often played on the machine. Paul's family is not poor. But this is 1980 and money isn't squandered. A bigger music centre is some way off. Not a priority. Not a sensible move for his dad. He and Paul's mam have six kids to raise on one income, albeit a decent one. A music centre would be lovely but, for now, frivolous.

Paul leaves the radio on, waiting for the commentary to begin. The match has already been in progress for at least half an hour but this is 1980 and RTÉ will broadcast the end of the first half and all of the second. The game isn't being televised. And there won't be highlights. This is 1980. A very different time.

Paul leaves it on in the front room and returns to the breakfast room and the TV, considering his options – just in case something goes wrong … the circuit dies or there's a power cut. Only the week before, there had been freezing rain and snow in Dublin. The storm had cut the power. Good thing his mam had batteries stored away. Batteries would maintain the broadcast if need be.

Still, Paul is only nine. And this is suburban Dublin, so there are TV attractions and distractions – and crucially not just Irish ones but British stations also, BBC1, BBC2 and UTV. Options. And there was one boy in green that evening, a big one at that, who could divert Paul's attention from the radio. *The Incredible Hulk*, the unfortunate Dr David Banner, had been on since 6.40pm. Paul had been keeping tabs. Dr Banner had taken what seemed like an innocent lift on a motorbike as he continued his efforts to stay a step ahead of his many pursuers – the military, journalists and nefarious government agencies – only to become unwittingly embroiled in a nasty gang conflict. Would the poor man ever find peace? Not on this evening's evidence.

Still, the *Hulk* provides a nice diversion after the early evening news. Paul is always encouraged to look at the news, even if he doesn't always understand it. His mother also encourages Paul and his siblings to read the newspaper each day after school – and circle in red words they do not understand. To improve their vocabulary and get a sense of the world around them.

The news today is the usual mix of the depressing, sad and unsettling. Paul couldn't claim to grasp it all. But the solemn tones gave him much of the picture. Things were grim all over. A man was holding a family hostage in Dundalk. They appeared to be related. According to the bulletin, he was a Republican who the Garda had been looking for. He had a grenade and a gun. The house was surrounded.

A good man, an archbishop called Romero, had been shot saying mass in a country called El Salvador. There was discussion on whether Ireland should send a team to the Olympic Games in Moscow in the summer. The British had decided to send a team, much to the annoyance of their prime minister, Margaret Thatcher. She had wanted a boycott to make plain her government's displeasure at the Soviet Union's invasion of poor Afghanistan. The prevailing view, it seemed, was that the Irish public wanted us to go too.

In Iran, American hostages were still being held at the United States Embassy in Tehran. They had been stuck there for 14 months and no one seemed to know what to do about it. In Northern Ireland, prisoners in the Maze Prison were protesting their treatment.

Grim all over. And grim for Dr David Banner too. But hopefully things wouldn't be grim for John Giles's Republic of Ireland in Nicosia against Cyprus. Paul returns to the front room to find out.

* * *

John Giles is tense on the touchline of the Makarios Stadium pitch. The game is much tighter than it should've been. The Cypriots should be dead and buried. The Republic of Ireland should've been out of sight, cruising. Instead, they're struggling to hold their narrow lead as the game enters its dying moments.

Giles had picked a 4-3-3 formation for the game against the Mediterranean islanders. Preparations had been disrupted by a number of enforced withdrawals. First-choice full-backs Chris Hughton of Spurs and John Devine of Arsenal withdrew two days before the game. Hughton had picked up an ankle injury in his club's English First Division win over Bolton Wanderers at the weekend. Devine withdrew with a groin strain.

John Giles had decided against bringing in reinforcements – he had built contingency in his squad for such eventualities. And, anyway, John Giles's Republic of Ireland should've had more than enough class to deal with a Cypriot side boasting only one professional player. A nation with just one win in World Cup qualifying since their first appearance in 1962. A country that had won just five of 62 internationals in total.

So, the dependable and adaptable Luton Town player Tony Grealish moved from his usual midfield berth to right-back – a position he'd filled on his international debut. Jerry Murphy of Crystal Palace was selected in the centre of the park, earning his second cap, with Arsenal's Liam Brady and Derby County's Gerry Daly on either side of him.

Brady had been nursing a cut on his right foot that required three stitches, picked up in the previous weekend's bruising clash with Murphy's Palace side. The injury was more irritating than serious, said Giles ahead of the Nicosia game. So Brady started as captain – at 24, the youngest player ever to do so.

The impressive Mark Lawrenson of Brighton & Hove Albion partnered Arsenal's David O'Leary in the heart of defence while Ashley Grimes of Manchester United was asked to fill in at left-back.

Up front, Preston North End's Paul McGee, dropped for the February European Championship defeat at Wembley, returned to partner Frank Stapleton while Liverpool's Steve Heighway was asked to trouble Cyprus out wide and in behind.

John Giles watched on as Ireland dominated from the off, Liam Brady making light of his injury and running the show, despite Cypriot efforts to flood midfield and deny him space and time. And the Irish skipper was involved as the Republic of Ireland took an eighth-minute lead. Brady floated a wonderful ball to Frank Stapleton wide right and his cross was hooked home gleefully by Paul McGee.

Fifteen minutes later, it was 2-0. Lawrenson, having broken up a Cypriot attack, glided forward in what was now trademark fashion, played a slick one-two with Brady, then held his nerve to score past keeper Fanos.

Cruise control. Complete dominance. But then, on 27 minutes, much to the annoyance of John Giles, the heretofore outclassed home side are allowed back into the game. A lapse of concentration and defensive sloppiness as the Irish fail to clear their lines convincingly saw Cypriot skipper Sotiris Kaiafas win a header and Nikos Pantziaras finish to halve the Republic of Ireland's lead.

But the visitors continued to pour forward. And, on 37 minutes, they deservedly restored their two-goal advantage. Brady picked out O'Leary with a sumptuous cross and McGee was on hand to dispatch the centre-back's knockdown for his second goal of the evening.

When Israeli referee Zvi Sharir blew for half-time, the talk was of how many the visitors could add to that tally. The Irish dominated the first 25 minutes of the second half and it seemed only a matter of time before the dam would burst. Stapleton wasted two presentable opportunities, twice shooting over Fanos's crossbar. Daly then saw an effort rebound off the woodwork before Fanos saved brilliantly from McGee's header to deny him a hat-trick. Jerry Murphy then cannoned a left-footed drive off the upright from the resulting corner.

It was the last action for Murphy, who hobbled off after a heavy challenge from Stefanos, and John Giles's Republic of Ireland seemed to lose their way in the disruption. They continued to push for goals, but missed chances seemed to sap confidence. And too often, they were wide open when possession was lost and had become increasingly careless and ragged at the back and through midfield. The home side and the home crowd sensed the change. And, with 15 minutes left to play, Cyprus were back in the game.

O'Leary tangled with Kaiafas in the Irish area. Israeli referee Zvi Sharir initially indicated an indirect free kick but then, to the bemusement of John Giles and his team, changed his mind and awarded Cyprus a penalty instead. Kaiafas didn't miss.

Fifteen minutes left and the Irish continue to unravel as they lose their discipline and organisation. The Republic of Ireland haven't won an away game for four years and that knowledge seems to now weigh upon them. Cyprus, roared on by the vast majority of the 10,000 fans in a stadium that had been for so long in quiet admiration of the visiting side, push for an equaliser that, fortunately for John Giles's Republic of Ireland, doesn't come.

Relieved, the Irish manager and his players head to the dressing room after ref Sharir calls time. Two points on the board. Two points on the road. Relieved and delighted, nine-year-old Paul switches off the radio and rejoins the rest of his family, who are watching *The Four Musketeers* with Raquel Welch, Oliver Reed and Richard Chamberlain on UTV. He gives a brief report on the game's outcome to the interested and disinterested alike ('Silly football,' his older sister says, rolling her eyes). Then stays quiet so as not to draw attention to himself and to try and squeeze as much TV out of the rest of the evening as he can.

* * *

John Giles talks to the assembled press in the bowels of the Makarios Stadium after the match. John Giles has decided he is going but he's not letting anyone know just yet. Now is not the time.

We let things get a bit out of hand and it was something of a sweat towards the end, he admits. However, points, rather than goals, are the priority, he tells the media. Ultimately, John Giles professes himself to be happy. Some of the football in what were difficult, gusty conditions on a bumpy pitch was superb, he contends, but the breaks that might have killed off the Cypriots went against his men at critical stages of the game. In time, he feels, the win may be placed in better perspective after Belgium, France and the Netherlands have played there.

Liam Brady echoes his manager's assessment. Liam Brady feels that the final score isn't a real reflection of the match. With a little luck, the Republic of Ireland would've been 5-1 up before the Cypriots were awarded their penalty. The penalty decision turned the game around for Cyprus, Liam Brady believes, but, overall, he doesn't think anyone in the stadium would deny that the visitors deserved their win.

Four days later, John Giles has had some time to reflect. In the 'Johnny Giles Column' in the *Sunday Independent*, he admits that the last 15 minutes of the game in Nicosia were among the most nerve-racking he has had in football. The erratic performance of the referee and the unpredictability of the surface unnerved his players. The decision to award a penalty to the home side was bizarre. So, from a position of almost unchallenged superiority, the Republic of Ireland were forced to cling on to the points.

But it wasn't all down to the ref or the pitch. John Giles says that his players didn't manage the game well in the last quarter of an hour. Crucially, they didn't take control in midfield in the way that they should have at that stage of the game. He uses Liam Brady as an example.

Every time Liam Brady got the ball in the last 15 minutes, he found vast acres of space in front of him and was understandably tempted to push forward to exploit this freedom. This, explains John Giles, one of the greatest midfield players to have played the game, is the natural response of players at the top level of football for whom such spaces rarely occur. However, according to the Republic of Ireland manager, in the circumstances, it would've been wiser to have simply stood on the ball, strung a few passes together and lowered the tempo of the game.

John Giles puts his team's failure to do so down to a lack of experience. This is the youngest side he has ever fielded. Hopefully, lessons will have been learned. However, overall, John Giles says the performance of this Irish side was commendable. The win and the points were all that mattered.

Had Ireland been deprived, no one would've wanted to hear their hard-luck story.

John Giles finishes his piece by brushing off criticism that his team have passed up an opportunity to enhance their goal difference. He can't see the two qualification places from the group being filled on any other basis than points totals.

And so, the Republic of Ireland have two points on the board in UEFA World Cup qualifying Group Two. They are on the way. And two weeks later, so is Johnny Giles. Like Dr Banner, John Giles – the biggest of green legends – turns and walks away. Cue the *Hulk* theme, piano rising to an emotive crescendo. John Giles has improved things for these people. He has done what he can. Now, it's time to move on.

# 4.

# Succession

JOHN GILES has gone. But John Giles offers to stay on for the summer friendlies against the Swiss, world champions Argentina and European champions Czechoslovakia. He offers to hold the fort until the FAI find a suitable replacement. The FAI thank John Giles but decide against his offer. It's time to move on.

On 17 April 1980, Peter Byrne of *The Irish Times* reports that the association have asked John Giles's long-time Ireland assistant, Alan Kelly, to look after the team for the friendly matches. Consideration will still be given to Giles's long-term replacement but the feeling is that if the Republic of Ireland perform well in the three upcoming games, Kelly, Nobby Stiles's No.2 at Preston North End and capped 47 times in goal for Ireland, will be offered the job.

The initial interpretation of the proposed temporary appointment, reports Byrne, is that the position of Republic of Ireland team manager will continue to be filled on a part-time basis. However, there's scope for that position to change. Byrne writes that there's still a body of opinion within the FAI that holds that if the responsibilities of managing youth, Under-21 and the senior sides are to be discharged properly, then a full-time manager, resident in the country, is the direction to go.

Byrne says that, if that were to be the case, former internationals Paddy Mulligan, Eamon Dunphy and Eoin Hand may come into the reckoning.

Mulligan, who'd played for Chelsea and Crystal Palace amongst others and earned 50 caps for Ireland, has recently hung up his boots after a stint under John Giles at Shamrock

Rovers. Hand is the current manager of Limerick United – a club whose fortunes he has revived in his first season on Shannonside. Dunphy has worked with Giles at Rovers, featuring as both a player and a youth coach. Sports journalism is now his main focus but, for some, he'd be the favourite to land the job if it became a full-time position. No wonder, perhaps, that he appealed for respect and patience for whomever succeeded John Giles when analysing his friend's departure in the *Sunday Independent*!

But if a week is a long time in politics, then the same can be said for football. Seven days later, Peter Byrne reports that Alan Kelly has been offered the Republic of Ireland job. The position will remain part-time. The probationary period has been shelved. Kelly, should he take the job, would be in charge at least until the end of the World Cup campaign; a clause, reportedly, that met one of his conditions for accepting the position.

Alan Kelly's employers at Preston North End are reported to have no objection to him accepting the position on a part-time basis. For the FAI, the appointment would make sense; a smooth transition, with John Giles handing the baton to his assistant. Byrne reports that Kelly will select his assistant and physio in the next 48 hours. His first job will be to name a squad ahead of the meeting with the Swiss at Lansdowne Road on 30 April.

Alan Kelly does so the Friday before the match, having been quickly introduced to one of the big headaches of the international game, especially for smaller nations. Alan Kelly can't name players from Liverpool or, more crucially, Arsenal in his selection. The two clubs are headed for a second replay of their FA Cup semi-final. Liverpool and Arsenal drew 0-0 after extra time on 12 April at Hillsborough. Liverpool and Arsenal drew 1-1 after extra time on 16 April at Villa Park. And the two teams were set to meet again two days before the Republic of Ireland's meeting with the Swiss. Steve Heighway of Liverpool won't be available. And nor will Liam Brady, David O'Leary, John Devine and Frank Stapleton of Arsenal.

Alan Kelly puts the players he can choose through their paces in the Maccabi grounds in Kimmage on the Monday before the game, then loses Crystal Palace linkman Jerry Murphy. The ankle injury he picked up in his impressive midfield display in Nicosia is still troubling Murphy and had seen him struggle at the weekend in Palace's league meeting with Liverpool. But that's the lot of the international manager.

The missing, however, allow opportunity to knock for other players. One of those is former Dublin Gaelic football star Kevin Moran, who has recently broken into the Manchester United side and has been keeping Scottish international Gordon McQueen out of the Red Devils' first XI with his aggressive, combative style. Indeed, his approach to the game was more than apparent at the Maccabi grounds as Paul McGee left the field pressing an ice pack to a swelling over his eye after a tangle with the centre-half.

This is Kevin Moran's first call-up and the All-Ireland Gaelic Football Championship winner can't quite believe it. He tells the press that he'd love to wear the green jersey, even for just part of the game. But with Alan Kelly's options restricted, Kevin Moran looks likely to earn his first cap from the off against the visiting Swiss.

Alan Kelly names Eoin Hand as his assistant and the Limerick United manager is also delighted to be part of the set-up. His last involvement had been as a player five years before. Another man delighted to make a return is Derby County full-back Dave Langan. Having fallen out of favour in the Giles era, Alan Kelly recalls him and shows that he intends to be his own man.

After the session, Alan Kelly talks to the assembled press. John Giles, he says, did a tremendous job in getting Irish football to its present level. Now, he and his coaching team have to build on that and make further progress. Alan Kelly believes he's capable of doing a similar job. The Preston North End assistant manager aims, at the very least, to maintain the respect the Republic of Ireland international side has gained, not just from opponents but, perhaps more importantly, from club managers across the water. This is crucial in ensuring that the Republic of Ireland will continue to see players released for international duty, except, of course, in exceptional circumstances.

The Liverpool-Arsenal FA Cup semi-final is just such a circumstance. But Alan Kelly says that you have to be able to cope with situations like this, adding that the absence of the Arsenal and Liverpool players should take nothing away from those who've answered the call to replace them. They are all good players, he says, and, like him, they want to better the image of the Republic of Ireland international football team.

Alan Kelly then lays out his manifesto. The 42-year-old says that he can't promise anything but he can say that he'll be trying to think and act positively at all times. And if he makes mistakes – and it is inevitable that he will – then at least they will be honest and educational ones.

And Alan Kelly will not ape anyone's style or try to be someone he's not. He has his own ideas as to how the Irish team can progress and the upcoming friendlies will give him an opportunity of putting them into practice in preparation for the next World Cup qualifier at home to the Netherlands in September.

*  *  *

Paul gets home from school around three o'clock on Wednesday, 30 April. Matchday. He's spent that last three quarters of an hour of the school day willing the clock on the wall to get a move on. Why do those last 45 minutes drag so, so much?

Once home, he cracks on with his homework while his mam sorts dinner. The plan: get the homework out of the way quick, get the dinner in – and then get outside. Dinner is Campbell's Meatballs, mashed potatoes and peas. His grimace at the mention of the meatballs is hopefully not too obvious. With eight mouths to feed, sometimes needs must. Sometimes it must be canned meatballs.

Homework in the bag, meatballs dispatched, Paul is ready for the outside world but Mam halts his gallop. What about the newspapers? Newspapers, then outside to muck about. First up, the *Irish Independent* and a quick read of the previews of the evening's match. The new man in charge has gone with

Gerry Peyton of Fulham in goal. A centre-back pairing of Mark Lawrenson and debutant Kevin Moran. Langan occupies the right-back slot, with Chris Hughton on the left.

Tony Grealish, ever dependable, is named captain in Liam Brady's absence. It will be the first time the 23-year-old Londoner will have captained a team of any description. He is surprised and delighted. He tells the press that he thought the captaincy might have gone to Mark Lawrenson or Don Givens, the squad's senior player. But it's a great honour to be asked and he will do his very best.

Grealish will be accompanied in the engine room by the experienced Gerry Daly and teenager Gary Waddock of Queens Park Rangers. Born in the shadow of Wembley Stadium, 18-year-old Waddock impressed for the Irish youth sides and Under-21s and has played 18 times for his club in this, his first season in senior football.

Up front, Alan Kelly has gone with Paul McGee through the middle with Birmingham City's Givens and Gerry Ryan of Brighton & Hove Albion in support.

The Swiss, according to the paper, will be no pushovers. They've beaten two of the qualifiers for the upcoming European Championships – Czechoslovakia and Greece – in recent friendlies. Their two top club sides, Grasshoppers and FC Zürich, have performed impressively in recent European competitions. Both clubs will be well represented in the Swiss side on the night.

While it may not seem like it, Paul is reminded by his mother that there's more to life than football and she suggests that he take a look at the other pages in the paper and at the weekend's *Sunday Independent* before he hits the streets. Perhaps she had seen the meatball grimace after all! Unsurprisingly, however, outside of sport, the papers make for grim, troubling reading.

Violence continues in Northern Ireland. A German woman and her two-year-old child were injured on Tuesday when a bomb exploded in a hotel car park in Larne. Thankfully, a 15-minute warning had been phoned in to the Samaritans in

Belfast by the perpetrators and the area had been cleared. Still, the force of the explosion was enough to see the mother and daughter injured and rushed to hospital.

Tensions between the United States and Iran were at an alarming high after an attempt to rescue the hostages held in the US Embassy in Tehran since the previous November ended in failure over the weekend. Eight US servicemen died in the raid as their helicopter crashed in an Iranian desert.

According to a report in the *Irish Independent*, a squad of 90 commandos, helped by sympathetic locals, aimed to gain access to the embassy disguised as Iranian military personnel after hiding out in Tehran on the Friday. They planned to overpower the guards and load the 50 hostages on to US Navy helicopters, also disguised in Iranian livery, and whisk them away to safety.

Unfortunately for the rescuers, the mission had to be aborted when a number of the helicopters broke down. Tragically, as the Americans withdrew, an airplane struck one of the choppers and the eight servicemen died. Shockingly, some of their bodies were brought to the US Embassy in the Iranian capital and displayed for all to see.

In another development, on Monday, Iranian aircraft from its Persian Gulf base at Bandar Abbas were involved in a skirmish over the Straits of Hormuz with US fighter planes from the aircraft carrier *Nimitz*.

The ship was the base of operations for the failed rescue attempt. It was in the region not just because of the hostage crisis but also due to the recent Soviet invasion of Afghanistan, which threatened to turn the Cold War into a considerably hotter affair. Tension between the world's two superpowers overshadows all news. The fear that one day it could ignite and consume everyone and everything was a real fear for nine-year-old Paul. The sense of foreboding would often seep into his dreams, which, seemingly innocuous for the most part, would often end suddenly and frighteningly with a mushroom cloud rising in the distance.

The news wasn't too rosy for the Soviets either, mind you. The *Sunday Independent* reported that the invading force had suffered heavy losses in Hazarajat, a mountainous region in central Afghanistan, in recent days. Local leaders reported that some 650 Soviet soldiers had been killed and 40 tanks destroyed as they sent a force to try and relieve the city of Bamian, the provincial capital.

Meanwhile, in South Africa, almost 400 schoolkids were arrested after a protest involving some 2,000 children outside a school in a Johannesburg suburb. The children were part of widespread protests about the disparity between the apartheid regime's spending on schools for the ruling white minority and its outlay on those for the majority black population. According to the report in the *Irish Independent*, the government spent nearly four times more on the white kids! Shockingly, Paul read that the student protesters weren't just arrested – many were beaten with batons and tear-gassed.

Paul would circle plenty of words and his mam would attempt to explain their meaning. But what was much harder to explain was a scary world seemingly full of tragedy and danger at every turn. Still, she would allay his fears and all would soon be forgotten during a few games of kerbs, wall ball and three-and-in on the green with his friends in the suburban cul-de-sac in which he lived.

Annoyingly, the Swiss match isn't being televised. But then friendly internationals rarely, if ever, are. That said, there will be radio coverage. However, Paul's older brother has control of that valuable resource this evening, so the TV, after everyone has been called in for tea, looks the best option. Paul will have to get the result later.

Unsurprisingly, Dr Banner is in trouble once more. Will he be forever tormented? Will he ever find a way to reverse the effects of that accidental overdose of gamma rays? Sadly, not in the post-teatime episode, 'Falling Angels', on RTÉ1. The good doctor, still on the run on suspicion of murder, has pitched up at the Chesley Heights orphanage. Working as a handyman, he's grown fond of the kids there and of two in particular. But Dr Banner is perturbed to find that the two girls in question are being schooled in the arts of pick-pocketing and safe cracking!

Needless to say, he takes on the criminals behind the enterprise, they make him angry (they shouldn't have made him angry), he turns green and matters are quickly settled. Sadly, as ever, having helped those deserving of assistance, Dr Banner has to move on before reports of a super-powered green giant draw unwanted attention.

With no one outside for a game of something, there's talk of watching the World Championship snooker over on BBC2, which is now at the quarter-final stage. The mesmerising Alex Higgins is battling it out that evening with the unflappable Steve Davis. But coverage doesn't start until 8.25pm. So, the decision is made to watch *The Rockford Files* on RTÉ1 at 8pm in the meantime.

This evening, in 'Nice Guys Finish Dead', Jim Rockford finds himself unwittingly trying to solve the mystery of the murder of a state senator who was a special guest at a convention dinner for private investigators. The victim is found murdered in the toilets. Suffice to say, Jim, with his natural charm and brass neck, wraps it all up with a nice little bow to the satisfaction of the local police department.

Nine o'clock and time for bed. Paul's been lucky enough to get to see the Rockford denouement. He doesn't push his luck.

At 9.30, his dad sticks his head round Paul's bedroom door and gives him a quick rundown of events at Lansdowne Road.

* * *

Despite the absence of key personnel, Alan Kelly's Republic of Ireland start with gusto against the visiting Swiss. Sixty seconds in, the returning Dave Langan pushes down the right and picks out debutant Gary Waddock 20 yards from goal. The young QPR midfielder takes a touch before firing in a blistering effort that just clears the Swiss crossbar. The tone is set. Alan Kelly's youthful Republic of Ireland side swarm all over their visitors. Don Givens is the only player in the starting XI aged over 30. Next oldest is Gerry Daly, at 26. This is a young side. A hungry side. The better side. And best in the first half, during which they give the Swiss a serious examination.

Twelve minutes in and it's Dave Langan leading the charge again. The Derby County full-back has been in the international wilderness for two years after John Giles lost faith in his abilities. But Dave Langan is back tonight and, socks down round his ankles, as is his trademark, he is flying. Twelve minutes on the clock and he puts his clubmate Gerry Daly away down the right flank with a precise pass a yard in from the touchline. Daly carries the ball to within 15 yards of the byline and his beautiful cross is met powerfully by the soaring Don Givens at the far post, the striker heading the ball into the corner of the net from ten yards.

Roared on by the enthusiastic 20,000-strong attendance at Lansdowne Road, who are warmed by the show of attacking intent by the men in green, Dave Langan goes again! This time, he swings over another superb right-wing cross but Gerry Ryan, with the goal at his mercy, just fails to make contact.

No matter, because a second goal is coming. The crowd can feel it, such is the Irish dominance. Then, with 40 minutes gone, captain Tony Grealish, with his proud parents listening in on the radio, finds Daly on the right with a terrific 40-yard pass. Daly knocks it down to the supporting Langan and then makes for the Swiss penalty area. Langan swings in the ball to Ryan, who heads down for the onrushing Daly, arriving untracked. Daly, with time and space, takes the ball down, turns and scores from eight yards. Class.

The second half is a quieter affair. The Swiss reorganise and half-time and a two-goal lead seem to sap the Irish of momentum. That said, they should be three up on 48 minutes when an unmarked Kevin Moran heads wildly from a nicely flighted set piece from Daly. Daly then almost adds to his tally on the night, fizzing a free kick at the Swiss goal that keeper Engel does well to divert. The visitors, who have barely mustered a response, think, out of the blue, that they are back in the game on 70 minutes. Pfister's probing ball seems to catch Moran unbalanced. The ball clips the Manchester United's man's head and sails past Peyton into the Irish goal. Thankfully for the Republic of Ireland, the linesman's flag was already up for an offside. No goal.

Spurred back into life, Gary Waddock and Tony Grealish regain control of the midfield and the home side almost make it three in the final minutes. Waddock wins his umpteenth tackle in the middle of the park, then sets Paul McGee in on goal. But the Preston forward shoots just wide in what is to be the last meaningful action on a good night for Alan Kelly and the Republic of Ireland.

Alan Kelly tells the press after the game that he thought his team played very well, although he is a tad disappointed that they didn't score more goals from the chances they created. That said, Alan Kelly is more than pleased with how his side went about their business and how they made the Swiss side look very ordinary.

When asked about the Republic of Ireland job, Alan Kelly explains that he has had several discussions with the FAI in recent days and that he'll be making a decision tomorrow.

\* \* \*

The following morning, Thursday, 1 May, Brendan McKenna in the *Irish Press* reports that Alan Kelly will give his decision in the evening. Later in the day, Con Houlihan of the *Evening Press* expresses satisfaction with the performance of Alan Kelly's Republic of Ireland from the night before. Accepting that it's dangerous to put too much store in friendly games, he writes that there was much that pleased in the Irish display. Alan Kelly had promised his side would attack, writes Con Houlihan, and only those reared on a diet of Errol Flynn or Roy of the Rovers would've been disappointed at his attempt to match word with deed.

While the majority of the Irish side acquitted themselves well, Mark Lawrenson and Chris Hughton particularly shone for Con Houlihan. Lawrenson, writes Con, has a cornucopia of skills, a fine physique and always seems to have time on the ball. Indeed, Con Houlihan reports that during the game he heard sober men compare Mark Lawrenson to Franz Beckenbauer! They exaggerated, writes the newspaper man, but understandably.

And Con Houlihan was very taken by Chris Hughton's positive outlook, adding that some of the Spurs man's assaults on the night made the Charge of the Light Brigade look like an extremely cautious operation.

All in all, concludes the *Evening Press* man, Alan Kelly's Republic of Ireland team won and not without style.

\* \* \*

Despite reports that Alan Kelly would give his decision on whether he'll be John Giles's replacement on Thursday, 1 May, no decision is forthcoming. Indeed, the news now is that no decision will be made until the weekend, at the earliest. Alan Kelly has had to defer his decision until he gets the expected go-ahead from the Preston North End board. Some board members have been unavailable in recent days, so everyone has to be patient.

But Saturday and Sunday come and go and still there is no news. Finally, on Monday, a decision has been made but it's not the decision everyone was expecting. Alan Kelly will not be succeeding John Giles as the Republic of Ireland manager. The decision is a blow to the FAI and a surprise to all, given Alan Kelly had suggested that only minor hitches were holding up approval from his club. In the end, those hitches are not minor.

The board members at Deepdale are unhappy with the level of commitment involved in what is still a part-time post. Alan Kelly accepts that this is an issue. Alan Kelly is a man of principle. Alan Kelly, the 41-year-old ex-Drumcondra goalkeeper, turns down the position of Republic of Ireland football team manager.

Now, the FAI must look elsewhere. For now, Alan Kelly's assistant for the Swiss game and manager of Limerick United, Eoin Hand, will take up the reins in a caretaker capacity, taking charge of the international side for the upcoming games against Argentina and Czechoslovakia. The FAI will then advertise the post of national team manager at the end of the month.

On the same evening, in the south Dublin suburb of Templeogue, no one in Paul's household is aware of the FAI's problems. Most are watching the Embassy World Snooker Final between Cliff Thorburn and Alex 'Hurricane' Higgins. It is tense and close and, by seven in the evening, there's agreement – and pressure from his older sister – that this game will go on for quite a while yet and that maybe switching over to BBC1 to watch their bank holiday movie offering, *Rio Lobo*, with John Wayne, would be fair. They can come back to the snooker later.

Over on BBC, John Wayne isn't happy. His friend has been killed and he's determined to exact retribution on those involved. But before John Wayne can properly undertake this task, the world crashes into Paul's living room. John Wayne is interrupted by a newsflash and an extraordinary moment in television begins to unfold before the eyes of Paul and his family.

In London, there are more hostages, this time in the Iranian Embassy. They've been held there since the previous Wednesday when, around lunchtime, a group of armed Iranian Arabs took control of the building, demanding that their comrades in an Iranian prison be released. They also demanded independence for the oil-rich province of Khuzestan in the south-west of the country.

Twenty-one hostages are being held. Four are Britons, who were either visiting or working at the embassy. The rest are Iranian. Given the escalating tensions between the West and Tehran and the ongoing US Embassy hostage crisis in the Iranian capital, it was fair to say the London siege has been a serious, precarious and delicate situation.

The British authorities were naturally initially hopeful of a peaceful resolution. The Iranians informed the British government that they could handle it as they saw fit, while making it clear that they would hold the British responsible for the outcome. However, the situation was made more complicated by the hard line coming from Tehran. Not only would none of the prisoners in their jails be freed in response to the hostage takers' demands but for every hostage killed the Iranian regime would execute a comrade of the gunmen.

The British government has declared that it will not give in to terrorism. And its negotiators have had some success over the intervening days in convincing the gunmen to release five of their captives in return for some minor concessions, raising hopes that all might be well.

But matters turn deadly on that Monday evening, when two hostages are killed. The body of one is pushed out of the front door at 7pm as a macabre and dreadful show of intent. A threat to execute a hostage every half hour is then received and the British authorities feel they are left with no alternative but to act.

And act they do, the SAS storming the building live on TV screens in living rooms across Britain and Ireland to the amazement of unsuspecting viewers. As the TV crews film, masked men appear on balconies either side of the embassy building. There is an explosion, gunfire and the building itself takes light. Operation Nimrod. Police marksmen duck behind cars. Helicopters fly low overhead. The façade of the building and the billowing smoke hide the frightening events inside – but screams, a stun grenade and more gunfire are heard. Then a hostage, BBC soundman Simeon Harris, makes his escape. He'd been visiting the embassy the previous Wednesday looking to a secure a visa to travel to Iran. An SAS man is gesticulating, calling someone Paul can't see from a balcony beside the embassy. Suddenly, up pops Harris, who seems to have escaped the building during the confusion through the window where the SAS threw the first grenade. He's been crouching down, unsure where to go next. He then clambers over the side of the balcony, flames roaring above his head, and is directed into the next building by one of his rescuers.

Fire engines arrive as the flames take hold. Police carrying a victim on a stretcher run from the side of the building and around the corner. Four more policemen bravely dash in the opposite direction with stretchers to try and retrieve more of the injured. Minutes later, they re-emerge, stretchers laden. The fire engines pull up across the street and start to hose the front of the building as more police race into the fray, bringing out yet more people.

After six days of siege, the storming of the Iranian Embassy in London takes just 17 minutes. Paul and his family, who'd by then all gathered to watch this most extraordinary event, are flabbergasted. Normal programming eventually resumes but on the news later, Paul hears that five of the gunmen were killed, with one arrested. Nineteen hostages were rescued but, tragically, one more died in the crossfire.

And then from one embassy to another, as viewers are returned to the Embassy World Snooker Championships in Sheffield. A return to bank holiday normality. And Cliff Thorburn defeats Alex Higgins, 18-16, in a tense final session.

The FAI may have their succession problems but they don't amount to a hill of beans in such a stormy, uncertain world.

\* \* \*

On Tuesday, 7 May, Eoin Hand assumes the caretaker manager position in charge of the Republic of Ireland senior international side. In *The Irish Times*, Peter Byrne reports that not only did Preston not want Alan Kelly to become the part-time manager of the Irish international side, they'd also offered him an improved contract to make their feelings doubly clear. Preston, explains Byrne, were conscious of the impositions of the Republic of Ireland post and clearly deemed it prudent to intervene in the long-term interests of their club.

The irony is that Alan Kelly's first act as manager of the national team had been to appoint Eoin Hand as his assistant. Eoin Hand is informed that he has the position the night the SAS storm the Iranian Embassy. He's told a few hours before receiving the 1979/80 Soccer Writers' Association of Ireland soccer Personality of the Year award in Dublin. The association's president, Jimmy Magee, hands over the award to Eoin Hand, with the FAI president, Charlie Cahill, in attendance. Eoin Hand is the soccer writers' choice because, as player-manager, he has performed wonders at Limerick United, guiding them to their first League of Ireland title in 20 years. Naturally, Eoin Hand is enthused by the prospect of managing the senior international side. Eoin Hand tells those present that he's pleased and honoured to be asked to take charge of the side and that he's looking forward to the cooperation of all the players involved.

With doubts raised over the proposed visit of Czechoslovakia later in the month because of a clash with their domestic season denouement, Peter Byrne says that Eoin Hand's appointment is not expected to last beyond the Argentina game.

\* \* \*

On the same day as Eoin Hand's appointment to the caretaker role is announced, his squad for the Argentina match just over a week later is released. Arsenal players David O'Leary, John Devine, Liam Brady and Frank Stapleton are missing once more, unavailable due to their FA Cup Final, European Cup Winners' Cup Final and league commitments. Should they become available over the coming weeks, Hand promises to include them in his plans for the Czech game, should it go ahead.

Jerry Murphy and Ashley Grimes miss out on the enticing tie with the world champions through injury. But Gerry Daly is available after his participation had been in doubt in odd circumstances. Daly had been in the United States in talks with Boston club New England Tea Men, for whom he had appeared in the previous two summers to earn some useful dollars. However, talks about a third summer stateside had broken down, leaving the Derby man available for selection for the Lansdowne Road tie.

Daly has shrugged off suggestions that his involvement with both Derby and the Tea Men saw his form dip across the current season. He tells *The Irish Times* that such assertions are entirely inaccurate, explaining that a player in his mid-20s should easily be able to involve himself in competition all year round. Any perceived drop off in form, he says, was down to a series of injuries he picked up at the start of the season. Daly says those injuries are now behind him and that his recent performances for the Republic of Ireland bear out the point.

Given the squad available and the encouraging performance against the Swiss, Eoin Hand is expected to stick with the same XI that started in Alan Kelly's one game in charge.

But then Mark Lawrenson withdraws, resulting in a change at the back. In comes David O'Leary's younger brother, Pierce of

Shamrock Rovers, at centre-half. Pierce O'Leary has performed well in his previous appearances in green. But he'll be paired on the night with Kevin Moran and, between them, they will have six caps, their inexperience surely to be of interest to the Argentine attack.

Paul isn't going to the game. A 7pm kick-off on Friday, 16 May does not suit his dad, who'd be much happier to just get home from work and take it easy anyway. The game isn't on TV either. It's only a friendly, after all. Annoyingly, though, RTÉ One is due to show live horse racing from the Curragh that evening. Hard to imagine that is what people would prefer.

Live horse racing on a Friday night. There's already hours of it across the national broadcaster's *Sports Stadium* programme on a Saturday afternoon. And on the BBC's *Grandstand*. And on ITV's *World of Sport*. Racing from Haydock. Racing from Newbury. Racing from Leopardstown. Racing from bloody everywhere, thinks Paul. Now racing on a Friday evening too.

Still, at least it's Friday. And at least it's nice outside. School sorted. No homework. Get the dinner into you, then see who emerges for whatever game the kids of the cul-de-sac fancy. Or whatever games. There's often more than one option.

No point really listening into the game on the radio, not if there's a match on the green. Or a game of bulldogs charge. Or kick the can. Paul's estate has about 40 semi-detached houses with a circle of green grass at its centre. A few mandatory cherry blossoms across the sward. A pain at times or goals at others. The 'can' also resides there, a tree set almost in the middle of the green, probably down a little right from Paul's house. The circle of houses offers ample hiding opportunities. As do the few cars parked round the circle. One car per household, by and large. This isn't California, you know!

Most families are of a decent size. There'll be at least three kids in almost every house. Four to six in many. Activities across the small estate will feature a range of ages. Seven and eight-year-olds in games of rounders or bulldog with kids in their mid-teens. That mix is a beautiful thing – the big ones knowing the capabilities of the small, accepting them, putting up with them, sometimes pretending not to see the little ones in kick the can or diving forlornly and comically as they *try* to catch them in bulldogs.

In football, however, whether it be a match or three-and-in or Spanish football (World Cup in every other estate – but always, mysteriously and somewhat romantically, called Spanish in Paul's), it's every kid for himself. Football is the great leveller.

But it's early and it's teatime for most. No one outside yet. So a bit of *Captain Pugwash* on BBC at 5.30. Then a quick switch to *Holmes and Yoyo* on RTÉ at 5.35. The first five minutes missed, in deference to the good captain.

Not much to keep a child indoors on an early summer's evening after that. Not even the news that coverage of the horse racing has been cancelled due to an industrial dispute at RTÉ. It will be replaced by two hours featuring the work of officers Jon Baker and Frank 'Ponch' Poncherello of the California Highway Patrol. Back-to-back episodes of *CHIPs*. An hour of the motorcycle cop show wouldn't normally have held Paul's interest. So two hours, well … outside on the green was always the more likely option. And with a game of bulldogs charge gradually taking shape as the gangs of kids of all ages pass out through their front doors, not even the thought of the Ireland game on the radio is enough of a pull that evening. The match report in Saturday's paper will suffice.

\* \* \*

Five of the Argentine side that lifted the World Cup two summers previously – Fillol, Olguin, Passarella, Tarantini and Gallego – line up for the touring side at Lansdowne Road as the match kicks off at 7pm on the dot. Also among their number is 19-year-old Diego Maradona, the most prized and talked-about football talent in the world. Barcelona are reported to be willing to part with £3m (sterling) for the services of the Argentinos Juniors attacker. Many in the 30,000-strong crowd in Dublin 4 are there to run the rule over this new wonderkid.

Eoin Hand fields a weakened Republic of Ireland side. He has little option. And from the off, it appears that this could be a chastening night for the home side. The visitors look streets ahead in terms of technique and skill, with Maradona at the heart of their best moments. Early on, he finds space to take a beautiful ball in his stride from the menacing Olguin before flashing a dipping left-footer just over Gerry Peyton's bar. On 19 minutes, he plays a delightful flick on the left touchline between the bamboozled Dave Langan and Tony Grealish to Santamaria, before dashing for the return pass and forcing a decent save from the Irish keeper with an angled drive.

Argentina dominate, despite the tigerish efforts of Grealish and Gary Waddock in the middle of the park and the aggression of Langan on the right. But the Republic of Ireland are struggling to lay a glove on the world champions, who, despite the gulf in class, appear to be playing well within themselves.

On 28 minutes, Maradona is upended by Grealish 12 yards from the byline on the Irish right. The teenager takes charge of the set piece and finds the head of winger Valencia with a cleverly angled free kick. Valencia stoops and directs the ball past the surprised Peyton. One-nil to Argentina.

Four minutes later, Maradona strikes a cracking free kick around the Republic of Ireland wall but Peyton parries the ball to safety. The Argentines control possession up to half-time. The 1-0 scoreline at the interval doesn't reflect their domination of the game. Ultimately, their finishing has failed to match their attractively incisive approach play.

In the second half, the visitors' intensity drops off, perhaps feeling the effects of their bruising meeting with England at Wembley on the previous Tuesday evening. And perhaps because of the ease with which they controlled proceedings in the first half.

But the Irish remain dogged and stay in the game. And, in the last ten minutes, they threaten on three occasions to nick an unlikely draw. Firstly, Gerry Daly sees his shot saved by the Argentine keeper. Then Don Givens, a hapless figure for much of the evening, mistimes a more than presentable header from Langan's cross to let the visitors off the hook. And finally, with time almost up, Paul McGee's adroit header releases Daly once more on the Argentine goal but the Derby man hooks wide and the chance is gone.

\* \* \*

Post-match, Eoin Hand is proud of his side's efforts. He couldn't have asked for more from the lads, he says. The fact that many of them were suffering from cramp in the dressing room exemplified the shift they put in. Eoin Hand is especially pleased with how his team handled Diego Maradona. Eoin Hand doesn't believe Diego Maradona was as impressive as he'd been in their 3-1 defeat by England at Wembley earlier in the week and suggests that Argentina didn't create as many chances against his side as they did against the English. And Eoin Hand believes his lads deserve credit for that.

The caretaker manager naturally takes a positive view of his charges but he's well aware that without the missing Arsenal players, and without Mark Lawrenson, there was a clear gulf in class.

Noel Dunne of the *Irish Independent* underlines the point in his match report on Saturday. While the result will bear a very respectable look indeed in the record books, he writes, the Republic of Ireland can obviously ill afford to do without the men who were missing last night.

Noel Dunne is also concerned that the Republic of Ireland will struggle in their World Cup qualification group unless they can find a convincing combination up front and at least a few men who can consistently put the ball in the back of the net.

All that said, Noel Dunne praises Eoin Hand's Republic of Ireland team for staying in a game that always looked beyond them. Indeed, post-match, Argentina manager César Luis Menotti also offers praise for their efforts, telling the media that he was amazed at the performance of the Irish side. They kept at his team for the whole match, he explains, and, so, he was very happy with the exercise they gave his travelling side.

Of the men in green, Peter Byrne of *The Irish Times* singles out Dave Langan at right-back and Gerry Daly in midfield for praise. Langan emerged as one of the most effective players in the home team, writes Byrne, with a performance that gives him a real hope of retaining the right-back position for the World Cup games in September. For Peter Byrne, Gerry Daly was the only Irish player with the flair and the confidence to match the visitors.

Con Houlihan in the *Evening Press* feels that the rookie centre-half pairing of Pierce O'Leary and Kevin Moran acquitted themselves well, forming a fine central bastion. Gerry Daly also caught his eye in a largely prosaic Irish midfield. This was the Gerry Daly of old, he writes, full of fight, skill and ideas.

But Con Houlihan is also worried about the Republic of Ireland's current attacking options, especially when Frank Stapleton is not available. The lack of invention was all too familiar. Don Givens worked tirelessly but too often did the obvious. Paul McGee spoiled much good work by being caught offside time and again. And Steve Heighway put on an odd display, brilliant and confident at times but hesitant and fumbling at others.

Ultimately, however, the Irish team were cast in a supporting role on the evening for the 30,000 present. Diego Maradona was, naturally, the focus of the majority of those in attendance. Con Houlihan was certainly impressed.

If you believe that there are footballers who can make the ball talk, he writes, then you must believe that Diego Maradona can make it sing. The little man's performance, in Con Houlihan's opinion, served to underline just why the world's biggest clubs are prepared to risk bankruptcy to secure his services.

\* \* \*

For Eoin Hand, the reviews are also positive, if not quite so fulsome. David Walsh in Saturday's edition of the *Evening Press* believes that Hand got a real tune from his players, with his team playing to the limit of its ability. The performance will give the FAI food for thought, Walsh believes. Indeed, he thinks Eoin Hand may now be the favourite for the Republic of Ireland manager's job, which the association will be advertising publicly on Tuesday, 20 May. Walsh says that, as well as the current caretaker, Frank O'Farrell, Tony Dunne, Paddy Mulligan and Liam Tuohy all have backers within the FAI.

The ad for the position is simple when it appears in *The Irish Times* appointment section.

---

## FOOTBALL ASSOCIATION OF IRELAND
## NATIONAL TEAM MANAGER

Applications are invited for the above position. Salary and conditions negotiable.

Applications should be made in writing not later than June 2nd 1980, to:

The Secretary,
FOOTBALL ASSOCIATION OF IRELAND
80 Merrion Square
Dublin 2.

---

A fortnight later, Peter Byrne reports in the same paper that FAI Council members will be told at their meeting on 7 June that there have been a dozen applicants. Among them, amusingly, is a man attached to a junior club in Longford, who phoned in his interest to the FAI offices, putting his services at the disposal of the national team. The unnamed man is not likely to be considered.

Paddy Mulligan and Eoin Hand are known to have their hats in the ring. But the FAI is tight-lipped on the other interested parties. Byrne says that a decision is unlikely to be made for at least a month. But a week later, the decision is made.

Six candidates are called for interview at the Burlington Hotel in Dublin. Former Manchester United player Paddy Crerand flies in from the UK. Hand, Mulligan, former boss Liam Tuohy and former Irish internationals Theo Foley and Ray Treacy are also in the shake-up. Paddy Crerand is already on a plane bound for London by the time the last candidate, Liam Tuohy, is interviewed.

The Scot Crerand, former Charlton manager Foley and Treacy are first to be eliminated from the process on the night. The FAI executive then vote on the remaining candidates.

Eoin Hand gets seven votes. Paddy Mulligan gets six votes and Liam Tuohy gets three votes. Tuohy is eliminated and the FAI executive vote again on the two remaining options, Hand and Mulligan. This time, Eoin Hand gets nine votes. Paddy Mulligan seven.

So, on 14 June 1980, Eoin Hand officially succeeds John Giles as the Republic of Ireland manager.

Eoin Hand tells Bill Kelly of the *Sunday Press* that he's delighted and honoured. He says that being the manager of your country's international football team is one of the highest honours in the game and he'll do everything that can be done to qualify for the World Cup finals.

Bill Kelly adds that, while Paddy Mulligan was viewed as the most likely candidate by many in the press, Eoin Hand was a popular choice amongst the international players. David Walsh, in the *Evening Presss*, reports that the Irish job is still a part-time position, so Hand is likely to remain at the helm of Limerick United.

The new manager's first major test will come in September when the Irish take on the 1978 World Cup finalists, the Netherlands. In the meantime, Eoin Hand is off to Italy to run the rule over the Dutch and another of our other qualifying opponents, Belgium, at the European Championships.

# 5.

# New Beginnings – the Dutch in Dublin

THREE WEEKS before the visit of the Netherlands to Dublin, Eoin Hand names his first squad for a competitive international fixture. There are 23 names in his panel and no real surprises as Hand banks on experience for the 10 September meeting with one of the powerhouses of European football. The squad will be reduced to 18 players closer to the game. Eoin Hand has named his strongest-possible group of players and is confident that if he has Liam Brady, if he has David O'Leary, if he has Mark Lawrenson, Frank Stapleton, Tony Grealish and Gerry Daly, if he has Steve Heighway, then Ireland will be able to take the game to the visitors. And Eoin Hand is confident that he'll have his star player, Liam Brady, who has recently broken new ground by signing for Juventus in Italy. Eoin Hand is sure that Brady's move to Serie A will not affect his availability for the Republic of Ireland.

Eoin Hand also names his assistant for the upcoming World Cup qualifying games, his old international team-mate Terry Conroy, once of Stoke but now plying his trade with Crewe Alexandra. With Hand resident in Ireland, Conroy will run the rule over Irish players across the water.

One player who Conroy will be watching soon is 20-year-old Celtic goalkeeper Packie Bonner. The Donegal man has sprung to prominence in recent months, although he isn't selected in Eoin Hand's squad. And he won't be until Terry has had a proper look at him.

In the Netherlands, the winds of change are forecasted to blow hard through manager Jan Zwartkruis's squad. The Dutch had an underwhelming European Championships campaign in the summer. They struggled to beat a moderate Greek side in Naples in their opener, with only Kees Kist's second-half penalty separating the two sides. And while they only lost by the odd goal in five against West Germany in their next game, the score didn't reflect the course of a game dominated by the Germans and lit up by Bernd Schuster. The Dutch were as insipid and disappointing as they had been against the Greeks.

And their meeting with the Czechs in their last group game at the cavernous and largely empty San Siro in Milan had been rendered somewhat meaningless because of the tournament format, which saw only the top side from each of the competition's two groups progressing to the final. With neither the Dutch nor the Czechs in a position to realistically do so, the uninspiring and somewhat half-hearted game that ensued wasn't a surprise to anyone.

The subsequent post-mortem questioned whether the side that had struck fear into opposition sides since the early 1970s had run out of steam or whether manager Zwartkruis had prepared the squad poorly for Italy by over-training them. Whatever the truth, Zwartkruis's selection for the World Cup qualifier against the Republic of Ireland renders Eoin Hand's scouting trip to see the Dutch in the Euros in June largely meaningless. For when the Dutch squad arrive in Dublin on the eve of the game, only Ernie Brandts and Willy van der Kerkhof from the side that played in the World Cup Final in Buenos Aires two years previously are included. Gone are many of the Dutch masters that had thrilled watchers of the game. Gone are Rudi Krol, Johan Neeskens and Rob Rensenbrink. Gone is Arie Haan. Gone are Rene van der Kerkhof, Jan Poortvliet, Dirk Nanninga and Johnny Rep. Indeed, Zwartkruis's transitionary axe means that only Brandts, Willy van der Kerkhof and Jan Peters can boast more than ten international appearances.

The Dutch side that will figure against Eoin Hand's team will contain many names unfamiliar to Irish ears. The churn in the Dutch squad must surely offer serious hope of a home win. But the Dutch football factory has a production line admired across the game. Maybe the likes of Simon Tahamata of Standard Liege, Johnny Metgod of AZ 67 Alkmaar, Dick Schoenaker of Ajax and Pierre Vermeulen of Feyenoord are set to herald the dawn of a new era for the Netherlands?

A week and a half before the game, Eoin Hand trims his squad from 23 to 18. Out go Notts County full-back Ray O'Brien, Aston Villa forward Terry Donovan, Ashley Grimes of Manchester United, John Anderson of Newcastle United and Gary Waddock of QPR. The omissions are not a surprise on form and based on previous performances in green. The squad is trimmed but, crucially, Eoin Hand still has Stapleton, still has O'Leary, still has Lawrenson, Daly, Heighway, Moran and Grealish. He still has the core of his side – the best of his side. And, most crucially of all, perhaps, he has the jewel in the Irish crown – he still has Liam Brady.

Eoin Hand is assured by Juventus, European Economic Community regulations on the transfer of players within member countries and the player's contract itself that Liam Brady, one of Europe's finest midfield schemers, will be available for the Netherlands test – and for the tests to come.

Liam Brady is set to play in the Turin derby just three days before the World Cup qualifier with the Dutch. But a Juventus spokesperson assures Eoin Hand, assures the FAI and assures Ireland that special arrangements have been put in place to get Liam Brady to Dublin immediately after the Torino match.

Liam Brady is seen as one of the coming superstars of European football. And, as such, his participation, despite his enduring desire to play for his country, will come at a cost to the FAI. The insurance premium for his appearance is estimated to be around £3,000 (Irish punts), according to Peter Byrne of *The Irish Times*. The figure is based on the £150,000 Juve are reported to be paying him annually for his services. The insurance premium is eye-watering in a country where the figure is almost 30 times what the average worker earns in a week. But then Liam Brady is not an average worker. Liam Brady is not an average footballer. And the average worker will surely be happy to see Liam Brady in green because Liam Brady shows us what is possible and what is beautiful.

Liam Brady is special and hence there are special arrangements. Eoin Hand reschedules the traditional Monday morning training session at the Maccabi grounds in Kimmage to Monday afternoon, so that Liam Brady can take part.

Interestingly, Eoin Hand only has three midfield players in his trimmed-down squad of 18. Daly, Brady and Grealish. That would suggest that all three will play. It also hints that Brighton's increasingly influential and impressive central defender Mark Lawrenson may figure in midfield. Manchester United's combative centre-half Kevin Moran will also be available, despite a recent knock. Arsenal's classy footballing centre-half David O'Leary looks sure to be the bedrock of Eoin Hand's defensive axis. And he is joined in the squad by his brother, Pierce, of Shamrock Rovers, the only domestic player in the 18, and may well be paired with him come matchday. Eoin Hand has an embarrassment of riches at centre-half.

And Eoin Hand also has an embarrassment of riches at full-back in Chris Hughton of Spurs, Arsenal's John Devine, and Dave Langan, now at Birmingham City and making his return to a competitive international squad for the first time in two years.

But, for now, Eoin Hand doesn't quite have an embarrassment of riches in forward positions. Twenty-four-year-old Frank Stapleton will be one of the first names on the team sheet but it's not certain who'll join him. The Republic of Ireland's record scorer, Don Givens, is in the squad but age and workload have taken their toll. He's no longer the threat of yore. Preston's Paul McGee, who scored two in Nicosia, has pressed his claim. Liverpool's Steve Heighway, at 33, has probably left his best days behind him – but the wide man will surely figure in Eoin Hand's thinking. FC Porto's Mick Walsh is also an option, as is Brighton's Gerry Ryan. But with only two goals in the Irish shirt between them, their best hope of an appearance would likely be off the bench.

Two days before the match, one selection decision related to his attacking options is taken out of the Republic of Ireland manager's hands and he is not happy about the circumstances.

As with the rest of the squad, Steve Heighway is expected to arrive in Dublin on the Sunday as preparations ramp up. But Steve Heighway does not arrive. Steve Heighway isn't in Dublin. Steve Heighway is still in England because Steve Heighway is injured. Indeed, Steve Heighway has been injured for several weeks. The Liverpool winger tore ankle ligaments on his last visit to Dublin back in August when playing in Paddy Mulligan's testimonial. Steve Heighway has been receiving daily treatment on Merseyside for his injury since but Steve Heighway never had any chance of playing for the Republic of Ireland against the Dutch.

Liverpool didn't notify the FAI about Steve Heighway's ankle ligaments. But the FAI never sought to confirm his availability. Eoin Hand is embarrassed, and Eoin Hand is angry. But there's little or nothing that Eoin Hand can do about it other than voice his displeasure. Bad news at the 11th hour is always hard to swallow.

Liam Brady doesn't arrive on Sunday either. And he doesn't arrive on Monday morning to take part in the rescheduled training session. And Liam Brady doesn't make the team talk in the evening. Eoin Hand admits he doesn't know the exact whereabouts of his star midfield player but assumes that everything is all right. Eoin Hand seeks to allay any fears over Liam Brady by insisting that he believes the Juventus man would've gotten word to the camp if there was an issue. Thankfully, Liam Brady flies into Dublin late on Monday night.

Also absent from Monday's training is David O'Leary. The Arsenal defender sits out the session to rest a slight tendon strain. But David O'Leary is expected to take part in Tuesday's training session and should be cleared to play against the Dutch on Wednesday.

Jan Zwartkruis's squad arrive in Dublin on Monday. They arrive later than they had hoped, having had their flight rerouted to Cork for an unscheduled stop. Their late arrival meant their planned training session at University College Dublin's Belfield ground was abandoned. Instead, they trained at Dalkey United's Hyde Park pitches, given their proximity to the Dutch hotel in the coastal Dublin suburb of Killiney.

\* \* \*

Eoin Hand names his Republic of Ireland XI on Tuesday afternoon after training. Eoin Hand promised when he took the job that he'd look to play expansive, attacking football and his team sheet suggests he aims to be as good as his word.

Eoin Hand explains that his formation will morph between a 4-3-3 when Ireland are out of possession and an aggressive, attacking 4-2-4 when they have the ball. Eoin Hand selects Gerry Peyton between the sticks. His back four will feature the O'Leary brothers in the heart of defence, Dave Langan at right-back and Chris Hughton on the left. Midfield contains something of a surprise. Mark Lawrenson will be deployed in the middle of the park. He has, at times, prospered there with Brighton but not as yet for Ireland. Tony Grealish will be in the engine room with him, with Liam Brady on the left and Gerry Daly on the right. Eoin Hand hints that the midfield may take on a lopsided look at times as he hopes to give Brady a freer role, starting notionally on the left but with the expectation that he will offer close support and ammunition for Frank Stapleton and Don Givens up front.

Under John Giles, Liam Brady tended to prompt from deep positions but a more attacking role won't be too strange for him. In his last season with Arsenal, Terry Neill had, from time to time, pushed Brady into a forward role as a partner for Frank Stapleton. Basically, the Juventus man's role will be a loose one, dictated in part by the flow of the game, Eoin Hand explains, but he hopes that Brady will go forward as often as possible. In the sense that all our team will be attackers when they have the ball, Eoin Hand says, Liam Brady will be no different to the rest of the side but, obviously, perhaps uniquely in the Irish set-up, the midfielder has special skills to trouble the opposition. And

Eoin Hand hopes his formation will give Brady the freedom to use those skills to best effect.

The O'Leary brothers will play together in the centre of defence for the third time, having performed competently as a pair against Bulgaria and Northern Ireland under John Giles. The Mark Lawrenson-David O'Leary central defensive axis has been extremely impressive in recent seasons but Eoin Hand is hoping that shifting the Brighton man into midfield will add running power in that crucial area. Moreover, Lawrenson's reading of the game, defensive talents and ability to cover the ground should allow the older of the two O'Learys to break forward from the back, commit opposition midfielders and open up the game, safe in the knowledge that Lawrenson will plug any resultant defensive gaps.

John Devine is bitterly disappointed to miss out at right-back. But Dave Langan's adventurous performances against Argentina and Switzerland advanced his cause ahead of that of the Arsenal man.

Jan Zwartkruis, who's betrayed a sense of uncertainty since the Dutch arrival in Dublin, has decided not to name his team until a final workout on the morning of the match. His situation is potentially a treacherous one. With such an inexperienced squad at his disposal – excluding Willy van der Kerkhof's 39 caps, the remaining 15 players have no more than 80 between them – there is the risk that his new-look team could unravel should the Irish score early. But on the flipside, the injection of youthful vigour and of players vying to be part of Jan Zwartkruis's rebuilding programme for the future should see a competitive and dangerous Dutch side take the pitch on Wednesday evening. The departure of so many household names may also present the home side with something of a voyage into the unknown.

Eoin Hand, while wary of the latter, is banking on the former – and hence has set up his side to attack the Dutch and test their mettle from the first whistle.

\* \* \*

Nine-year-old Paul is a clock-watcher. In school, it can be a cruel affliction – that interminable period after the lunchtime runabout until freedom at a quarter to three. Paul doesn't really mind being in school. He revels especially in the football at breaktimes – be it with a tennis ball in a small-sided game played on a 'pitch' with a 90-degree angle, the bars of two shelters acting as the goals, or with a proper size five plastic ball across the big yard, played through seemingly hundreds of kids wandering across the tarmac pitch playing their own games and in their own worlds. Paul loves all that but he loves going home more.

But *Time* knows Ireland face the Netherlands in a World Cup qualifier at 6pm today. And *Time* senses Paul's excitement. So *Time* decides to have a little fun at Paul's expense – slowing the school classroom clock, persuading the second and the minute hands to amble, at best. But *Time* can only hold itself back for so long and 2.45pm eventually comes, the sweetest of releases, and Paul is out the gate for the 15-minute walk home and his pre-match preparations.

Once in the door, it's snack, homework and throw his eyes over the news of the day to placate his mam. He's only been back to school just over a week since the summer, so the homework is mercifully light.

The newspaper provides a brief diversion to help pass the time – six double-decker buses were burnt out in an apparent arson attack in the Summerhill depot in Dublin city centre. Many Irish holidaymakers have been caught up in a French trawlermen's protest that effectively shut the port of Cherbourg. Six toilets for the thousands of tourists and others hoping to get away via ferry has brought misery, discomfort and anger. At least the holidaymakers aren't actually hostages, thinks Paul, as he reads of some possible positive movement in relation to the American hostages still languishing in the US Embassy in Tehran. And then a bizarre story from the mysterious lands of Libya and Syria, separated by some 700 miles, according to the report in the *Irish Press*, who have proclaimed a merger into a single Arab nation and hinted at fostering closer ties with the Soviet Union.

Paper scanned, Mam happy, two and a half hours to kick-off. No one outside on the green, so telly it is. *HOW* on ITV or *Hong Kong Phooey* on BBC? The latter, for the fun of it and for the brilliant opening credits song, for sure. Anyway, Johnny Ball will be along just after with *Think of a Number*, which will satisfy the continuing quest for knowledge. Ball is more fun than the *HOW* crew anyway. And then *John Craven's Newsround* at 5pm, just before dinner. The gap bridged, *Time* defeated. The game will soon be afoot.

\* \* \*

With the usual pre-match niceties conducted, the World Cup qualifier between the Republic of Ireland and the Netherlands kicks off at 6pm on Wednesday, 10 September. A crowd close on 30,000 is in attendance. As Eoin Hand had promised, his Republic of Ireland team open up full of fire, aggression and endeavour. Forcing their will on the game.

Two minutes in, Gerry Daly finds Liam Brady, who has drifted over to Ireland's right side, with a throw-in, ten yards from the byline. Brady controls under pressure from two Dutch defenders before slipping a pass inside to Daly, who has moved infield to receive the pass. Gerry Daly drives for the byline and swings over a cross that deflects off two backtracking players in orange before landing at the feet of Frank Stapleton at the far post. Stapleton crashes an effort across goal but it's charged down by Dick Schoenaker.

However, the ball comes back to the Arsenal forward once more and, with the second bite of the cherry, Frank Stapleton smashes the rebound right-footed against the outside of the stanchion from 12 yards. Minutes later, 30 yards out on the left, Chris Hughton plays the ball infield to Tony Grealish. Grealish, with the Dutch defence pushing out, tries one from range but the ball cannons up into the air off a Dutch body. Grealish, tigerish in his play, wins the loose ball and this time plays a delicate pass through to Liam Brady, who strikes from the edge of the area, but Dutch keeper Joop Hiele saves comfortably down to his left.

The football is breathless, the intensity high as Eoin Hand's Republic of Ireland search for openings. The game settles briefly as the Dutch begin to find their bearings. They're mobile, quick and disciplined and they smother the home side for a time as they pull everyone behind the ball to gain a foothold and disrupt the Irish team's initial brio. And then they show their teeth. On 14 minutes, Ipswich Town's Frans Thijssen outpaces and out-thinks the Irish defence to get a flick on to Peters's free kick some 40 yards out. With both O'Learys caught flat-footed, the ball clips the crossbar and the Irish fans breathe a collective sigh of relief.

The midfield is especially congested, with Mark Lawrenson looking a fish out of water at times, struggling to deal with the traffic and the lack of space. But Eoin Hand's Republic of Ireland persist and they begin to dominate once more. On the half hour, Pierce O'Leary strides gracefully out of defence and through midfield, finding Stapleton. Stapleton holds the ball up, as he does so well, then picks out Don Givens, who has drifted wide left. Givens draws the Dutch defence before slipping the ball back to Lawrenson, who crosses to the far post, where Daly is arriving. But Michel van de Korput of Torino just beats the Irish midfielder to the ball. Appeals for a penalty are waved away by Danish referee Henning Lund-Sørensen.

Seconds later, the Republic of Ireland have a free kick within range of the Dutch goal. Liam Brady shapes to strike but, instead, runs over the ball, leaving it to Daly, who clips it into Frank Stapleton. Meanwhile, Brady has continued his run and Stapleton flicks it into his path but Hiele dives in bravely to grab the ball as the Juve man prepares to pull the trigger.

The home crowd roar encouragement and their approval of the imagination and verve being shown by Eoin Hand's men. The personnel may be largely the same as under John Giles but the intent and directness of their play is different.

On 36 minutes, Brady finds Stapleton once more in the box. Stapleton heads for goal but the harassed Hiele palms the ball to safety. Five minutes later, Chris Hughton throws to Brady, who picks out Stapleton once more. Stapleton spies Lawrenson in front of goal, just inside the area, and nods the ball down to the Brighton man. Lawrenson has a clear sight of the Dutch goal but shoots wildly and the chance is gone.

Nil-nil at half-time. Liam Brady dazzled and Eoin Hand's Republic of Ireland dominated but the Netherlands survived and are much the happier side to hear Mr Lund-Sørensen's half-time whistle.

Jan Zwartkruis's side play a little higher from the off in the second period, lifting the tempo, committing more of their forces forward. Clearly, the manager has directed a change in approach during the interval. Frans Thijssen and Feyenoord's Jan van Deinsen become increasingly dominant in midfield and Eoin Hand's Republic of Ireland find themselves deprived of possession and very much on the back foot.

On 50 minutes, Standard Liege winger Tahamata, 40 yards from goal on the Irish left, turns inside and finds Ronald Spelbos. Spelbos touches the ball forward quickly to Jan Peters who has found space behind the Irish midfield. Peters plays a delightful wall pass back to Spelbos, who drives at the Irish box just to the left of the 'D' before unleashing a shot that Peyton struggles to scramble around his right-hand upright. Tahamata takes the ensuing corner. Peyton punches, under pressure, to the edge of the area. Van Deinsen beats Daly to the dropping ball, directing it towards Peters, who strikes a volley from 20 yards, but Peyton, alert to the danger, shovels the ball to his left and safety.

Ireland respond. Liam Brady picks up possession once more on the Irish right and curls a ball into the area for Stapleton's head. Stapleton is beaten to the ball and Van de Korput boots it unceremoniously away towards the centre circle. Pierce O'Leary meets it, punting it high back towards the Dutch defensive line as they push out to try to spring the offside trap. But Gerry Daly times his run perfectly and then tangles with the onrushing Hiele. The Derby man pounces on the breaking ball, rounds the keeper, who is prostrate at his feet, and shoots for goal. But seemingly from nowhere, the ubiquitous Thijssen blocks and the Dutch survive.

Regaining their composure, the Netherlands wrestle for control. Profiting from a lovely double one-two down their right, Toine van Mierlo picks up the ball 40 yards from goal and drives toward and then across the Irish penalty area – careering past Langan, away from Lawrenson and evading David O'Leary. But his last touch is heavy and Peyton dashes from his goal and dives to grab the ball on the penalty spot. But the orb squirms free of his grasp – perhaps he's momentarily distracted by Langan, who is also arriving to try to snuff out the danger – comes back off the Dutch runner's ankles and rolls softly into the path of Tahamata, who gleefully rolls the ball into the empty net. This may not be the Dutch side of old – but they still have quality. They still have bite. The Netherlands lead on 57 minutes.

The silence is deafening. Irish shoulders slump as the goalscorer and Van Mierlo wheel away in delight. In Templeogue, Paul falls back on the couch, his hands covering his eyes. There's silence and then some muttered oaths from his brothers. Paul looks at the clock. Where earlier in the day, he had wished away *Time*, now he implores it to slow its inevitable advance.

But Tony Grealish's shoulders do not slump. Tony Grealish will not capitulate. And Tony Grealish takes the fight to the Dutch once more. With the visitors sitting back, hoping to soak up the expected Irish response, Pierce O'Leary drives through the centre circle unmolested and passes the ball left to Gerry Daly 25 yards out. Daly dips his shoulder and then plays a short square ball to Grealish on his right. The bearded No.10 quickly sets himself, then unleashes a stinging shot high to Hiele's right – but the Dutch keeper saves brilliantly, flying through the air to pull off an outstanding stop.

But Tony Grealish isn't finished and Tony Grealish refuses to be denied. On 79 minutes, the Luton Town man accepts a delightful, clipped pass from Brady between two of the visiting midfielders in the centre of the Dutch half, 40 yards from goal. Tony Grealish trades passes with Frank Stapleton and drives at the Dutch 18-yard line. The Dutch scramble to repel the danger, and a despairing defensive challenge on the edge of the area ends Grealish's surge. But the danger isn't cleared and the ball runs to Gerry Daly, lurking in the clear, 12 yards out. And Gerry Daly, Ireland's No.7, sweeps the ball, right-footed, into the net.

The roar around Lansdowne Road that greets the leveller is of both joy and relief. The equaliser is no more than Eoin Hand's Republic of Ireland deserve. Gerry Daly salutes the South Terrace and then runs to salute Tony Grealish, who lies crumpled at the edge of the area, having been dumped on the turf by that panic-stricken Dutch challenge. The pain doesn't cloud the joy.

But the men in green believe they deserve more and they are intent on getting more. And the players in orange, so disciplined throughout, are reeling in the Lansdowne din. Five minutes are left on the clock as the Irish push forward in search of a winner. The indefatigable Dave Langan dashes over the halfway line down the right and demands someone show for the ball. Givens obliges and Langan pings a 20-yard pass into the veteran forward's feet. A Dutch foot diverts the ball to Givens's right side, where Gerry Daly collects, only to be cut down by Ben Wijnstekers. Mr Lund-Sørensen blows for a free kick, 25 yards from goal, just left of centre. Well within range for Liam Brady. Grealish and Daly join him over the ball as the Dutch construct a barrier in front of Hiele. The six-man wall leaves them with just four outfield players to pick up the Irish players converging on their penalty area. One goes to Chris Hughton, who has stationed himself on the left angle of the penalty area. One goes to Frank Stapleton, Ireland's biggest aerial threat. But no one in orange seems to see Mark Lawrenson, ambling toward the edge of the area. But Liam Brady sees Mark Lawrenson. And Liam Brady picks out Mark Lawrenson, who has begun to run, with a chipped ball toward the penalty spot. And Mark Lawrenson throws himself and Mark Lawrenson connects with a wonderful diving header that gently curls around Hiele and into the Dutch net.

Pandemonium. Pandemonium on the pitch as the men in green celebrate. Pandemonium on the terraces and in the stands. Pandemonium on the roads outside, where fans who'd left early join the celebrations. And pandemonium in Paul's sitting room in Templeogue!

Paul's views on *Time* do a full about-turn as soon as the ball nestles in the back of the Netherlands' net. Now the end can't come quick enough. *Blow it up!* he implores of Mr Lund-Sørensen of Denmark. *Blow it bleedin' up!* And then, as the clock ticks past the 90, Mr Lund-Sørensen of Denmark obliges and the Republic of Ireland have beaten the Netherlands in one of their greatest ever results, in one of their greatest ever displays. Maybe not the Netherlands of Cruyff and 1974. Nor the Netherlands of 1978 of Neeskens, Rep and Haan but the Netherlands, one of the powerhouses of European football, all the same.

\* \* \*

Eoin Hand tells the press post-match that he believes his Republic of Ireland team were full value for their win. They were the better team. But he admits that there were times across the game when he feared the worst. Missed chances in both halves gave the Dutch belief they could come away from the trip with something – and they very nearly did. But Eoin Hand says his side never deserved to lose one point let alone two. To their eternal credit, says Eoin Hand, the players never gave up and both goals were the product of skill rather than good fortune.

The bespectacled Jan Zwartkruis sees things in a different light. He believes his inexperienced and experimental side should have taken at least a point from the game. He doesn't believe that Eoin Hand's Republic of Ireland dominated proceedings. Doesn't believe the Irish were the better side. The Irish enjoyed five great minutes, he says, and in that time, they made us pay for our mistakes. Jan Zwartkruis adds that he is full of admiration for the courage of his young side and that he won't be falling back in the aftermath of the defeat on the players he discarded after the European Championship finals in Italy.

But it doesn't really matter for today. Because today, Eoin Hand's Republic of Ireland have beaten Jan Zwartkruis's Netherlands. Eoin Hand's Republic of Ireland have four points from their two opening games. Eoin Hand says there is every reason to feel optimistic about the World Cup qualifying campaign. Liam Brady agrees. We must be in with a real chance, he says. The Republic of Ireland's World Cup dream is very much alive.

## 1982 FIFA World Cup qualification: UEFA Group Two

|  | P | W | D | L | F | A | Pts |
|---|---|---|---|---|---|---|---|
| Republic of Ireland | 2 | 2 | 0 | 0 | 5 | 3 | 4 |
| Cyprus | 1 | 0 | 0 | 1 | 2 | 3 | 0 |
| Netherlands | 1 | 0 | 0 | 1 | 1 | 2 | 0 |
| Belgium | 0 | 0 | 0 | 0 | 0 | 0 | 0 |
| France | 0 | 0 | 0 | 0 | 0 | 0 | 0 |

# 6:

# 'Here Come the Belgians!'

'HERE COME the Belgians!' The BBC commentary team's refrain, while in paroxysms of laughter during coverage of *International It's a Knockout*, is in Paul's head when he reads the Belgian squad for the upcoming World Cup qualifier. He never did quite know why the arrival of the Belgians would cause so much mirth. After all, they didn't appear to slip and slide or fall over more or less than the other plucky contestants or bring any more mayhem to the party. But for some reason, the arrival of the Belgian representatives in oversized shoes, or dressed as giant penguins or whatever used to reduce the BBC commentators to a quivering mess.

But the Belgians who are coming to Dublin to play Eoin Hand's Republic of Ireland on Wednesday, 15 October 1980 are not going to slip and slide and fall over for everyone's entertainment. They aren't going to be wearing oversized comedy shoes and daft foam rubber costumes. They aren't going to be firing water-filled balloons at their opponents. And they wouldn't give a BBC light-entertainment commentary team cause to even crack a smile were they to be present on the occasion.

The Belgians who are coming to play the Eoin Hand's Republic of Ireland are not some light-entertainment feature. No, the Belgians who are coming to Lansdowne Road are one of the most serious outfits in European football. The Belgians who are coming to play Eoin Hand's Republic of Ireland feature some of the most feared and respected players in football. The Belgians who are coming to play the Republic of Ireland in the 15 October World Cup qualifier are coming off the back of the greatest football tournament campaign result in their history. The Belgians who are coming to play Eoin Hand's Republic of Ireland are the second-best international side in Europe, having lost narrowly to West Germany in the final of the European Championship in Rome in June.

Guy Thys's side had surprised many commentators on the game with their performance in the European Championship in the summer. But their performance didn't surprise the Belgians. They had been planning for just such a breakthrough ever since they failed to qualify for the 1974 World Cup. Missing out prompted a plan to rebuild their international side by focusing on the development and screening of young talent. Crucially, pathways to senior football were created, aimed at giving young players better opportunities to graduate to senior sides earlier in their careers. The plan began to pay dividends as early as 1977 when their Under-18 side won the UEFA youth championship hosted, as it happened, by the Belgian FA. And the plan's success was brilliantly realised in the European Championship in Italy in the summer of 1980 when five of those who played with the youth side figured in the final against Horst Hrubesch and Co.

Drawn in a group containing England, Spain and tournament hosts Italy, Belgium were expected to simply make up the numbers. Thys had proclaimed England as tournament favourites before his team came from behind to earn a hard-fought draw against Ron Greenwood's men in Turin. Victory in their second game against a technically superior Spain side meant the Belgians only needed a point against Italy to top the group. This they achieved with a 0-0 draw in Rome, grimly strangling the life out of the hosts with a defensive display borne of hard work, discipline, more than a dose of cynical play and an offside trap that could reduce any opponent to tears.

But Belgium had quality too. Centre-forward Erwin Vandenbergh was the holder of the European Golden Boot, having scored 39 league goals for Lierse in the 1979/80 season. The hulking Jan Ceulemans was one of the most feared attackers in Europe. Behind him sat the highly regarded Eric Gerets –

an attack-minded, teak-tough defender and one of the most respected right-backs in the game. And in veteran midfield schemer Wilfried van Moer, Belgium possessed one of the best football brains in the world, according to Manchester United and England midfielder Ray Wilkins, who had faced the Belgian playmaker in Turin.

Guy Thys names his squad a week and a half out from the Lansdowne Road clash – and, ominously, it contains all of the players who featured in the European Championship Final. Eoin Hand names his 22-man preliminary squad on the same day. The most notable difference from the squad for the Dutch game is the inclusion of Manchester United keeper Paddy Roche, who is recalled to the international fold for the first time in five years. Roche, who plays second fiddle to Alex Stepney at Old Trafford, comes in, according to Eoin Hand, because of his experience.

Intriguingly, the squad released to the press includes 'A.N. Other' – reportedly the powerful Brighton & Hove Albion forward Michael Robinson. Robinson expressed an interest in playing in green several years previously while at Preston, qualifying by virtue of his Corkonian grandparents. But he then recanted, saying he wanted to keep his options open should England come calling. But that call never came and so he pressed on with getting clearance to play for the Republic of Ireland. A space is left in the squad for him but when it becomes apparent that he won't gain international clearance in time to figure against Belgium, Aston Villa's Terry Donovan is added to the squad in his stead.

Two days later, Hand reduces the squad to 18. Almost as soon as he is in, then Terry Donovan is out again. And out with him goes Porto's Mick Walsh, who's been enjoying a new lease of life in Portugal; his axing reportedly leaving him very disappointed.

Manchester United duo Roche and Kevin Moran are also dropped from the squad. That said, Moran's omission may prove temporary given the injury problems faced by David O'Leary, still troubled by a lingering Achilles problem. The Arsenal man hasn't trained for a fortnight after aggravating the injury against Nottingham Forest in the league. The Gunners face Manchester United the Saturday before the Belgium game. If David O'Leary doesn't figure in that game, then he won't figure for the Republic of Ireland the following Wednesday. Eoin Hand is already considering pulling Mark Lawrenson back into the centre of defence.

And as if Eoin Hand didn't have enough to worry about, a potentially bigger problem has been bubbling up ahead of the Republic of Ireland's qualifier in Paris against the French at the end of the month. That game, set for Tuesday, 28 October, is set to clash with the fourth round of the English League Cup. Five of the eight ties will involve Irish players. FIFA has confirmed that the FAI have no power to compel the clubs to release their players, presenting Eoin Hand with a major headache. Four key members of his squad – Hughton, Stapleton, Devine and O'Leary – are set to feature in the clash of the two north London giants, Tottenham Hotspur and Arsenal. Both clubs had considered rearranging the game in light of the Irish fixture – but the game has now been set for 27 October, the night before the France game!

Both Spurs and Arsenal are willing to let their players travel straight to Paris after the cup tie is settled. But Eoin Hand and the FAI are extremely unhappy with the prospect of the players having such a short turnaround before the France clash.

Gerry Daly, now at Coventry, is in the same boat, and Gerry Daly hopes that he won't be put in a position where he must choose between club and country. It's a great honour to play for your country, he tells the press, but, on the other hand, Coventry pay his wages and he will have to abide by the club's decision, whichever way it goes.

It's a major worry for Eoin Hand. But there's little or nothing he can do about it. It's one for the men in blazers to debate and rule on. For now, Eoin Hand has the second-best team in European football to concern himself with.

\* \* \*

On the Saturday before the clash with Belgium, David O'Leary, as expected, is ruled out of the World Cup qualifier. Kevin Moran is drafted back into the squad. That evening, France enter the qualification fray – travelling to Limassol to play Cyprus. Eoin Hand hoped to be in attendance but, with Limerick United due to play Thurles Town the following day, the scouting mission was abandoned. In his absence, France put seven past the hapless Cypriots and lay down a marker. After the Republic of Ireland's narrow win in Nicosia, John Giles said he believed the qualifying positions would be settled by points rather than goal difference. Given the French tally, the Irish camp hope this isn't a prediction that comes back to haunt them. But for now, with plenty of points to play for, points simply have to be the priority.

\* \* \*

Eoin Hand names his Republic of Ireland side to face Belgium on the eve of the game. There are two changes – veteran Liverpool winger Steve Heighway returns to patrol Ireland's right flank. And Kevin Moran, who hadn't made the original trimmed-down squad of 18, replaces Pierce O'Leary at centre-back. It's a hard few days for the O'Leary clan.

There's also one positional change – Mark Lawrenson dropping back into central defence beside Moran in place of Pierce's injured older brother, David. Lawrenson is relieved, having by his own admission struggled in midfield against the technical Dutch, despite scoring the winning goal. That said, his athleticism in the middle of the park and his willingness to cover for the forward forays of the O'Leary brothers had brought both a stability and a flexibility to the Irish play. And, crucially, it allowed Brady, Grealish and Daly to get about the Dutch higher up the pitch.

Eoin Hand explains his thinking on Moran to the press after Tuesday's training session. If his team were setting out to contain the Belgians, then Pierce O'Leary would be playing. But with the onus on his side to attack and win, he believes that Moran's aggression could be a key factor. The more so as he's likely to be squaring up to the muscular Jan Ceulemans. Moran's involvement is also likely to allow Lawrenson to occasionally make the long, penetrating runs from central defence that have increasingly become his trademark. If the Irish are to unlock the Belgian defence, Lawrenson's ability to commit opposition midfielders could prove an important weapon.

Heighway's return is also welcome, offering the promise of width and service for Givens and Stapleton and much-needed big game experience against a side of rude quality. Peter Byrne of *The Irish Times* believes that the Belgians may well be the outstanding team to visit Dublin in the last 15 years. Ominously, eight of Guy Thys's matchday selection figured in the European Championship Final.

\* \* \*

With kick-off set for 4.15pm, Paul has little time to play with when he gets home from school at three. His teacher has good-naturedly let them off homework, given the importance of the late afternoon qualifier, so it is dinner and then his daily trawl of the newspaper, red pen in hand.

As ever, the world seems as gloomy and sorry as could be expected. The Irish news was dominated by the capture of a suspect believed to have been involved in the murder of a Garda, Seamus Quaid, in a quarry in County Wexford two days previous. Detective Garda Quaid and his partner, detective Garda Donal Lyttleton, had been out on the Monday evening checking on the movement of possible suspects after a bank robbery earlier in the day in Kilkenny. They had happened upon a van driven by Peter Rogers, who had history with the Provisional IRA. When they went to check the van's contents, they realised that it contained a quantity of guns and explosives. On challenging Rogers, a shoot-out ensued, in which Garda Quaid was mortally wounded. Rogers, with a gunshot wound to his left foot, took flight but was eventually apprehended on the Tuesday evening in a pub in Wexford town.

Garda Quaid was the third member of the force to die violently since July. John Morley and Henry Byrne were killed in a gun battle after a bank raid in Roscommon in July. There was a general sense of outrage in the country – with calls for the death penalty for the perpetrators. When talking to the media on the Tuesday night, justice minister Gerry Collins wouldn't rule out such an eventuality. He confirmed that the law presently on the statute books made provision for the death penalty in certain circumstances. Indeed, he pointed out that the death penalty for conviction of a person found guilty of the murder of a Garda acting in the course of their duty was the 'law of the land'. Dark days.

Away in the Middle East, the Iran-Iraq War raged on into its second month. The Iraqis had launched a large ground offensive towards the Iranian city of Abadan, home to the region's largest oil refinery and close to the border between the two warring countries. The Iraqis were reportedly trying to cut off fuel lines to Tehran further north in the hope of forcing their foes to the negotiating table. In response, the Iranians launched an air raid on the Iraqi capital of Baghdad, using their American-built aircraft, and reportedly crushed a rebellion by Iraqi-backed Kurds in the north-west of the country. They also claimed to have shot down five Iraqi planes, MiG fighters supplied by the Soviet Union, that had attacked Iranian oil refineries on Kharg Island in the Persian Gulf.

And for a little more grimness, Paul read of the dreadful aftermath of an earthquake that levelled the Algerian city of Al-Asnam. Latest estimates suggested that the quake had killed more than 20,000 people and had left 200,000 without homes. As the Algerian government struggled to provide food and shelter to the victims, looting had, unsurprisingly, broken out in the remains of the city. And as if things couldn't be worse for those caught up in this natural disaster, the government had given troops orders to shoot looters on sight.

Meanwhile, over in the USA, former movie actor Ronald Reagan was now the favourite to win the upcoming presidential election in November. A poll run by the *Associated Press* and *NBC* had Reagan eight points clear of the incumbent president, Jimmy Carter. The story raises Paul's eyebrows. But his dad says that while the Americans can be a little crazy, even they won't be crazy enough to elect a former Hollywood actor to the White House.

Anyway, with words he didn't know marked in red and their requisite meaning supplied by his mother, Paul sticks on the TV at 4.10pm, where RTÉ's match coverage had just begun. In a world so often sorry and sad, at least there was football.

\* \* \*

On the eve of the game, Eoin Hand calls on Irish football fans to get behind the side and lift the roof off Lansdowne Road. And when the game kicks off, they duly oblige. A crowd of some 40,000 is present, a record for a football match at the stadium, some 10,000 more than saw the Dutch game the month before. Eoin Hand's Republic of Ireland team have captured the imagination and Lansdowne Road is rocking.

The conventional wisdom is that the best route to qualification is to win all your home games, win away to the Cypriots and pick up a point from each other rival when travelling. This will give you 13 points and almost certainly plane tickets to Spain. And so, Eoin Hand's Republic of Ireland know they must win this game and Guy Thys's men know that anything they take from Dublin could be crucial to their own hopes.

The Irish probe and press from the off and, nine minutes in, Tony Grealish, running on to a Brady chip, beats the Belgian offside trap but left-back Michel Renquin is alert to the danger and scrambles the ball out for a corner, which comes to nothing. Two minutes later, the same combination sets the Luton Town midfielder through on goal again. This time, he tangles with Belgian keeper Jean-Marie Pfaff and goes to ground. The home crowd bay for a penalty as Mr Norbert Rolles of Luxembourg blows his whistle. But the home crowd do not get their penalty. Mr Rolles has blown for an offside, even though his linesman did not flag.

Despite the Irish pressure and intensity on the pitch and from the terraces and stands, Belgium, coolly marshalled by Luc

Millecamps and Walter Meeuws at the heart of their defence, stand firm. And then, on 13 minutes, there is silence then muffled oaths and curses at Lansdowne Road. And silence then muffled oaths in sitting rooms all round Ireland.

'He'll have to try again, Moran,' says RTÉ commentator Jimmy Magee, as an aerial duel between Kevin Moran and the tall, elegant figure of Erwin Vandenbergh sees the ball shoot high into the air 40 yards from the Irish goal in the centre of the park.

The two men duel once again but it's the Belgian who wins the battle, the ball arcing over the covering Mark Lawrenson. 'Breaking through to Cluytens!' Magee sounds the alarm as Albert Cluytens, who has drifted infield from the right wing, bursts on to the ball. Cluytens accelerates. 'He's got the pace on Hughton,' warns Magee as Cluytens leaves the Spurs full-back for dead with an electric burst. 'Ah, it's great play by Cluytens,' shouts Magee as the midfielder careers left of the desperate, sprawling Peyton and puts the ball in the back of the net from the acutest of angles with the outside of his right foot. The midfielder wheels away in delight at the foot of the stunned South Terrace. 'Ah, that's a superb score ... an absolutely beautiful goal by the Belgians,' admits Magee. And it is. A beautiful goal of power, pace and no little skill. A beautiful goal met by silence and muffled oaths in Lansdowne Road. Silence and muffled oaths in sitting rooms around the land.

Eoin Hand's Republic of Ireland team look shell-shocked. And for the next 25 minutes, Belgium outplay them. Belgium outclass them. The 36-year-old Van Moer, despite his age, despite the efforts of Brady, Daly and Grealish, is running the show, pulling the strings. This is Belgium at their controlled, aggressive best. Hard, combative, fluent and accurate. The home side struggle to win and hold possession and, when they do, are too often reduced to a long ball down the middle, hoping, often in vain, to find the isolated Frank Stapleton or Don Givens.

Belgium gobble up possession, then open up the Republic of Ireland defence. Peyton does well to deny Vandenbergh with his legs. On the half hour, Van Moer plays a delicious ball to the striker, who nods down for his partner Ceulemans, leaving him with a clear sight of goal, but the burly forward, to the relief of the Lansdowne masses, shoots wide. Liam Brady looks to release Dave Langan, who has pushed down the right, but Vandenbergh, who appears to be everywhere, intercepts and plays Ceulemans into the space the Irish right-back has left behind him but, again, the big man shoots wide, letting the home side off the hook.

The Republic of Ireland may be reeling, but they are still fighting. Fighting to stay in the game. On 37 minutes, Kevin Moran's cross finds Gerry Daly, who has timed his run to perfection. His diving header also seems judged to perfection. The crowd leans in to acclaim what looks a spectacular equaliser. But Belgian custodian Jean-Marie Pfaff springs athletically, gymnastically across his goal to claw the ball round for a corner.

A roar comes down from the stands and terraces of Lansdowne Road in response to the fight shown by the men in green. Willing them on. Urging them on. And suddenly the Belgians don't look so assured. Not so certain. Then Dave Langan, who epitomises all the endeavour and spirit of the Irish team, gathers the ball in the shadow of the East Stand, right on halfway. Dave Langan clips a ball down the right wing toward Don Givens but the Irish forward is beaten to the ball by Michel Renquin. However, Renquin can only divert the ball to Gerry Daly, just in from the touchline, 20 yards into Belgian territory.

The Coventry man cuts inside, skips past a tackle and plays a short ball toward Tony Grealish. But Brady gets there first and Grealish redirects his run toward the heart of the advancing Belgian back line. Brady, 35 yards out, reads Grealish's intent and chips a ball toward the Luton Town man. The Belgians converge to intercept but, somehow, the ball pops out goalside and Grealish is away. Some of the visiting defenders stop, expecting a flag – they are used to getting a flag – but Tony Grealish doesn't stop. Tony Grealish continues his run. And Tony Grealish, holding his nerve, rounds the advancing Pfaff and slides the ball home from an acute angle, despite the desperate efforts of the retreating Eric Gerets.

Lansdowne roars. Roars oaths. Roars curses. Pfaff rushes to Mr Rolles of Luxembourg. Roars and remonstrates with Mr Rolles of Luxembourg, while his team-mates look to the linesman in disbelief. But the linesman has shown no flag and the linesman is quite correct. Liam Brady's pass has come off a Belgian player, so Tony Grealish is not offside. The goal stands. Eoin Hand's Republic of Ireland are level. They may have been outplayed for much of the first half. They may have been out-thought for much of the first half. They may have been outclassed for much of the first half. But they have not been outfought.

Choice words and a regroup at half-time, Eoin Hand's Republic of Ireland emerge a different team in the second period. Brady, Grealish and Daly up the industry and intensity in midfield. The ball is moved quicker. The ball is moved wider. Stapleton's starting position is also a little wider – and he begins to make use of the space to probe and prompt and link up more effectively with those behind him.

Eight minutes into the second period, interplay between Daly, Stapleton and Brady creates an opening for Daly on the fringe of the Belgian area. It's the Republic of Ireland's best passage of play so far. Gerry Daly then trades passes with Tony Grealish and is free inside the box. But a poor touch allows a grateful Pfaff to smother the ball at his feet.

Long balls to the frontmen are eschewed. Hughton, Langan and Heighway on the flanks become the main avenues of attack. On 64 minutes, Brady intercepts the ball and releases Steve Heighway down the right and, for once, he skips past the impressive Gerets. Steve Heighway then whips over a cross perfectly for the incoming Frank Stapleton. But the Arsenal man just can't find the power with his header and the Belgian keeper saves comfortably.

The Republic of Ireland have a stranglehold on the game. So much so that the visitors can only manage two half-chances in the second period. Eoin Hand's midfield dominate. Dave

Langan is marvellous at right-back – all tenacity and attacking intent. Kevin Moran quietens Ceulemans. Mark Lawrenson subdues Vandenbergh. But Eoin Hand's Republic of Ireland seem toothless up front. Givens and Heighway are not the players they were and fail to exert consistent influence. Fail to penetrate. Stapleton is the most likely route to goal as the clock ticks but, in truth, there are precious few openings.

The Belgians, having bent and broken once, will not bend and break again. They're intent on taking a point from Dublin and take a point they do. Mr Rolles's final whistle is met with a mixture of relief and regret, and no little pride, from the 40,000 assembled, the many watching at home and the men in green.

Relief, because it could certainly have been worse. The Belgians could've put Eoin Hand's team away in their imperious first half. Pride, because the Belgians are the second-best team in Europe, one of the most fearsome sides in the world game. But the Republic of Ireland showed that they can compete. Showed that they can have a say in this group. And regret. Regret that Eoin Hand's men in green couldn't convert their second-half supremacy into one more goal and two points.

* * *

As Eoin Hand and Guy Thys perform their post-match media duties, Paul and family consider their post-match TV options. *This Is Your Life* is on at 7pm on UTV. Paul's mam asks if she can see the start of it, just in case it's someone worth watching. They never announce beforehand who is to get the surprise Eamonn Andrews treatment, so it always makes sense just to check. Just in case someone really good is on. This evening, it's the turn of Joe Loss, leader of the big band era Joe Loss Orchestra. The name means nothing to Paul and his brothers. The groans are enough for his mam to relent and let the lads switch over to BBC1 where *The Goodies* are just starting. Tim Brooke-Taylor has fallen in love with Olivia Newton-John and has replaced his portrait of the Queen with one of the Australian star. He's also started going to discos and dressing like John Travolta. Housemates Graeme Garden and Bill Oddie decide to go along too. Chaos and hilarity ensue. Joe Loss could never live with this.

Meanwhile, in the bowels of Lansdowne Road, Eoin Hand lauds the efforts and character of his team in how they recovered from their early setback and came back to force the pace. Belgium were playing for a draw in the second half, which says much for his side's performance against the second-best side in Europe, he tells the assembled media. Eoin Hand professes to be pleased with a point, all things considered. Five points from six, having played both the Dutch and the Belgians, gives cause for hope for the rest of the campaign.

Eoin Hand also praises Belgium's extraordinary use of the offside trap. A feature of the Belgians' run to the summer's European Championship Final and a feature of their performance in Dublin. Indeed, much to the frustration of the Irish players, they found themselves caught offside no fewer than 14 times across the 90 minutes. Eoin Hand has never seen the ploy used so efficiently by any side. His lasting impression of the Belgians, though, was of their impressive physical strength. They are a very fine side, he concludes.

Guy Thys feels the result was a fair one. He admits a sense of surprise at the strength of the Irish challenge displayed thus far in the group. But, having seen the Irish victory over the Dutch, he knew this was going to be a difficult fixture. Guy Thys singles out Liam Brady, Tony Grealish and Gerry Daly for praise, admitting surprise at just how good the latter two were. The Belgian charms the assembled Irish media by suggesting that the Republic's next opponents, France, will struggle to pick up the points from the upcoming clash in Paris. Winningly, Guy Thys suggests that Eoin Hand's team have a strong chance of taking the second qualifying place ahead of the French and the Dutch. It goes without saying that he believes that Belgium will be top of the pile.

Notably, both managers roundly condemn the quality of the pitch. Both say the grass was much too long for international football. Of course, the pitch belongs to the Irish Rugby Football Union (IRFU) and the FAI are but tenants. That said, given that the gate receipts for the game were expected to be around £200,000 (Irish punts) and the IRFU was expecting to pocket as much as £40,000 of that figure, Eoin Hand and his team should surely have been afforded a better surface on which to play. An angry Liam Brady agrees and labels the sward 'disgusting'. The Juventus playmaker says that if people want the team to do well in the campaign, then he and his team-mates need to be given every help to do so. The grass was simply too long, he complains, causing the players' legs to eventually give way to cramp and fatigue.

The pitch aside, Republic of Ireland captain Liam Brady thinks his side achieved a very good result. And in response to a question as to whether he thinks the dropped home point and goal difference may prove pivotal in how qualification is decided, Brady replies sharply and rather spikily that he is interested in football, not mathematics.

## 1982 FIFA World Cup qualification: UEFA Group Two

|  | P | W | D | L | F | A | Pts |
|---|---|---|---|---|---|---|---|
| Republic of Ireland | 3 | 2 | 1 | 0 | 6 | 4 | 5 |
| France | 1 | 1 | 0 | 0 | 7 | 0 | 2 |
| Belgium | 1 | 0 | 1 | 0 | 1 | 1 | 1 |
| Netherlands | 1 | 0 | 0 | 1 | 1 | 2 | 0 |
| Cyprus | 2 | 0 | 0 | 2 | 2 | 10 | 0 |

# 7.

# Paris in the Fall

EOIN HAND'S 22-man squad for the clash with France in Paris on Tuesday, 28 October is released to the press five days after the exhausting draw with Belgium. Eoin Hand adds two newcomers to the group – Celtic's young goalkeeper Pat Bonner and Brighton's powerful and pacy forward Michael Robinson, who has received international clearance to play for the Republic of Ireland. David O'Leary is also selected, having missed the Belgian game through injury.

Eoin Hand picks his strongest-possible squad for his first away test as manager of the international side. But Eoin Hand faces more than the usual uncertainty in terms of player availability. Eight days out from the Republic of Ireland's massive date with the French, player availability issues regarding the fixture clash with the English League Cup have still not been settled. Eight days out from this critical game, Eoin Hand doesn't know if he will have the services of David O'Leary, Frank Stapleton, John Devine, Chris Hughton, Gerry Daly, Dave Langan and Don Givens. The players' clubs are involved in League Cup action, either on the eve of the Paris game, on the same night or on the night after.

The fixture clash has been known about since before the Belgium game. The FAI had hoped that some agreement with Spurs, Arsenal, Coventry and Birmingham about the release of the players or the rescheduling of matches could have been agreed well in advance of Hand's squad announcement to allow him certainty in his plans.

But eight days out from the Republic of Ireland's clash with France in Paris in a vital World Cup qualification game, Eoin Hand has no such certainty.

Spurs are proving the main obstacle. They're set to meet Arsenal the night before the France game. This would mean that the four Irish players likely to be involved in the League Cup tie would only have a 24-hour turnaround before lining up at the Parc des Princes for the Republic of Ireland. This would clearly not suit Eoin Hand or the FAI. The French would pose a serious challenge to the Republic of Ireland's hopes even if the Irish players were to rest for a whole week. The situation is simply not acceptable.

Spurs are actually open to the postponement of the cup tie until the following Monday, 3 November. Moving the tie isn't actually the problem. Their problem relates to the date of any possible replay. Arsenal are happy to play a replay, if needed, on Thursday, 6 November. Spurs aren't happy with that date and, so, refuse to budge. Consequently, without agreement between the two north London clubs, the League Cup tie is set to go ahead the on the eve of the Paris game.

Coventry manager Gordon Milne is also causing Eoin Hand a headache. He's refusing to release Gerry Daly from Coventry's League Cup tie with Cambridge United on the night of the French game. Gerry Daly has probably been the Republic of Ireland's best player, their most consistent attacking and creative threat in the three qualification games so far. He's central to Ireland's hopes.

Meanwhile, Birmingham City manager Jim Smith's stance also poses a problem for Eoin Hand and the FAI. Birmingham are due to meet Ipswich Town the night after the France game. Jim Smith is prepared to let Don Givens travel to Paris. But Jim Smith doesn't want Dave Langan to do likewise.

The indifference of the English clubs has created unneeded pressure and uncertainty for Eoin Hand and his squad. The intransigence of the English clubs threatens the Republic of Ireland's World Cup dreams. The situation can't be allowed to stand. And, so, the FAI take action – informing the English

FA and the Football League that they're invoking Article 2 of the UEFA regulations governing the release of players for international games. And, in so doing, the FAI are making football history, being the first national association to seek an official ruling on such a matter.

Article 2, as applied to member countries of the European Economic Community (EEC), makes it imperative that clubs release players to national squads not less than 48 hours before a competitive international fixture. Dr Brendan Menton, FAI president, says that the association would've preferred to have reached agreement in negotiation with the clubs involved. But with no such agreement or goodwill forthcoming, the FAI has had no choice but to seek UEFA intervention. Dr Menton adds that the FAI is determined to apply the regulations as necessary. In the FAI's view, the World Cup should take precedence over the English League Cup.

Eoin Hand is optimistic. He tells the Irish media that he has picked the strongest squad possible and the FAI has assured him that he is entitled to have all the players named, barring injury.

A cable is sent to UEFA stating the FAI's intent on Monday, 20 October. Copies of the cable are sent to the English FA and English Football League. But no reply or reaction is received that day. UEFA officials contact the English FA on Tuesday morning to resolve the matter. But English FA secretary Ted Croker isn't available for comment, as he's away in the Netherlands on business. However, a spokesman for the English association says that Mr Croker is being kept informed of the matter and there will hopefully be some news later in the day.

Ken Friar, Arsenal secretary, says that the club has a duty to its season ticket holders, its shareholders and the public in general to play the League Cup game with the strongest side possible. Arsenal aren't against their Irish players figuring in Paris on the Tuesday but they'll have to play the League Cup game against Spurs the night before. The League Cup is a major competition, explains Friar, and the clash with Tottenham means a lot, financially, to both clubs. Moreover, the League Cup offers a lucrative place in Europe for the winners, so Arsenal can't countenance facing their north London rivals without their Irish internationals.

The FAI plans to make further overtures to English Football League secretary Graham Kelly on Tuesday, 21 October, as he is due in Dublin for a meeting of the International League Board. The FAI will try and convince him to call for the League Cup games to be postponed.

The same day, in a whirlwind of football diplomacy, UEFA contacts the FAI and asks it to investigate the contracts of the Irish players in question. The UEFA regulation that the FAI hopes to invoke states that players who've signed a contract in a foreign country since 5 October 1978 must be released for competitive internationals with their home nations. The regulation pertains to clubs in the member states of the EEC. A UEFA spokesman explains that if the FAI finds that the contracts are covered by the regulation, the clubs must release the players 48 hours before the World Cup qualifier. If the contracts aren't covered, then a special UEFA committee will convene to rule on the matter. On Wednesday, a week before the Paris clash, it becomes clear that there is uncertainty over the application of the regulation to some of the player contracts, meaning the UEFA committee will have to convene. The English FA believes that, as all the players involved were already in England before the regulation came into force, it does not apply.

Meanwhile, other questions are being asked of the FAI. The League Cup draw had been made a month ago. So, if the FAI knew of the regulation, why did it leave it until a week before such a crucial match before invoking it? Naturally, it's understood that the association would've been hopeful that an agreement could've been reached to the satisfaction of all parties. But when it became clear that the clubs were unwilling to budge, shouldn't the FAI have acted sooner?

Birmingham City's Don Givens, the Republic of Ireland's record goalscorer, is severely critical of his own football association. Don Givens says that it's a terrible situation for players to be in. Don Givens says that it's obvious that the players desperately want to play in Paris but it's the clubs who pay their wages. Don Givens says the whole debacle should never have happened. The FAI should never have let it happen. Don Givens says that Irish football has progressed tremendously on the pitch in recent years but that this isn't the case when it comes to off-the-field matters.

The English Football League is also critical of the FAI. It feels that the Irish association is largely responsible for the problem, as the timing of the fixture it agreed with the French is outside of the designated international dates the English FA would've agreed. While the English League may have a point, it's arguably unfair to suggest that the FAI must always set its games based on when England are playing. Nevertheless, had the FAI done so, then, the English League says, there would've been no problem to fix. No clash to deal with. Either way, none of this is very helpful for Eoin Hand's preparations.

The word in the Irish media is that UEFA won't issue a decision until Friday at the earliest. Tensions continue to rise. FAI secretary Peadar O'Driscoll says the association is simply amazed at the lack of cooperation it has received from across the water. He considers the attitude of some of the clubs to have been extraordinary. Peadar O'Driscoll says the association may well respond by looking at ways in which to stem the flow of quality Irish youngsters into English football if there's no reconciliation between the parties. The FAI secretary says the association will look at ways to protect such youngsters to ensure that playing for their country will come first in future. Peadar O'Driscoll says that the France match is vitally important to Irish football. Qualification is within our reach, he says, and all of Irish football wants it desperately.

The UEFA committee meet at noon on Friday, four days before Eoin Hand's Republic of Ireland are due in Paris. The three-man committee meeting in Rome consists of René van Den Bulcke (Luxembourg), Professor Paulo Barile (Italy) and Hans Bangerter, the general secretary of the organisation. Speaking in Berne, UEFA official Rene Eberle says that everyone is anxiously awaiting the outcome, noting that it is the first case of its kind to have come before the association. That fact makes it a case of serious interest across the continent. Eberle will not prejudge the outcome. It's a matter for the committee. He doesn't believe a statement will be issued by UEFA until Saturday, although the associations involved may hear something beforehand.

Meanwhile, in London, David O'Leary is preparing to test a tendon injury to see if he'll be fit to play for club and country, depending on the outcome of the FAI's case. He has been resting for 20 days but admits that he's not especially confident. An operation may be required to rectify the problem. David O'Leary says he'll be very sorry to miss the Paris game. The side badly needs to be at full strength. The clash of dates, even if he were to be passed fit, was a real pity, he believes. He suggests that, going forward, regardless of UEFA's ruling, the FAI should look to make sure its international dates line up with England's so that there will never be a future problem over the release of players.

Late on Friday night, the FAI receives the news it is hoping for. UEFA's committee unanimously rules in its favour and directs the English clubs at the heart of the disagreement to release the Irish players for the qualifier with France.

There is delight at FAI headquarters in Merrion Square. Peadar O'Driscoll, the FAI secretary, says the association is pleased and relieved. The only pity, he says, is that the FAI had to take the issue to UEFA rather than reach a settlement with the English clubs. A souring of relations is the likely outcome. FAI president Dr Brendan Menton also expresses his delight but adds that he was always confident that UEFA would rule in favour of the Irish case. After being subject to a lot of criticism, he feels the FAI has been fully vindicated and that the English clubs had misinterpreted the UEFA rule in question.

The misinterpretation revolves around contract renewals. The English clubs believed that players who had signed for clubs before the 1978 UEFA rule came into being weren't covered by said rule. But UEFA has ruled against that interpretation, stressing that players renewing their contracts in the intervening period are covered by the rule and, indeed, provision for said rule should've been included in their renewed contracts. The case and the ruling are a landmark in the game. From now on, the

FAI (and other associations) will have first call on their players whenever there is a club versus country clash.

So, David O'Leary, Frank Stapleton and John Devine of Arsenal, Chris Hughton of Spurs, Dave Langan of Birmingham City and Gerry Daly of Coventry City are free to join up with the rest of Eoin Hand's squad for the big game in Paris. Unfortunately for Eoin Hand, however, the good news is quickly tempered by bad. O'Leary pulls out of the squad – his fears about his injury realised on the same day as the UEFA ruling.

Then on Sunday, Gerry Daly, who had pulled out of Coventry's game at the weekend with an ankle injury, also withdraws from the squad. The Lord giveth, and the Lord taketh away, Paul's dad smiles philosophically as they hear the news on the radio. Eoin Hand is also in philosophical mood. It's a pity, he says, that his team will be without two such good players but the picture was a lot less encouraging a week ago.

\* \* \*

Eoin Hand and Michel Hidalgo name their sides on the day before the game. Eoin Hand brings in the experienced Mick Martin of Newcastle United to replace the injured Gerry Daly. Martin hasn't figured in an Irish shirt since November 1979 in the European Championship qualifier with Northern Ireland at Windsor Park. Injury has played a big part in him missing games in that period. A serious knee injury had seen him out of the game for six months. But Mick Martin is fully fit at an opportune time. His versatility, work rate and know-how in the middle of the park should compensate for the absence of Daly.

However, Eoin Hand is keen to dispel the notion that Martin may ultimately play as an auxiliary defender, perhaps just in front or between Ireland's centre-halves. People will interpret the selection as they will, Eoin Hand tells the press, but, as he sees it, Ireland would be dicing with disaster if they went to Paris just looking for a point. He believes that French teams, even one of this quality, can be brittle mentally. So if he instructs his players to chase both points from the off, it is probable that they can come home with at least one.

Kevin Moran will once again deputise for the injured O'Leary. It will be the Manchester United man's first away international. The former Dublin GAA star impressed in his match-up with Jan Ceulemans in the Belgium game and he's likely to be similarly tested by the aggressive and speedy Bernard Lacombe. Much may depend on how Moran fares.

But the biggest talking point is a debut for 22-year-old Michael Robinson in place of Don Givens. The Brighton forward, who once figured in England's Under-21 set-up, has settled well on the south coast since his £400,000 (sterling) summer move from Manchester City. That transfer could well have seen his confidence knocked, having signed for City only the year before from Second Division Preston for £750,000. It was an eye-watering sum for a forward with no First Division experience, a sum that made him the second most expensive English player of all time. But he struggled under the weight of expectation at Maine Road. And he struggled under the management of Malcolm Allison.

But Michael Robinson has been reinvigorated by his Brighton move. He has begun confidently with the Seagulls, scoring six times already for his new club. And Eoin Hand is hopeful the striker will bring the power, pace and explosiveness he's been displaying for the Goldstone Ground outfit to the Irish front line.

For his part, Michael Robinson, aware that some may question the tenuous nature of his Irish allegiance – he qualifies by virtue of his Corkonian grandparents – is anxious to quell any concerns over his commitment to the cause. International football is the goal of every player, he says, and he has promised Eoin Hand that nobody will be running harder for him on the field in Paris on Tuesday night.

The young striker also feels he has a personal point to prove. Malcolm Allison has rather cruelly stated that the signing of Robinson was the biggest mistake he had ever made. But Michael Robinson is backing himself and says he wants to repay the faith shown in him by Eoin Hand by grabbing a goal or two in the French capital.

Michel Hidalgo's France team is founded very much on the side that won admirers with their swashbuckling play in the World Cup in Argentina. Eight of the side that lost narrowly to the hosts and eventual champions – Dominique Dropsy, Patrick Battiston, Christian Lopez, Maxime Bossis, Michel Platini, Dominique Rocheteau, Bernard Lacombe and Didier Six – will play against Eoin Hand's Republic of Ireland on Tuesday evening. The French missed out on Euro 80, beaten to qualification by a point by the Czechs. They are determined not to miss out on tournament football again, determined to show their quality again on the world stage, to prove that their flair can bring tangible results. There's a growing sense that Michel Hidalgo's men are a coming force in international football. The 50,000 sell-out at the Parc des Princes suggests the French public sense it too.

* * *

On matchday, the big news coming out of Templeogue, Dublin is that Paul will be allowed to stay up for the entire game. Speaking to his friends on the road in the afternoon, he stated that he had expected it would be the case but, given that the game wouldn't be ending until after 9pm, there had been some uncertainty. With the game kicking off at 7.30pm, the final whistle would be blown not too long after the usual 9pm cutoff. Recognising the importance of the occasion, Paul's parents had come to the decision without the need for a prolonged period of negotiation. The key stipulation in the agreement was that Paul be in his bed no later than 9.30pm on the night and that any post-mortems could be left at least until breakfast the next morning. Satisfied with the deal, all parties were pleased there was no need for UEFA to convene a special committee to adjudicate on the issue.

Elsewhere, there was also what appeared to be good news in the *Irish Independent* for the American hostages in the US Embassy in Tehran – although Paul's parents had no hand, act or part in it. Rather, the news was emerging from a special envoy of the Ayatollah Khomeini during a visit to Beirut. The envoy said that a message had been conveyed by the Iranian prime minister, Mohammad-Ali Rajai, via UN secretary general Kurt Waldheim to president Jimmy Carter that the Ayatollah was interested in bringing an end to the hostage issue but wanted to wait until after the upcoming US presidential elections.

Reports suggest that Khomeini has finally decided to release the hostages, as they are no longer useful to him in the domestic political game in Iran. The hostages had been used to defeat remaining pro-US and pro-Western factions in the country – something the Ayatollah now believed he'd achieved. The hostages were now a burden and an unneeded distraction, especially as the country had the more pressing matter of the war with Iraq to attend to.

Meanwhile, in Northern Ireland, tensions were being dialled up after seven prisoners in the Maze Prison had just completed the first day of a hunger strike. The Republican prisoners were demanding that they no longer be treated as normal inmates and be given political status. Paul's dad explains that, essentially, they want to be treated as prisoners of war rather than as criminals. It is a demand that the British government are unlikely to accept. And, in truth, there's little sympathy anywhere for the group, outside of immediate Republican circles, given that a number of the hunger strikers were in prison for murder.

The *Irish Independent* editorial suggests that the prisoners had miscalculated the feelings of the general public down south who see in those inmates men who have committed terrible crimes: 'They are counting on the hunger strike and attendant publicity provoking a wave of emotion and possibly drawing more recruits to their organisation. In many ways, it is a final card to play – support for the Provisionals has been waning and this campaign is meant to halt the drain. If it does not, nothing will.'

\* \* \*

France begin at a ferocious pace at the Parc des Princes on Tuesday evening, stretching and turning Eoin Hand's Republic of Ireland all over the pitch as they look to find wide men Didier Six and Dominique Rocheteau. Jean Tigana, in only his second appearance for Les Bleus, makes an early statement of intent, dancing around the lunging Liam Brady and accelerating away from Frank Stapleton in the middle of the park and setting the French on a path towards the Irish goal. The visitors are chasing shadows, unable to get a foot on the ball. When they do in those first few minutes, back passes to Gerry Peyton are a feature as they look to break the French rhythm, which has been set unerringly early.

Michael Robinson is upended by Patrick Battiston on nine minutes – welcome to international football. Twelve minutes in, Lacombe gets away France's first shot in anger. Christian Lopez sweeps a long pass to the French left to find Six in space; one touch to control with his right and then a left-footed ball into the box for the onrushing centre-forward who gets a touch before Kevin Moran, but Peyton gathers comfortably.

A minute later, Six plays a lovely one-two with Platini and is in on goal but a fine challenge by Dave Langan robs the French winger as he prepares to shoot. France take the resulting throw-in quickly. Tigana crosses, Moran and Hughton can't reach it and Platini, lurking ten yards out and right of centre, kills the ball with his chest and passes it into the net past Gerry Peyton. Les Bleus lead.

The visitors try to be positive but their inability to retain possession sees France time and again exploit spaces in the Irish rearguard and midfield as they attempt to push into a more attacking posture. Eoin Hand's side's problems are compounded by being outnumbered in midfield as the French full-backs, Bossis and Battiston, push into the middle of the park at every opportunity.

On 16 minutes, a sumptuous pass from Platini finds Lacombe seven yards from goal. But the forward fluffs the chance and Peyton gathers gratefully. A minute later, the imperious Tigana finds Lacombe again in the Irish box, this time to the right of goal, but the overworked Irish keeper hustles ball and man out of play for a corner. However, the Republic of

Ireland fail to clear the set piece and Tigana once again picks up the ball in midfield, drives at the right-hand side of the Irish defence between Moran and Hughton and whips in a cross that barely evades Lacombe. The Irish fans breathe a sigh of relief.

But Eoin Hand's Republic of Ireland aren't in the City of Light as mere sacrificial lambs and, suddenly, the siege is lifted. Langan back near the corner flag finds Mick Martin 20 yards further forward in a little space. Martin turns, carries the ball over halfway and switches it inside to the supporting Mark Lawrenson, who immediately transfers it to the right wing and the overlapping Langan once more. The Birmingham full-back cuts inside and accelerates, running directly towards the French 18-yard box to the surprise of the French cover. Langan slips the ball to his left to Robinson, who, with his back to goal, lays it back to the onrushing Tony Grealish 20 yards out in a central position. The Luton man strikes cleanly and Dominique Dropsy is forced into making a fine save at full stretch to push the ball to safety.

Lawrenson's increasingly regular forays into midfield from his centre-half position are helping the Irish cause, redressing the midfield balance. The French storm abates and Eoin Hand's Republic of Ireland haven't been blown away. Balls to Robinson and Stapleton, who've been on the end of some meaty challenges from Léonard Specht and Christian Lopez, are now sticking. Grealish, Brady and Martin have wrested a greater say in the midfield battleground.

On 35 minutes, Martin once again picks out Langan's run. The full-back plays a lovely clipped ball into the feet of Stapleton to the right of the penalty spot. Stapleton shields the ball, then lays it off to the onrushing Martin, who chips it to the far post for the waiting Robinson. But Dropsy claws it off the striker's head. Robinson chases the clearance to the corner flag and turns it back to Brady, who crosses to the far post where Stapleton challenges and Martin plays the loose ball back across the six-yard box –and there's Robinson again! He beats Battiston to the header but he can't generate enough power and Dropsy gathers.

The game has been turned on its head. The boisterous crackle of the vociferous home crowd has been reduced, replaced by an uncertain hubbub. Early thoughts that the Republic of Ireland would go the way of the hapless Cypriots are replaced by a realisation that Eoin Hand's team have no intention of rolling over. Indeed, they are emboldened, pushing higher up the pitch in their efforts to harass their hosts, closing space, their tackling taking on an increasingly uncompromising nature. And then Liam Brady comes to life on the Irish left. He beats Tigana on the corner of the 18-yard box, leaves Battiston on his backside and beats Tigana again before curling in a delicious right-footed cross that Robinson and Moran (where did he come from?) are within a whisker of converting, with Dropsy stranded.

Lacombe lets his frustration at the Irish dominance boil over, scything down Lawrenson in the centre circle with a late, high tackle that leaves the defender in a crumpled heap and the Irish players and staff enraged. Two years previous, Lacombe had seriously injured David O'Leary in similar vein. He could count himself lucky to only receive a yellow here.

Lacombe's foul is the last meaningful action of a first half in which Eoin Hand's Republic of Ireland looked as if they might be swept away by a flood of French flair and flamboyance. But the nature of their recovery gives cause for both admiration and optimism as both sides depart down the tunnel.

The second period starts where the first ended. Eoin Hand's men are first to every ball and strong in every tackle. Didier Six is left in no doubt of the presence and determination of Dave Langan, the Irish defender upending the winger just after the restart and, minutes later, threatening to clear the Frenchman into the crowd along with the ball. The 1,500 Irish fans in the stadium find their voice in response.

Ten minutes in, the French launch their first attack in anger. Platini dribbles into the Irish penalty area and flings himself to the ground as Grealish challenges. The French captain implores the ref to consider awarding him a penalty but Augusto Lamo Castillo waves play on and the Irish launch a counter.

Langan feeds Robinson up the right, ten yards inside the Irish half. The Brighton man knocks the ball off for Stapleton, who drives forward 20 yards into the heart of the French half, before slipping the ball to his left and Brady. Brady, aware of the onrushing Hughton on his outside, draws Tigana before feeding the Spurs full-back, who is running at full tilt. Hughton sprints to the edge of the French area and unleashes a ferocious strike with his right foot but Dropsy beats it away.

And then it's the French who are on the attack. Lacombe comes deep to collect the ball, turns and finds Rocheteau free on the right. The winger moves inside, slips a pass to his right to Tigana and continues his run into the box. Tigana spots the run and finds Rocheteau with a magnificent return ball. But Langan reads their intentions. Covering across on to the penalty spot, the tigerish Irish full-back gets a vital tackle to clear the danger.

Fifty-seven minutes on the clock and the Republic of Ireland build another attack. Hughton feeds Heighway just inside the Irish half on the left. The Liverpool winger turns and attacks the space ahead, the French seemingly content to let him run deep into their half before challenging him. Heighway knocks a short ball to Grealish in centre field, 45 yards out. Grealish looks for the one-two but Heighway's heels are clipped by Battiston and the Irish have a free kick ten yards closer to the French goal.

Grealish and Brady stand over it but decide it's too far out for a shot, so Brady passes the ball right to Langan. The full-back crosses into the area but it's headed clear to the left-hand side. Heighway recovers the ball and returns it swiftly to the far post, where Kevin Moran challenges Bossis, wins the header, knocking it down to the waiting Robinson, who gleefully cracks it past Dropsy for the equaliser!

The small knot of Irish fans behind the goal dance as the Irish players celebrate what seems just reward. But then, no! Ref Augusto Lamo Castillo is pointing to his linesman and, to the disbelief of the Irish players, he disallows the goal.

There seems no obvious reason. But before the Irish players can remonstrate with the officials, France take a quick free kick

– for whatever infringement was deemed to have occurred – and make their way quickly towards Gerry Peyton's goal.

Rocheteau finds Platini, who feeds Tigana first time on the right of the Irish half while the visitors try desperately to get back goalside. Larios picks it up and runs across the edge of the penalty area, with the Irish still in disarray, but Lawrenson tackles magnificently and the men in green survive. Seconds later, though, Platini has possession again, just inside the Irish half. He spies the run of Six inside Langan and finds him. Six crosses low, Lacombe takes it on the penalty spot with his back to goal but there is Lawrenson again and his tackle prevents the French striker from getting a shot away, although it sends the ball past Peyton and off the foot of the Irish post and out for a corner.

A crazy, exhilarating two minutes of football that should see the visitors level but instead leaves them scratching their heads and very nearly two goals down. What was wrong with Robinson's goal? No time to ponder. To their credit, Brady and Co. don't let their heads drop and continue to search for a way back into the game. But as they continue to press forward, a pattern is emerging. As the visitors push more men into attacking positions, France look to counter with rapier-like thrusts, exposing gaps in the Irish cover as players get caught ahead of the ball.

On 66 minutes, Michel Hidalgo makes his first change – Jacques Zimako for Lacombe. The change electrifies the home side and reignites the crowd. The Saint-Étienne forward's pace, trickery and direct running unsettle the tiring and increasingly desperate Irish. On 75 minutes, he embarks on a mazy dribble down the left and into the Irish penalty area, Tony Grealish in hot pursuit. With Zimako about to strike, Grealish lunges. Zimako goes down. To a man – on the field and in the stands – the French appeal for a penalty. But Lama Castillo says no and play continues. Replays are inconclusive, although, had a penalty been given, the Irish could scarcely have complained.

Seconds later, Larios releases Rocheteau as France break up another failed Irish attack. But Peyton sees the danger and smothers the ball at the Frenchman's feet. The Irish keeper quickly releases Hughton and the Republic of Ireland go again. Lawrenson feeds Grealish and then continues his run forward to join the attack. Grealish trades passes with Moran, who is also staying well forward, and carries the ball to within 30 yards of the French goal. Grealish to Moran once more, then Moran cuts inside and finds Martin, who tries to find Brady just inside the box. But the ball is stolen by Jean Petit, who has come on for Platini. Tigana picks it up and releases Six just short of halfway on the right and the Irish are in deep trouble, with only Grealish and Langan trying to cover.

Six carries the ball 40 yards before slipping a lovely pass to his right to Zimako, who dinks a delicious finish over the sprawling Peyton and into the back of the net. Heartbreak for Eoin Hand's Republic of Ireland and surely no way back. They battle manfully right to the end. Peyton denies Larios and Zimako, Robinson forces a fine save from Dropsy and Gerry Ryan, on for Martin, prods the ball against the foot of the French post. But they're just the last vestiges of Irish defiance and they change nothing.

Mr Lamo Castillo blows the final whistle. The French players and fans celebrate. The Irish are left to wonder at what might have been. How might the evening have turned out if Robinson's equalising goal had been allowed when the Irish team were clearly in the ascendancy?

But there's also a sense of pride. Pride at how the Republic of Ireland didn't go under when the French were at their fluid best in that opening half an hour. At how they wrested back control of the game and tested the mettle of their extravagantly gifted hosts. Pride. Pride and regret.

\* \* \*

In the aftermath, Eoin Hand tells the press that, having controlled the last 15 minutes of the first half and the first 15 of the second, he is disappointed with the outcome. He's naturally bitterly disappointed about the disallowed goal. Eoin Hand is also somewhat bewildered, as he could see no obvious infringement. There was no question of offside and as to the suggestion of handball, the Irish manager maintains that the TV footage doesn't seem to support that idea either.

Kevin Moran, who'd challenged Battiston at the far post, denies that he handled the ball, insisting it was a clean header. The defender, who excelled on his first away night with the Irish team, sees the incident as pivotal in the game. Had the goal been allowed in a period when the team were on top, Moran argues, then an Irish victory wouldn't have been out of the question. Eoin Hand agrees. Anything could've happened had the goal been given.

But the Irish are getting used to it. Four years previously, the Republic of Ireland met France at the same venue in a World Cup qualifier and, trailing one to nil, saw a Frank Stapleton effort inexplicably chalked off. A year later in Sofia, John Giles was similarly penalised. In games and qualification groups of fine margins, such moments can change fortunes. The Irish view is that Tuesday night's decision by the Spanish referee may come back to haunt them when the final points are tallied.

But Eoin Hand isn't giving up. Eoin Hand has seen enough from his charges to believe that qualification isn't beyond them, despite the difficult task ahead. France boss Michel Hidalgo concurs. Expressing surprise at the attacking approach and spirit of the Irish team, he says he has nothing but respect for them and that they can still qualify if they attack the other teams in the group as they did here.

Eoin Hand admits that the margin for error for his side is narrowing all the time but he insists that there's a lot of football yet to be played in Group Two. For Eoin Hand, 11 points is the realistic target for the second qualifying spot and, with four games to go, that isn't an impossible tally for his side to amass. After all, there are eight points still to play for.

However, to achieve the 11-point target, Eoin Hand's Republic of Ireland will need to win both remaining home games, against Cyprus in November and France the following October, and take at least a point from each of their two away trips, to Belgium in March and the Netherlands in September.

Realistically, the task is an enormous one but, then, so is the prize. But on the evidence of the Irish performances thus far in the group, where they've gone toe-to-toe with three of European football's powerhouse nations, there's still plenty of cause for optimism.

## 1982 FIFA World Cup qualification: UEFA Group Two

|  | P | W | D | L | F | A | Pts |
|---|---|---|---|---|---|---|---|
| Republic of Ireland | 4 | 2 | 1 | 1 | 6 | 6 | 5 |
| France | 2 | 2 | 0 | 0 | 9 | 0 | 4 |
| Belgium | 1 | 0 | 1 | 0 | 1 | 1 | 1 |
| Netherlands | 1 | 0 | 0 | 1 | 1 | 2 | 0 |
| Cyprus | 2 | 0 | 0 | 2 | 2 | 10 | 0 |

# 8.

# Feasting on Minnows

JOHN GILES may not have believed that World Cup qualifying Group Two would be settled on goal difference after he oversaw the Republic of Ireland's 3-2 win in Nicosia in the first match of the qualifiers. But France's 7-0 win away to Cyprus in what looks like being a very tight group has brought the issue of goals into sharp focus for all concerned. And for Eoin Hand's Republic of Ireland, the need to inflate their 'goals for' column just in case is a key area of discussion ahead of the visit of the Cypriots on 19 November.

Details of the squad are released 12 days before the game. Most interest is focused on the inclusion of 24-year-old Pat Nolan of Limerick United. Eoin Hand, as player-manager of the club, has plenty of first-hand experience of the full-back, who has been capped twice for the Under-23s and had been a player of interest for both Blackpool and Wolves in recent years. Despite how prominently he has figured in the rise of the Shannonsiders, Nolan's inclusion in the squad at the expense of Arsenal's John Devine does, nevertheless, raise eyebrows.

Eoin Hand explains that Nolan's performances have been deserving of recognition. And with Chris Hughton and Dave Langan established as his first-choice full-backs, the Limerick player's inclusion means Devine has to make way. Heads are scratched all the same. John Devine has, after all, been figuring in Arsenal's first XI.

The only other uncapped player in the initial squad is Celtic's Packie Bonner. The 20-year-old keeper has displaced Peter Latchford as No.1 at Parkhead and has played more than 20 games in the first team.

Eoin Hand has also named Gerry Daly and David O'Leary in the panel. Both missed the Paris game and both are struggling with Achilles issues. Eoin Hand is hopeful that they'll be available for selection come the visit of Cyprus but will closely monitor both in the interim.

Daly's return, given the opposition and the midfield linkman's creativity and quality in front of goal, will be especially welcome for Hand. Over the last five seasons, the Coventry man ranks only second to Don Givens as the Republic of Ireland's top marksman.

On the Friday night before the squad announcement, Daly calls Hand to discuss his availability and his recovery from injury … and to clear the air. The next day he talks to the press. It was reported in the English media during the storm surrounding the FAI's UEFA appeal before the France game that Gerry Daly's priority was to play for Coventry City and that his interest in the international side was secondary.

Gerry Daly was upset that some fans believed what they read and heard, reporting that he was inundated with letters from fans expressing dismay and disappointment at his reported attitude.

Gerry Daly wants to make it very clear to Irish soccer fans that he's always keen to play for his country. That's been the case for the last seven years and nothing has happened to change his outlook.

Gerry Daly says that an interview he did with a local radio station in Coventry at the time of the World Cup wrangle had been seriously misinterpreted. He says that, in the radio interview, he did feel the need to explain that he felt a commitment to Coventry City, as they pay his wages. But his comments were distorted in a later newspaper article. Gerry Daly believes that he's always had a very good relationship with the Irish fans and that, deep down, they know he always gives 100 per cent to the cause. But he accepts that, given recent reports, some may have had their doubts.

However, Eoin Hand has no such concerns. He says that he's more than satisfied that the player's comments were taken out of context. He adds that anyone who's seen Gerry Daly in the green of Ireland would never have had any doubts as to his commitment.

The only question now is whether Gerry Daly will be fully fit to face Cyprus.

* * *

Eoin Hand trims his squad to 18 a week before the Cyprus fixture. Out go Limerick's Nolan, Paddy Roche of Manchester United, Palace's Gerry Murphy, and Mick Walsh of Porto. Walsh, who has been in scoring form after his move to Portugal, has probably the most cause to feel aggrieved. Two goals in three games, including a recent winner against Benfica, since his move from QPR left him hopeful of being part of Eoin Hand's matchday plans. But the big impression made by Michael Robinson on his debut and his own good form in front of goal have given the Brighton man the edge.

Roche's departure means that young Bonner will, at the very least, sit on the Irish bench for the game. Or, at least, that looked like being the plan until Celtic shed doubt over his selection. The Cyprus game clashes with Celtic's Scottish League Cup semi-final second leg against Dundee United on the same day and the Bhoys are reluctant to release Bonner for the World Cup qualifier.

Chaos and confusion reign in the week before the match. The FAI are reportedly ready to invoke UEFA regulations to ensure Bonner's availability. Eoin Hand, for his part, is somewhat reluctant to see the rule employed in this instance, preferring instead to discuss the issue with Celtic manager Billy McNeill and see it all resolved amicably. Celtic, for their part, appear somewhat unaware and then uncertain about the UEFA regulations, seemingly not having noticed the furore around player selection when the Republic of Ireland played France.

Meanwhile, the Scottish FA (SFA) is watching closely. They have suffered similar difficulties to the Irish in the past when looking for the release of players for international duty. Bill Richardson, the association's assistant secretary, says that the

SFA has every sympathy with the FAI and he hopes that they can get the player they want, as the application of the UEFA ruling would also help the Scottish cause in future.

Reportedly, Eoin Hand doesn't feel this is the best time to use the regulation as leverage, given that his side should overcome the Cypriot opposition regardless. However, the FAI, having fought so hard for the release of O'Leary, Stapleton, Daly and the others just a few weeks before, feel they must apply a consistent approach. After all, what would the English clubs think of them making an exception for Celtic in this instance?

On the Friday before Cyprus come calling, the matter is settled diplomatically. Eoin Hand decides to release Bonner to Celtic for their cup tie, recalling Paddy Roche in his place.

\* \* \*

David O'Leary is withdrawn from the Republic of Ireland squad the weekend before the qualifier. He'd missed both the Belgium and France games due to his protracted Achilles tendon injury. The player made a return for Arsenal on Saturday in their 2-2 draw with West Brom at Highbury and appeared to have come through the game unscathed. But Arsenal manager Terry Neill wasn't convinced and the player won't be released for international duty. Neill says it was apparent from the game at the weekend that O'Leary is not fully fit. And, so, he and the club felt it was advisable under the circumstances to withdraw him from the Irish squad.

Peter Byrne wonders in *The Irish Times* whether the decision was coloured by the recent sharp exchanges between club and country over player availability. But if there is an issue, no one in the Irish camp seems to want to raise it publicly. As with Bonner, maybe it's best left for another day. Maybe it's best to smooth things over. After all, Eoin Hand's Republic of Ireland are well capable of beating their visitors without both players.

In other slightly disquieting news, Mark Lawrenson has delayed his arrival in Dublin to see a specialist on a knee issue that has been causing him some discomfort in recent games.

However, Eoin Hand believes the issue won't be enough to see Lawrenson withdraw.

Liam Brady will also arrive late, missing Monday morning's training session at the Maccabi grounds. He played for Juventus on Sunday but is stopping over in London for a dental appointment before travelling on to join up with the Irish squad. There should be no issue as to his availability. Nevertheless, Eoin Hand won't announce his team to play Cyprus until after Tuesday morning's training session.

Meanwhile, a stone's throw from the Irish training base in Kimmage, there is consternation at Paul's house in Templeogue. Hopes that the game would be screened live have been dashed. Without floodlights, the FAI has had to schedule the game for a 2.30pm kick-off, right in the middle of the working day and 15 minutes before Paul gets out of school. The association recognise this isn't an ideal situation but the men in blazers are worried that putting the game live on the TV would further reduce the expected attendance, hence the TV blackout. And, so, Paul, without anyone to take him to the game, will have to settle for radio coverage and a highlights programme on RTÉ2 at 6.55pm.

Aged nine, Paul will readily confess that the FAI's coffers are not of especial interest to him. And he'll wonder loudly why on earth there are no floodlights to illuminate Lansdowne Road? But this is 1980. And this is the reality. Floodlights are an exotic adornment of just a few sports grounds around the country.

\* \* \*

Liam Brady and Mark Lawrenson arrive late Monday evening and train on Tuesday. Lawrenson allays any fears about his knee, explaining that the issue pertains to a cyst on the back of the joint. It can be uncomfortable at times but not enough to stop him playing. An operation may be required in the close season to remove it but, in the meantime, he plays on.

Frank Stapleton goes over on an already suspect ankle in the session. But after treatment, Eoin Hand is happy to include him in the team for Wednesday. There's only one change to the side that lost in France. Gerry Daly returns in place of the more defensive-minded Mick Martin. The Coventry's man's return could be seen as something of a risk, as he hasn't figured in his club's first team over the last three weeks. Indeed, he didn't figure in Gordon Milne's matchday side at the weekend. The Coventry manager felt Daly hadn't played sufficient minutes in the reserve side to convince him of his fitness. But with the Republic of Ireland chasing goals, Eoin Hand is prepared to take a chance on a player who has been a consistent scorer for the national team.

Notably, six of the players who figured in John Giles's side in their win over Cyprus in Nicosia – David O'Leary, Ashley Grimes, Jerry Murphy, Paul McGee, Gerry Ryan and Fran O'Brien – will not be in Eoin Hand's line-up at Lansdowne Road.

John Giles, however, has given his successor a full debrief on the opposition, who trained at University College Dublin on Monday and at Lansdowne Road on the eve of the match. The main team news of interest from the visitors' camp is that striker Kaiafas, who produced a goal and an assist when the sides met back in March, will figure. However, the Cypriots will be without centre-half Papadopoulos, a player who impressed in that first fixture and who often came between Cyprus and disaster that evening.

Very little is expected of the Cypriot side, however. After all, Cyprus have never won a World Cup qualifier away from home and have, in fact, only ever scored once on their travels. Naturally, there's an expectation that the Republic of Ireland should win the game convincingly. Eoin Hand knows the score but, on naming his side 24 hours before kick-off, he urges the fans and his players to be patient.

Too many people seem to think we should win by a bucketful of goals, he tells the assembled press. But the Cypriots will come prepared to defend in depth and, so, it may take time to break down their resistance. But if his players are patient enough to build methodically and the fans get behind them as they did against the Belgians and the Dutch, then Eoin Hand is confident that the goals will flow.

\* \* \*

Matchday and Paul is off school. Not very sick but sick enough. But while a day or two of recuperation from a heavy cold is probably required, he's not too unwell to perform his trawl of the paper. And he can do so before radio coverage of the match begins at 2.25pm. The midafternoon workday kick-off time due to the lack of floodlights is just one small symptom of the wider malaise that affects Ireland in 1980, a country and economy deep in a gloomy recession. Indeed, matters appear to be getting worse. Paul's matchday read of the paper under the watchful eye of his mother underlines that point.

*The Irish Times* reports that the number of people without a job was 28,000 more in October 1980 than it was in October 1979. Exacerbating the problem is the fact that voluntary emigration, so often the pressure release for the economy, isn't really an option, as labour markets are depressed in the traditional overseas destinations. And to make matters worse for those toiling to make ends meet, the inflation rate stands at 19 per cent. Paul has little idea what this means but he gathers from his mam that it's grim.

And there's yet more disquieting news from Northern Ireland. Paul wonders if there's any other kind of news from north of the border? It doesn't seem like it. *The Irish Times* reports that the British government is preparing for the possible deaths of the seven prisoners on hunger strike in the H-Block prison protests. A confidential assessment by the administration suggests that three of the seven will be at risk of death by around 6 December. Only a fortnight away. The condition of the other four is expected to be similarly critical around 16 December. Contingency plans have reportedly been drawn up to deploy greater numbers of security forces personnel to deal with widespread disturbances should the worst happen.

The ins and outs of the problems in the North are difficult for a nine-year-old in Dublin to comprehend. But the horror and the fear are not. The news on BBC Northern Ireland and on Ulster Television is always so full of tragedy, rancour and dreadful deeds. The juxtaposition to the news that you might sometimes see on HTV in Wales, when on holidays down in Wexford, for example, is startling. The news in Wales is so mundane. A strike. A robbery. A traffic accident. No murder and mayhem. No bombs and bullets.

Meanwhile, bombs and bullets continue to rain down depressingly in the dreadful Iran-Iraq war. And maybe worse still, chemical weapons. Iran has accused its neighbour of using these dreadful munitions in their attempt to seize the town of Susangerd, a key objective in the invading force's efforts to lay claim to the city of Ahvaz, capital of Iran's oil-producing Khuzestan province.

The war, like all wars, is characterised by claim and counter-claim. The Iranians claim to have cleared Susangerd of enemy forces. Baghdad claims to be tightening its grip on the town and to have destroyed three medium-sized Iranian warships in the Persian Gulf on the same day. Whatever the truth on the ground, the horror continues.

Meanwhile, former Swedish prime minister Olof Palme has arrived in Tehran on a special United Nations mission to listen, learn and clarify the positions of the two warring states. He'll later travel on to Baghdad. The war is only a couple of months old. Maybe he can find some formula for peace?

Maybe Mam shouldn't really make him read the paper, Paul thinks. Yes, he gets the point about improving one's vocabulary. But, God, the world seems such a miserable place when you get down to it. At least it is for so many, many people. But amongst all the sorrow and struggle, one story representing perhaps a tiny chink of light catches his eye. President Jimmy Carter has given the go-ahead for the export of equipment from United States company Caterpillar to the Soviet Union for the construction of an oil pipeline from Siberia to Western Europe. Not exactly the ending of the dread tension between the two superpowers but, with the world's future seemingly in the hands of the men in the Kremlin and those in Washington, news of any accommodation between both sides must be welcomed.

Then Paul reaches the sports pages and the football. Thank God for the football. At least there's that. The great escape. The great dreamscape. The troubles of the world put aside. Kick-off at 2.30pm on the radio and highlights after tea. Not the worst way to spend a sick day!

\* \* \*

The minnows of Cyprus start competently, winning the first corner of the game in the opening minutes. Playing a 5-3-2 system, they're clearly set to defend in numbers. But leaving two men forward suggests a certain optimism. Perhaps Eoin Hand's call for patience on the field of play and on the terraces was timely? The set piece comes to nothing and, almost immediately, the Republic of Ireland set about their task, taking control, stretching, twisting and turning their opponents.

Steve Heighway hugs the right touchline. Liam Brady plays at inside-left. Dave Langan and Chris Hughton push down the flanks as the Irish launch a series of attacks and press their opponents back. Brady has the first real opportunity nine minutes in, steering a Langan cross just wide. Seconds later, Michael Robinson spins on a ball from Heighway and is felled by the panicked Klitos Erotokritou. Referee Eysteinn Gudmundsson points immediately to the spot. The Cypriot defenders remonstrate angrily with the Icelandic official. Full-back Philippos Kalotheou is booked. He's restrained by keeper Constantino before he gets himself into more trouble. The Cypriot anger seems not to be at the actual penalty award but at the fact that one of their players had been lying injured in the box during the build-up.

Order is restored. Gerry Daly stands over the ball – a sea of expectant faces watches from behind the Cypriot goal on the South Terrace. Gerry Daly sends the keeper right and the ball left and the Republic of Ireland lead with ten minutes on the clock.

What composure the visitors showed in the opening exchanges evaporates. Cyprus struggle to cope with the strength and movement of Robinson and Frank Stapleton up front. They're struggling to track the runs of Hughton and Langan out wide. They're struggling to track the movements of Steve

Heighway, who appears to be everywhere. And they struggle with the Republic of Ireland's aerial prowess.

On 15 minutes, Liam Brady swings over a wicked corner. Kevin Moran, unchallenged, heads at goal. Constantino is stranded but Nikos Pantziaras heads the ball off the line. Two minutes later, Liam Brady sends over another wicked corner and Michael Robinson crashes a header off the crossbar.

The Republic of Ireland keep the pressure on. Twenty-four minutes in, Brady stands over another corner down the Irish right. He clips the ball to the near post, where Robinson is stationed. The Brighton man is beaten to the ball but it's cleared only as far as Dave Langan, 20 yards from goal. The Irish right-back heads the ball back into the box. Stapleton flicks it hopefully over his shoulder on the penalty spot. Pantziaras heads it straight up into the air. Gerry Daly wins the next header on the edge of the 18-yard box, Lawrenson has a swipe but the ball falls to Cypriot striker Sotiris Kaiafas, deep in his own area, to the left of goal. Kaiafas turns to knock the ball back to his keeper to relieve the pressure. But Daly, running from the edge of the area, somehow reads his intention, dashes to intercept and flicks the ball past Constantino. Two-nil. Daly, on the occasion of his 25th cap, takes the adulation of the South Terrace once more, his extraordinary anticipation deserving of their praise.

The Irish retrieve the ball from the Cypriot restart just a minute later. Brady, on the centre spot, turns and finds Chris Hughton to his left. The Spurs man attacks, accelerates past one challenge, slaloms past another, then another and then yet another and, in a thrice, he's at the byline, with the crowd roaring encouragement. His cutback is cut out in desperate fashion by the retreating Loucia, who clears, but only to Tony Grealish, 35 yards from goal with the midfield all to himself. The Luton man kills the ball with his first touch, shoots and scores with a rocket into the top right-hand corner of the visitors' net. What a goal! Three-nil to Eoin Hand's Republic of Ireland.

Cyprus are all at sea and are taking on a serious amount of water. They bail and pump as best they can but they're in danger of sinking without a trace. Ireland are remorseless in their quest for goals. On 28 minutes, Mark Lawrenson strides out of defence with the ball, 15 yards in from the right-hand touchline, and picks out Frank Stapleton with a slide-rule pass that cuts through the Cyprus midfield. The Arsenal forward, 40 yards from goal, controls and turns sharply before finding Michael Robinson moving toward the edge of the 'D'. Robinson, without breaking stride, cracks the ball into the roof of Constantino's net in spectacular fashion. What a way to open your international account! And what a way to win over the fans! Brilliant goal. Four-nil Ireland. And four-nil to Eoin Hand's Republic of Ireland at the break.

A minute into the second period, Liam Brady collects a pass from Hughton ten yards inside his own half, wide left. The Juventus man lifts his head, surveys the scene, then arcs a beautiful 45-yard diagonal ball from left to right on to Robinson's head. Robinson, displaying wonderful awareness and touch, guides the ball down to the onrushing Stapleton, who dinks a delightful lob from the edge of the area over the advancing keeper and into the net for number five. A partnership that showed promise in Paris is bearing fruit in Dublin.

The Republic of Ireland keep coming. The marauding Hughton curls one just wide of the far post, with Constantino rooted to the spot. From an incisive Heighway pass, Daly clips the crossbar when it looked easier to score. Then, in the 64th minute, Lawrenson, ten yards inside enemy territory, just past the centre circle, has time and space to pick out Brady 20 yards further forward. Brady, with his back to goal, spies Hughton in an advanced position to his right. The Spurs man gratefully accepts Brady's tidy knockdown and sets off on a mazy dribble, cutting inside the first challenge, driving through a second on the edge of the penalty area, shifting to his right to evade a third, before shooting low to Constantino's right for the Republic of Ireland's sixth!

Six-nil with 25 minutes to go. Eoin Hand's Republic of Ireland push on for more. Gerry Daly should bag his hat-trick on 74 minutes and then Steve Heighway cracks a sumptuous drive off the crossbar. But no more goals come. No matter, for the Republic of Ireland have recorded their biggest ever win in an international fixture, and dreams of the World Cup finals in Spain are reignited.

Eoin Hand praises his side for their discipline – both in defence and attack – in his post-match remarks. In such a game, it would be easy to take your eye off the ball, conceding a silly goal or two, as in Nicosia. And it would be easy to lose your focus at the opposite end of the field. If everyone tries to get on the scoresheet, then the scoresheet can suffer. If the game becomes too easy, you can stop doing the basics.

Obviously, Eoin Hand says, his team wanted to score as many goals as possible. But that requires tremendous discipline, so he was delighted with how his team responded to the challenge. If he did have a complaint, it was that the bumpy Lansdowne Road surface didn't help the home side in their endeavours. If anything, it favoured the visitors. This is the second home game in a row where the pitch has caused issues. Given the rent the FAI are paying the IRFU, the international football side might be entitled to expect better.

There is some disquiet amongst the media that the scoring stopped after Hughton's 64th-minute effort. However, Liverpool's Steve Heighway believes no one should underestimate the work required to amass such a tally, even against even a team of minnows when they stick every man behind the ball. To score a goal every 15 minutes on average, as the side did on the day, is a formidable achievement, he argues. With Liverpool, Steve Heighway explains, he's played against many weak sides in Europe and run up big scores but the players have had to work damn hard to do so. Steve Heighway believes that the Irish team completed a difficult task in a very satisfying manner.

Liam Brady is perhaps a little downbeat in his assessment. Or perhaps he just feels a realistic tone should be recorded. A team like Cyprus, he says, can make a mess of a World Cup group. The best time to assess the merit of the win and performance, the Juve man suggests, will be after the qualifying group has been completed.

Cyprus coach Kostas Talianos is proud of the efforts of his charges, despite the fact they have conceded 13 goals without reply in their last two matches. Kostas Talianos says that he thought his men did well considering they were facing an Irish side that, in his opinion, is a better than the French.

Later the same evening, Belgium beat the Dutch in a tight and tough affair in Brussels. Erwin Vandenbergh's 48th-minute penalty was all that separated the two sides in front of a raucous crowd of 58,000 in the Heysel Stadium. Despite picking up the two points, Guy Thys is seething after the match. He believes that the overly physical approach taken by the Dutch players crossed the line and was a 'disgrace to football'. Nevertheless, he believes the result puts his side on the road to Spain.

The Belgian manager also finds time in his post-match comments to praise the Irish performance against the Cypriots. He's looking forward to welcoming Eoin Hand's side to Brussels in the spring. They play football, he says, in the traditional way and the Belgian supporters will see a much more enjoyable game when the two sides meet than they just witnessed against their Dutch neighbours.

Back in Dublin, as the players and staff prepare to go their separate ways, there's a sense of satisfaction over a job well done. And with seven points from ten in a very competitive group containing three of Europe's giants, Eoin Hand's Republic of Ireland have grounds to be optimistic, even if, perhaps, the biggest challenges lay ahead.

In the four-horse race for qualification, the Dutch, with no points from their opening two fixtures, have the most ground to make up. But after five games, the Republic of Ireland are well in the mix. That's pretty much all anyone could ask for and more than many would've expected.

## 1982 FIFA World Cup qualification: UEFA Group Two

|                     | P | W | D | L | F  | A  | Pts |
|---------------------|---|---|---|---|----|----|-----|
| Republic of Ireland | 5 | 3 | 1 | 1 | 12 | 6  | 7   |
| France              | 2 | 2 | 0 | 0 | 9  | 0  | 4   |
| Belgium             | 2 | 1 | 1 | 0 | 2  | 1  | 3   |
| Netherlands         | 2 | 0 | 0 | 2 | 1  | 3  | 0   |
| Cyprus              | 3 | 0 | 0 | 3 | 2  | 16 | 0   |

# 9.

# A Stormy Night in Brussels

TO HELP Eoin Hand with preparations for the Republic of Ireland's crunch clash away to Belgium, the FAI arrange a friendly against Wales at Tolka Park on the north side of Dublin. The game is set for Tuesday, 24 February, an open date on the international calendar, one month before the game in Brussels.

However, a game designed to help fine-tune preparations for his side's most important qualification game to date becomes one of auditions. Injuries to and unavailability of players due to the friendly nature of the fixture – clubs are only required to release players for competitive games – sees Eoin Hand's side shorn of its stars. Brady, Stapleton, Robinson, O'Leary and Lawrenson, amongst others, don't travel to Dublin.

And while Hughton, Langan, Grealish, Givens and Daly all feature, the low-key fixture ends in a 3-1 defeat for the home side and an abject display. Grealish's 30-yard strike gives the Republic of Ireland a first-half lead and briefly illuminates the evening before Eoin Hand's makeshift side fall away alarmingly. None of those hoping to catch the manager's eye – among them Stoke City's Brendan O'Callaghan, Jimmy Holmes of Spurs and Everton's Eamonn O'Keefe – could fairly claim to have done so. It was a difficult night on which to perform and, in truth, the more established members of Hand's squad don't cover themselves in glory either.

All the auditionees must wait three weeks to find out if they might somehow have forced their way on to the plane bound for Brussels.

\* \* \*

The disappointment of the Wales display is tempered for Eoin Hand by the surprising efforts of Cyprus in three games they play between their 6-0 defeat in Dublin and late February 1981. Just before Christmas, Guys Thys's men travel to Nicosia hunting for goals. But the Cypriots are resolute defensively and Belgium labour to a 2-0 win with goals in either half from Vandenbergh and Ceulemans.

The sides meet again in Brussels on 18 February. And this time, the Belgians are really made to sweat. An all-out attacking approach sees them take a 2-0 lead, Gérard Plessers and Vandenbergh the scorers. But Cyprus dig in and score their first away goal of the qualifying group through Stefanos Lysandrou to leave it 2-1 at the break. Ceulemans restores the two-goal lead in the second period. But the home side just can't shake the predominantly part-time visitors, who grab their second goal, courtesy of Fivos Vrahimis, to set up a tense finish.

Four days later, Cyprus are in Groningen to face the Dutch, now under the guidance of caretaker manager Rob Baan after the January resignation of Jan Zwartkruis. And again, the Cypriots give a fine account of themselves. At half-time, they trail by a single goal – a lead and performance that see the Netherlands players booed off at the interval. Baan brings on Dick Nanninga, who scored for the Dutch in the 1978 World Cup Final, and the big striker turns the game, laying on of a goal for Cees Schapendonk on his international debut before adding a third ten minutes later.

The efforts of the Belgians and Dutch against the group's whipping boys give an entirely different complexion to the 3-2 win in Nicosia of John Giles's Republic of Ireland and, more importantly, to the 6-0 win in Dublin of Eoin Hand's side. The winter results see the Belgians draw level on points with the Irish, with a game in hand, and the Dutch pick up their first points. But Eoin Hand's Republic of Ireland have a superior goal difference. That said, with qualification looking like it will go right down to the wire, Eoin Hand knows that his team must come away with at least a point from Brussels to keep the pressure on their august rivals.

Cyprus have shown what can be done. Belgium must be respected. But they mustn't be feared.

## 1982 FIFA World Cup qualification: UEFA Group Two

|  | P | W | D | L | F | A | Pts |
|---|---|---|---|---|---|---|---|
| Republic of Ireland | 5 | 3 | 1 | 1 | 12 | 6 | 7 |
| Belgium | 4 | 3 | 1 | 0 | 7 | 3 | 7 |
| France | 2 | 2 | 0 | 0 | 9 | 0 | 4 |
| Netherlands | 3 | 1 | 0 | 2 | 4 | 3 | 2 |
| Cyprus | 6 | 0 | 0 | 6 | 4 | 24 | 0 |

Eoin Hand names his squad for the Belgium game on Monday, 16 March. The game is one of the most important in the history of Irish soccer and Eoin Hand is taking no chances. The emphasis is squarely on experience. The most notable changes to the squad that faced Cyprus are the return of Arsenal full-back John Devine and the inclusion of Everton keeper Jim McDonagh.

McDonagh has cemented his place as first-choice custodian with the Merseyside club over the course of the season. With Gerry Peyton having lost his form and his place between the sticks at Fulham, McDonagh must be considered as a serious contender in goal for the trip to Belgium. Clearly, Eoin Hand is looking beyond the Everton man's poor showing on his debut against Wales in what was a night to forget for almost everyone involved. And the fact that McDonagh has been performing well week in and week out at his club makes his inclusion sensible.

There'd been calls for the inclusion of young talents like Ipswich Town's Kevin O'Callaghan, an important part of his club's title challenge, and Liverpool youngster Kevin Sheedy, who had impressed in a recent Under-21 game against England. But Eoin Hand resists. Eoin Hand says such players will be in his thoughts for future games and campaigns but the game in

Brussels will be, in a football sense, one for men of experience. It will not be a game in which to experiment and, hence, Eoin Hand will be putting his trust in players with proven international credentials.

With the game just over a week away, the Irish manager will be keeping a pensive eye on the upcoming weekend fixtures in England, Italy and Portugal, hoping that the Republic of Ireland's key players come through unscathed.

As the players gather in the team hotel on the outskirts of a wet and windy Brussels on the Sunday before the game, news emerges that Gerry Peyton hasn't made the trip. The Fulham keeper injured his elbow in training with his club before the weekend and it has swollen alarmingly. Eoin Hand calls up Celtic's Pat Bonner as cover but it now seems nailed on that Jim McDonagh will make his competitive bow in the Heysel Stadium cauldron on Wednesday evening.

And there's concerning news about Brighton pair Mark Lawrenson and Michael Robinson and Arsenal duo David O'Leary (again) and Frank Stapleton. Lawrenson suffered knee ligament damage training with his club on Thursday. He didn't figure at the weekend against Stoke City and hasn't travelled to Brussels. However, there's hope, as the injury appears to have responded to treatment. Terry Conroy, Eoin Hand's assistant, tells the media that the player believes he's an 80-20 chance of making the game. However, for now, Lawrenson is staying in Brighton for more treatment. The plan is for him to have a fitness test on Monday morning, two days before the game, and if Seagulls manager Alan Mullery is satisfied the injury has cleared up sufficiently, the player will be on the first plane to Belgium.

Michael Robinson suffered a slight concussion against Leicester but he's expected to be okay for the game. Terry Conroy laughs it off. That sort of thing happens to Michael every other week, he jokes, as the forward is a very brave lad who sticks his head in when most players would think twice. He's hard as nails, says Conroy, and is very much looking forward to facing the Belgians.

O'Leary and Stapleton both played for the Gunners in their 1-1 draw with Norwich. Both were feeling a little sore but were expected to take part in the Irish training session on Monday morning. O'Leary reports that he's suffering from a niggling hamstring strain that he's had for a few months but he says it didn't really hinder him at the weekend and he expects to be good for selection.

Stapleton tweaked his knee in training the day before the Norwich game. However, he still played the full 90 and believes that by kick-off on Wednesday, he should be fine.

There is better news, however, in relation to the Republic of Ireland's continental contingent as Liam Brady and Mick Walsh arrive to join the squad on Monday afternoon, having come through their Sunday fixtures with Juve and Porto respectively. Brady is in ebullient form, having helped his club move to the top of the Serie A table. The Dubliner has settled in well in Italy and is currently the top foreign scorer in Serie A. He tells the press that he's very happy with his form of late and is really looking forward to the match on Wednesday night.

Meanwhile, it appears that the home side also have a goalkeeping issue. Jean-Marie Pfaff has been suspended until June for allegedly striking a linesman! In his stead, Belgium will be reliant on the efforts of Standard Liege's highly rated but inexperienced Michel Preud'homme, who'll be picking up only his second cap should Guy Thys give him the nod.

*　*　*

On Monday morning, Mark Lawrenson undergoes a fitness test at the Goldstone Ground under the watchful eye of manager Alan Mullery. It only lasts a couple of minutes. Lawrenson pulls up lame. Even in that time, Mullery reports, it was clear there was no way the player could hope to play on Wednesday. It's a bad blow for Ireland and a bad blow for Brighton. Mark Lawrenson is withdrawn from Eoin Hand's squad.

Monday also brings more worry in relation to David O'Leary's injury and some additional concerns in relation to Kevin Moran and Michael Robinson. All three sit out the

Republic of Ireland's two-hour training session some five miles outside of the Belgian capital.

The Arsenal defender's hamstring injury is worse than initially thought. He's undergone three sessions of treatment with physio Trevor Enderson in eight hours but the prognosis isn't encouraging. The injury is pretty serious at the moment, Enderson tells the media. And it's anybody's guess as to whether it will improve enough in time to let him play. Enderson puts O'Leary's chances at 50-50.

Moran is suffering from a badly bruised toe. But the feeling is that a painkilling injection before the game should see him right. Michael Robinson is nursing a tightness in his hamstring but his omission from the session is purely precautionary. The player himself assures reporters that even if the game had been on Monday, he would've played.

Irish spirits are lifted with news that Belgium's midfield general, the man who makes them tick, Wilfried van Moer, will miss the game. Van Moer won't recover in time from a rib injury suffered at the weekend with his club SK Beveren. As the Belgian side is built around the veteran, and their patterns of play rely heavily upon his presence, Guy Thys will be forced into a radical rethink.

For Eoin Hand, the news is a boost in a gloomy start to the week. The Belgians will definitely miss Van Moer, he says, and he's comforted by the thought that someone else has problems and that everything isn't entirely against his Republic of Ireland team. But it scarcely compensates for the loss of the increasingly influential Lawrenson.

\* \* \*

Gerry Peyton is out. Mark Lawrenson is out. And now David O'Leary is out. Eoin Hand's Republic of Ireland will have to play the crucial match against a formidable Belgian side in the forbidding Heysel Stadium without their first-choice goalkeeper and their preferred central defensive unit. It's a devastating blow, says Eoin Hand. Lady Luck, for reasons known only to herself, has decided to pull another stroke.

David O'Leary's left hamstring had undergone intensive treatment at the hands of team doctor Bob O'Driscoll and physio Trevor Enderson before he took to the training pitch outside of the stadium for a fitness test. Sprinting was a problem. Twisting and turning in a quickly convened five-a-side were also a problem. Eoin Hand tells the press that he wasn't happy with David O'Leary sprinting and turning, so he simply couldn't take a chance including him in the team.

Mick Martin and Kevin Moran will deputise. Had O'Leary been fit, Eoin Hand would've chosen Martin, rather than Moran, to fill in for Lawrenson. Eoin Hand explains that it was a case of judging Martin's experience and ability to read a game against Moran's strength and aggression. For this particular game, he felt Martin's strengths would be required most. But fate intervenes and both will play, the latter with the aid of a painkilling injection in his damaged toe.

Jim McDonagh and Martin are the only changes from the side that beat Cyprus in the Republic's last qualifier. The rest of the side have a clean bill of health.

On the eve of the game, the Belgian papers preach respect for the visitors but are confident of victory. *Le Soir* calls Eoin Hand's Republic of Ireland team a formidable side, using the fact that all 11 starting players play in the English First Division, which it dubs the hardest in the world, as evidence. *Le Soir* laments the absence of Van Moer and keeper Pfaff but it believes that having clubmates Gerets and Renquin with him in defence will help the talented but young Preud'homme in the Belgian goal.

Another paper, *La Derniere Heure*, offers blanket coverage of the game. It notes that it'll be a pivotal night in the qualification group, as the French and Dutch are also set to clash in Rotterdam. And should Belgium and France come out victorious, then the group may well be over as a contest.

In terms of the Heysel Stadium fixture, the Belgian paper picks out the Irish midfield for special mention, believing that Liam Brady, Gerry Daly and Tony Grealish have the ability to shock and compete with any opposition. Another player drawing the attention of the Belgian press is Michael Robinson. The burly striker didn't face Belgium in the first match-up and they admit to not knowing too much about him. That said, they are aware of his power and pace and the fact that he has notched 20 goals already this season for his club. His presence is causing a measure of apprehension.

Eoin Hand knows that securing a point could be vital. Losing wouldn't necessarily mean the end as far as his team's qualification ambitions are concerned but such a result would be damaging. But the Irish camp aren't thinking that way, Eoin Hand tells the media. They are targeting a point at least.

Liam Brady believes that, on the evidence of their recent struggle with Cyprus, Belgium can be beaten. He saw a video of that game and, in his opinion, Guy Thys's side certainly didn't look like the second-best team in Europe in that fixture. Yes, they are a supremely organised and disciplined team when allowed to sit in and play on the break. They showed this at Lansdowne Road, says Brady. But when they had to chase goals, as they did against Cyprus, Brady observes that they left themselves badly exposed at times. And being the home side on Wednesday evening, the onus will be on the Belgians to attack, something that Brady feels the Republic of Ireland can use to their advantage.

The Irish fans in Brussels seem to have an air of confidence about them also, writes Con Houlihan in the *Evening Press*. Some 6,000 are expected to descend on the stadium, a record travelling support and four times the number that visited Paris for the team's last away game. The swollen numbers suggest a growing belief in the capabilities of Eoin Hand's Republic of Ireland.

Houlihan notes that such is the confidence of some, they will not even hear talk of a draw! Their reasoning revolves around the current form of the Irish skipper with Juventus and the fact that Van Moer is sidelined. Steve Heighway's return to form and to the Liverpool first team also gives cause for positivity. And the involvement of new fan favourite Michael Robinson adds to the sense that a notable result can be achieved.

Con Houlihan reports, however, that the upswell in confidence may not be unconnected to the availability of the cheap and potent Stella Artois beer, which is being downed in copious amounts!

There's a general belief amongst the Irish football media present, amongst Con Houlihan, Peter Byrne of *The Irish Times* and Noel Dunne of the *Irish Independent*, that a draw is very much achievable. However, Mel Moffat of the *Evening Press* points to the Republic of Ireland's notoriously poor away record in competitive fixtures and suggests caution. The victory in Nicosia was the first such away win since Prague in 1967. And draws in such fixtures have been similarly thin on the ground.

Moffat does point out how there have been many hard-luck stories in the Republic's recent trips abroad, with disallowed goals ruining Irish hopes on foreign soil. Let's hope, he writes at the end of his pre-match preview, that tonight's tale is not one of similar woe.

\* \* \*

Paul reads the match previews in the *Evening Press* and then, as directed, the news. The front of the paper is dominated by a shocking attack on a British businessman in Trinity College, Dublin. Geoffrey Armstrong, an executive at British Leyland, had been speaking at a seminar organised by the Dublin Chamber of Commerce. Not long after he began, around 2.20pm on Tuesday, three gunmen wearing balaclavas burst into the university lecture theatre and shouted for everyone to freeze. One then approached Mr Armstrong and shouted that the action they were taking was on behalf of the H-Block prisoners and hunger strikers. He then shot the businessman three times in the legs before the gunmen made their getaway.

Thankfully, it seems, Mr Armstrong wasn't too seriously injured. But there is deep concern amongst the authorities about security ahead of the upcoming Eurovision Song Contest taking place at the Royal Dublin Society on Saturday, 4 April. Special security precautions are being put in place for the British entrants, a singing group by the name of Bucks Fizz.

There's also serious concern in tourism circles. The Irish hospitality industry had been expecting a massive inflow of visitors in the summer from Britain because of the favourable exchange rate for those across the water. But incidents like the attack on the unfortunate Mr Armstrong may cause many to rethink their plans.

One other story catches Paul's eye before he sets down the paper. Some of the Irish fans en route to Belgium hadn't been covering themselves in glory. Fighting broke out amongst groups of travelling fans on the boat arriving at Ostend and then on the streets of the town in the early hours of Wednesday morning. The local police arrived to deal with the trouble and reported that about 1,000 fans arrived on a ferry around 1am and that they were all drunk. The police quickly put them on a train to Brussels. Two Irish fans were arrested and kept in jail overnight but they were released without charge later on Wednesday morning so they could travel on to the game.

In another incident, the British Rail ferry the *St Columba*, which carried over 300 fans to Holyhead on the first leg of their journey to Brussels, was daubed with graffiti of, according to a company spokesperson, a very offensive nature. The spokesman remarked that the boat got more graffiti in one night than in the whole of the last three years! No one was apprehended for the incident.

With more and more Irish football fans following the team abroad, Paul's dad wonders whether they might get drawn into the scourge of hooliganism that has attached itself to the game in Britain. It'd be a shame if Irish fans were to end up going down the same route, he says. You'd like to think they'd be better than that. Anyway, compared to what Paul had seen on TV during the recent Euros in Italy, the incidents involving Irish fans seemed to be pretty tame stuff involving a few fools. Hopefully, that's all it would ever be.

To kill time after tea and before the match, Paul decides on a game of Subbuteo, featuring the Irish and the Belgians. Paul must play the part of both teams, as none of his brothers will play him. Paul recognises that this isn't ideal. But then the world is often less than ideal. Encouragingly, the Irish run out winners by two goals to one. Michael Robinson put the Irish in front on 36 minutes (Paul plays nine-minute halves, which he multiplies by five to help get realistic times). Belgium equalise through Ceulemans on 54 before Gerry Daly grabs what proves to be the winner on 72.

In fairness to the Belgians, they have had to play under difficult circumstances. Firstly, they were sporting the Liverpool kit, as Paul doesn't have Belgium. Secondly, some of them were carrying injuries, having been involved in a shocking recent incident where Paul's two-year-old cousin bit off and spat out the heads of a number of players before he was discovered and his rampage stopped. Gluing heads back on is tricky. The results not always as you might desire. But then the world and life can be that way. The Belgians just had to suck it up.

* * *

The din as the players emerge from the dressing rooms is deafening. A wall of noise, klaxons and air horns, the sound magnified by the Heysel Stadium bowl. But Eoin Hand's Republic of Ireland appear unfazed. Eoin Hand's Republic of Ireland are here on a mission. On the eve of the match, the Belgian paper *Le Soir* said that Belgium are the past masters at realising that it's the result that matters. Eoin Hand's Republic of Ireland may not be past masters in this regard but they, too, know the importance of the result. So they're not in Brussels to entertain. They're in Brussels to contain. To frustrate and, ideally, to strike. A point will do. And while they believe they can get two, a point will do.

The Belgians prod and probe. The Republic of Ireland are more than happy to use their keeper. Back passes to kill the crowd. Dampen the noise. Kill momentum. And for the opening quarter, nothing really happens. Then Belgium show their quality on 26 minutes. Anderlecht's Ludovic Coeck and Erwin Vandenbergh swap passes to release Jan Ceulemans but Jim McDonagh is alert and decisive and blocks for a corner. The resulting outswinger is attacked by the hulking figure of

Ceulemans once more. He arrives a fraction of a second ahead of Kevin Moran. It's not clear who redirects the ball but it is redirected and arrows for the left-hand corner of flat-footed McDonagh's goal. But Chris Hughton is there, on the post, to clear the ball to safety and elicit the first loud sigh of relief from the Irish fans in Brussels and the many glued to the TV coverage at home.

And the game slips into a lull once more. Eoin Hand's Republic of Ireland, superbly marshalled at the back by Mick Martin and directed in midfield by Liam Brady, hold possession of the ball for lengthy spells and are comfortable, much to the displeasure of the home crowd. They saw their side struggle against the lowly Cypriots and they're seeing their side struggle again. But the Irish are a different animal in terms of quality and this is becoming clear. Uneasiness is mixed with frustration all around the Heysel Stadium.

On 41 minutes, full-back Michel Renquin receives a quick throw from Raymond Mommens on the Belgian left, 20 yards inside the Irish half. He looks up and crosses deep into the Republic's penalty area. Hughton misjudges the flight of the ball and it sails over his head. Gerets, steaming in from the right wing, blindsides Heighway, steals the ball and shoots for the far corner. But, thankfully, he gets his angles wrong and the ball flies wide of McDonagh's right-hand post.

Just before half-time, Michael Robinson charges down the Republic of Ireland right but his dash is obstructed by Luc Millecamps on the right angle of the Belgium penalty area. Free kick Ireland. Brady, Daly and Grealish convene and discuss their options. Heighway hovers about 35 yards from goal in the centre of the park. Moran, Stapleton and Robinson are arranged across the Belgian 18-yard line. Referee Raul Fernandes Nazaré of Portugal walks along the edge of the penalty area past the Belgian two-man wall, tells them to stay ten yards back, then breaks into a trot toward the penalty area. Looking over his shoulder, Nazaré blows his whistle.

Daly and Grealish step away from the ball. Stapleton starts a run toward the penalty spot, clearly in a pre-planned move.

Brady clips the free kick just in front of his former Arsenal colleague and Stapleton gets there before the sprawling Preud'homme, diverting the ball past the keeper and into the goal before tumbling over the Belgian custodian.

The Belgians half-heartedly appeal for offside. The Belgians always appeal for offside. That's the professional thing to do. Walter Meeuws is lying prostrate on the turf. The Belgians then appeal for a foul on Meeuws. Referee Nazaré is in a spin. The ball is in the back of the net. Michael Robinson wheels away in delight. Stapleton stands up, arms aloft. Referee Nazaré turns to look at his linesman. It's clear the Portuguese official had positioned himself badly for the set piece and doesn't seem to really know what's going on or how the ball came to be nestled in the rigging. Raul Fernandes Nazaré looks quizzically at his linesman, who looks back just as quizzically. The linesman didn't signal for a foul or infringement as the ball rolled in. And then Nazaré makes his decision. The Portuguese referee disallows the goal. Bizarrely, his linesman raises his flag a split second later.

Stapleton's shoulders slump and he walks away disconsolate, almost as if he expected the referee's decision. Robinson, closest to Nazaré, is aghast and is first to remonstrate. He's joined quickly by Grealish, Daly and Moran. Brady turns his attention to the nearby linesman. They've been here before. We've been here before. Paris 1976, Sofia 1977, Paris again in October 1980 and now Brussels. Flustered Raul Fernandes Nazaré waves away the Republic of Ireland players and blows for the game to resume, while still surrounded by irate Irish faces. Belgium take their free kick and the Irish have no choice but to spring back into action, despite their disgust.

The beleaguered referee blows for half-time and becomes the besieged referee Raul Fernandes Nazaré as Eoin Hand's Republic of Ireland team and staff continue to question his decision.

As if to mirror Irish anger, booming thunder and spectacular lightning greet the second half. And Eoin Hand's Republic of Ireland take the field with renewed intent, with fire in their bellies but still, crucially, so crucially, with composure and skill. The disallowed goal shows that, officials aside, goals are possible. Belgium can be got at.

The brilliant Brady leads the charge. Receiving the ball wide left from Heighway, he pirouettes and skips away from Gerets's lunge, puts Millecamps on his backside and shoots low and hard from 20 yards. Preud'homme gathers safely and it is just as well for him, as Robinson arrives to punish any error. Belgium are on notice.

Minutes later, Langan's long free kick from just inside the Belgian half evades Millecamps. The ever-alert Robinson arrives behind him to volley from 14 yards but Preud'homme is there again to gather at the second attempt.

But the home side are one of Europe's best for a reason. They pick up the pace, the intensity and drive back Eoin Hand's Republic of Ireland. Kevin Moran is hurried into a clearance that only finds Meeuws in midfield. He spots Cluytens storming down the right and picks him out with a lovely arced pass. Cluytens takes it in his stride and swings over a wonderful cross, which is met by Ceulemans with a powerful header eight yards out. McDonagh reacts brilliantly and blocks with lightning quick reactions. Brady picks up the loose ball but is tackled and it cannons off his shins for a Belgian corner. The noise is deafening, the rain torrential. The Republic of Ireland defend their lines and survive.

But while the pressure mounts, Eoin Hand's Republic of Ireland hold firm and continue to threaten. On 73 minutes, Gerry Daly lifts the gathering siege with a perceptive ball down the right flank that picks out the rampaging Robinson. Sweeper Millecamps desperately tries to intercept but he can't live with the Brighton man and is brushed off as Robinson attacks the penalty area and shoots from an acute angle; Preud'homme, though, pushes his effort behind for a corner.

The Irish can make nothing of the set piece and are soon mounting a defiant defence of their goal as the time on the stadium scoreboard slips away. Ceulemans wins another header in the Irish area and Vandenbergh is primed to score but Langan gets his head in first and directs the ball over his own bar. From the corner, an almighty scramble. Cluytens toe-pokes for goal. McDonagh reacts brilliantly and Moran clears to touch out of the mud.

The rain hammers down. The decibel levels rise. Thunder and lightning abound. But Eoin Hand's Republic of Ireland refuse to yield. The clock ticks on. And still Belgium come. Ceulemans chases a ball to the left touchline and retrieves it, plays a quick one-two, evades Langan and sprints into the box away from the tiring Moran. The big Club Brugge forward spies his strike partner on the edge of the area and tees him up. Vandenbergh connects sharply but McDonagh saves superbly. The save of the night. Surely, Eoin Hand's Republic of Ireland have done enough. They certainly have given enough. No one could ask for more. But more is needed, as there's still three minutes left on the clock.

The home side, roared on by the frenzied Belgian fans, are increasingly desperate. Gerets attacks the Irish box to the right of the 'D' and launches himself into the area in an effort to win a penalty. The dive is extraordinary. The dive is comical. But Raul Fernandes Nazaré is convinced that a free kick 20 yards from the Irish goal is warranted.

McDonagh erects a five-man wall. The Belgians pack the box. The tall René Vandereycken stands over it. And then he clips one to McDonagh's left. The ball hits the crossbar and flies 20ft into the air above the six-yard box. The Belgians converge. Mick Martin and Chris Hughton try to challenge but, facing their own goal, the ball favours those in attack and the ball favours Jan Ceulemans. Mick Martin and Chris Hughton are powerless to stop him. Jan Ceulemans leaps highest and powers a header past the despairing Kevin Moran on the goal line.

Pandemonium and despair. The Belgians are a mass of celebration. The Heysel Stadium erupts. McDonagh, who had managed to regain his feet just as Ceulemans struck, collapses back to the turf. Mick Walsh chases the ref but it's not clear why. The rest of the Republic of Ireland players stand in shock and horror. Hands on hips. Heads in hands. On the Republic of Ireland bench, heads in hands. On the Heysel terraces, Irish heads in Irish hands. All over Ireland where the game is watched, the people sit and stand. Heads in hands. In Templeogue, Paul sits. Head in hands. Tears in his eyes.

A free kick in the last minute is surely the Republic of Ireland's last chance. Everyone is forward as Hughton fires in from the halfway line. Robinson leaps and connects but the ball soars harmlessly over Preud'homme's crossbar. The Belgians raise their arms aloft, the high flight of the ball a release. Triumph and release. The game isn't quite over but it feels over. And then it is over. Belgium find a way. Past masters.

The Republic of Ireland have lost matches before. But perhaps none stings like this one. Erwin Vandenbergh goes to shake Raul Fernandes Nazaré's hand. And then Dave Langan arrives. And then Mick Walsh. And then Liam Brady. The pain and anger spill out. The are no Irish handshakes for Raul Fernandes Nazaré. There is disgust instead. And disgust is voiced. Mick Walsh translates Liam Brady's choice words into Portuguese and the Juve man delivers those choice words in no uncertain terms. The anger is palpable. The anger is understandable.

\* \* \*

Eoin Hand is furious after the final whistle and berates referee Raul Fernandes Nazaré on the Heysel Stadium pitch. Eoin Hand is furious as he meets the press after the game and berates Raul Fernandes Nazaré once more. The press wonder what he said to the Portuguese official after the game. Eoin Hand says that first he asked Raul Fernandes Nazaré if he could speak English. When the ref nodded in the affirmative, Eoin Hand told him that he was the manager of the Republic of Ireland football team and that he thought he was a disgrace and a cheat. Eoin Hand can think of no reason for Frank Stapleton's goal to be disallowed. Any neutral in the stadium would agree that his players deserved to get something out of this game.

Eoin Hand says he believes it's more than a coincidence that this sort of thing keeps happening to the Republic of Ireland

and that he, his team and the FAI are sick and tired of having the dirty done to them.

Eoin Hand's players are also furious and upset. Gerry Daly tells the press that he's completely disillusioned. All the planning and the work counts for nothing when you come up against officials like those who oversaw the Brussels game, he laments. A dejected Tony Grealish says that no one should talk about the luck of the Irish any more after that game. He adds that it's been a long time since he's been reduced to tears after a game of football but he was on Wednesday night. Michael Robinson reveals similar frustration, tears flowing, he says, for the first time ever after a match.

Dave Langan is incensed. It's hard enough to beat 11 men away from home, he complains, but when that becomes 14, with the ref and the linesmen, then it makes a mockery of football at international level. The unfortunate Frank Stapleton tells the Irish media that, while playing with Liam Brady at Arsenal, he scored many goals like the one that was chalked off. Frank Stapleton believes the referee got himself in a muddle, was badly positioned for the free kick, didn't see the goal properly and then chickened out under the pressure.

Sheffield Wednesday manager Jack Charlton was also at the game. He was in Brussels scouting one of the Belgian players. The well-worked set-piece goal was as good as anything he'd seen this season, he says. Neither the referee nor the linesman indicated a foul when Stapleton put the ball in the net, Jack Charlton notes, so he can only assume that the referee panicked.

The Irish media are angry and sympathetic the day after the game. 'Rage Greets Belgian Farce' and 'Heartbreaking' are the headlines in the *Evening Press*. 'Robbed Again' laments the *Irish Press*. The *Irish Independent* goes with 'A Real Sickener', while *The Irish Times* headlines its front page with 'Cruel Disappointment in the Brussels Rain'. For the Belgian press, there's a sense of relief, admitting that it wasn't a good night for any Belgian with a weak heart. There is praise for Eoin Hand's team, with *La Derniere Heure* reporting that the Irish kept Belgian supporters in terror until the very last second.

Belgian manager Guy Thys is delighted with the result, if not the performance. And he is especially impressed by the midfield work of Irish trio Liam Brady, Tony Grealish and Gerry Daly. For him, though, Brady, in particular, stood out. He was often magnificent, Guy Thys tells the assembled press.

The compliments are generous. The compliments are correct. But they offer scant consolation for Eoin Hand's Republic of Ireland.

But a night of sorrow, anger and disgust for the players on the pitch and the staff on the bench was also a night of disgrace for some amongst the record travelling support. After the incidents in Ostend and on a ferry the previous night, there was worse to report, both during and after the game. Sadly, the *Irish Press* and *Evening Herald* record on Thursday that a section of the Irish crowd were involved in fighting on the broad expanses of the Heysel Stadium terraces. And, unfortunately, the bad behaviour continued afterwards in the city centre. Four Irish people were arrested in the stadium for assaulting Belgian supporters. A further 12 were arrested in Brussels after repeated clashes with locals. There were also reports of damage to hotel rooms in which some supporters stayed.

The *Evening Herald* report focuses on the actions of approximately 100 fans who chanted anti-British slogans throughout the game and seemed to be at the centre of much of the trouble. A hotelier in Ostend tells the paper that the Irish are the worst tourists they've ever seen in the city. A police spokesman in Brussels is similarly unimpressed. Belgium have had enough of the Irish soccer fans, he states, but rather than bring them to court, the Belgian authorities will tell them to vacate the country immediately.

Ignominy on top of heartache. A wretched night in Brussels in every conceivable way.

\* \* \*

As Eoin Hand's Republic of Ireland fall to defeat in Brussels, Michel Hidalgo's France suffer the same fate, with the same scoreline, in Rotterdam. Arnold Mühren's superbly taken free kick early in the second half condemns the French to their first defeat in the group and revives Dutch hopes after their poor start.

Now, to reach the 11-point total that Eoin Hand believes will be enough to book the passage to Spain, his team must win their remaining two games – away to the Dutch and home to the French. Even then, they'll likely need France, Belgium and the Netherlands to cancel each other out if they're to get over the line. That's still possible, given that Belgium and France must play each other twice and the Netherlands must play Belgium in Rotterdam and, in the group's penultimate game, France in Paris.

The sense that goal difference may settle the two qualification spots continues to grow. So, somewhat oddly, Cyprus may well be cast in the unlikely role of kingmakers, as they must play the Netherlands in Cyprus in late April and France in Paris in the group's final fixture in December.

## 1982 FIFA World Cup qualification: UEFA Group Two

|                     | P | W | D | L | F  | A  | Pts |
|---------------------|---|---|---|---|----|----|-----|
| Belgium             | 5 | 4 | 1 | 0 | 8  | 3  | 9   |
| Republic of Ireland | 6 | 3 | 1 | 2 | 12 | 7  | 7   |
| France              | 3 | 2 | 0 | 1 | 9  | 1  | 4   |
| Netherlands         | 4 | 2 | 0 | 2 | 5  | 3  | 4   |
| Cyprus              | 6 | 0 | 0 | 6 | 4  | 24 | 0   |

# 10.

# Staying Alive

EOIN HAND'S Republic of Ireland bounce back from Brussels in most impressive style a month later. A 3-1 win over Dr Jozef Venglos's Czechoslovakia, the reigning Olympic champions and the side that finished third in the Euros, reminds those present of just what the Irish side are capable of. The more so given it is achieved without Liam Brady, Tony Grealish, Mark Lawrenson and Michael Robinson.

Kevin Moran scores two headers on that April evening, with Frank Stapleton bagging the other goal. There are notable displays from squad players John Devine, Ashley Grimes and Mick Walsh. Young Ronnie Whelan of Liverpool makes his debut, as a replacement for Gerry Daly. And Ipswich Town's 19-year-old left-winger Kevin O'Callaghan, who has been playing his part in his club's Division One and UEFA Cup campaigns, plays a stormer.

However, the news from the Republic of Ireland's World Cup qualification group and the fixtures being played on the same evening is less encouraging. France beat Belgium 3-2 in Paris. A win for the Belgians, who took an early lead through Vandenbergh, would've put them on 11 points and within touching distance of qualification. Such a result would also have seriously dented French hopes, leaving them on four points from four games and with tough trips to Brussels and Dublin to come. At this stage, it would probably suit the Irish for Belgium to pull away and leave a three-way shoot-out for second place. But France's victory leaves them just a point behind Eoin Hand's Republic of Ireland with two games in hand and gives Michel Hidalgo's men hope that they can still top the group.

The Netherlands' narrow win in Cyprus also moves them to within a point of the Irish, having played one game less. But the 1-0 scoreline does little for their goal difference.

Ultimately, it looks as if the Republic of Ireland will need to win both of their remaining fixtures, away to the Netherlands and at home to France, if they are to qualify. Three points from those two games could be enough, if other results fall their way.

### 1982 FIFA World Cup qualification: UEFA Group Two

|  | P | W | D | L | F | A | Pts |
|---|---|---|---|---|---|---|---|
| Belgium | 6 | 4 | 1 | 1 | 10 | 6 | 9 |
| Republic of Ireland | 6 | 3 | 1 | 2 | 12 | 7 | 7 |
| France | 4 | 3 | 0 | 1 | 12 | 3 | 6 |
| Netherlands | 5 | 3 | 0 | 2 | 6 | 3 | 6 |
| Cyprus | 7 | 0 | 0 | 7 | 4 | 25 | 0 |

Eoin Hand names a strong squad for the short end-of-season tour to West Germany and behind the Iron Curtain to a Poland undergoing much social upheaval.

The Republic of Ireland manager picks a squad of 20, mindful that he'll be without Liam Brady, who'll be chasing Serie A glory with Juventus late into May. He expects others to cry off too. Eoin Hand picks his squad of 20 but the FAI blazers do not like his squad of 20. They question his selection, particularly the inclusion of Paul McGee and Gerry Ryan, two players who have rarely figured since Eoin Hand took charge.

The FAI blazers would prefer that he bring two younger players instead to gain experience. Eoin Hand disagrees. Eoin Hand insists on his squad of 20. This is the first time since taking the job that he's been questioned by his employers. But Eoin Hand took the job on the basis that he'd select his squads. He took the job after his predecessors had worked to give him such power. Eoin Hand isn't about to back down. And Eoin

Hand does not back down. Eoin Hand stands his ground. And the FAI blazers yield.

But that victory is about as good as it gets for Eoin Hand in relation to the tour. West Germany's second-string side comfortably beat Eoin Hand's Republic of Ireland 3-0 in Bremen on Thursday, 22 May. Indeed, it could well have been worse, so dominant were the home side and so lethargic the visitors. The performance was hard to credit given that the Irish side featured many of the players who so impressed against the Czechs three weeks earlier. In fact, only Brady, Hughton and Lawrenson are missing from the side that lost so cruelly in the Heysel Stadium. Eoin Hand doesn't sugarcoat things in his post-match comments, calling it the worst performance since he took over as manager and adding that his team failed to even execute the basics of the game.

Six days later, the Republic of Ireland are in Bydgoszcz to face a powerful Polish outfit. Lawrenson and Hughton return to the starting XI. But while the performance is marginally better, the result is the same and, again, the touring party are somewhat flattered by the scoreline.

One depressing display is bad enough, says Eoin Hand, but when it happens twice, it's too much of a coincidence. The Irish manager says that his players were completely flat, with no zest about their performance, and puts it down to end-of-season tiredness.

If the tour was aimed at building confidence ahead of the crucial World Cup qualifier in Rotterdam in September, then it failed. But there's no question this wasn't the Republic of Ireland side witnessed throughout the qualifying campaign. They looked mentally and physically jaded after a very long club and international season. The tour is best forgotten. Holidays are the order of the day.

* * *

When the football season resumes in late August 1981, several of Eoin Hand's squad have been on the move. Frank Stapleton and Mark Lawrenson have made big-money transfers to Manchester

United and Liverpool, respectively, for fees reportedly in the region of £900,000 (sterling). Tony Grealish has left Luton Town for Lawrenson's old club, Brighton. Steve Heighway is no longer at Liverpool. He's no longer even in England. Steve Heighway, at 34, is in the United States looking to prolong his career in the North American Soccer League (NASL) with Minnesota Kicks. Don Givens is also no longer in English football, having signed for Swiss side Neuchatel Xamax. Goalkeeper Jim McDonagh is no longer with Everton and is now back with Bolton Wanderers.

All of them are included in Eoin Hand's preliminary squad for the World Cup qualifier with the Netherlands when he names it on 31 August. Gerry Daly and Mick Walsh are the most notable absentees. Daly will miss the game through a one-match suspension – the result of an accumulation of bookings picked up through the campaign. Walsh has a cartilage problem. The former's absence is the biggest blow; his goals, creativity and work rate have been crucial to the progress of the Irish side. Young guns Kevin O'Callaghan, Ronnie Whelan and Gary Waddock, all just 19, are called up.

There is some doubt as to the availability of Steve Heighway. The FAI have contacted Minnesota Kicks seeking his release for the fixture but have heard nothing back. He's named in the squad, as the association seem happy that no news is good news and the US club should have no objections. Should his release not be agreed, O'Callaghan is an option to replace him wide left. However, so poor were the Ipswich youngster's showings in Bremen and Bydgoszcz that Hand was moved to suggest that perhaps he'd been introduced to senior international football just a little too soon. Then again, that should be balanced against O'Callaghan's impressive involvement in Ipswich Town's excellent 1980/81 season, during which he made 34 league and cup appearances as they finished runners-up to Division One champions Aston Villa and won the UEFA Cup.

Two days later, Eoin Hand reduces his squad to 18. O'Callaghan is one of the players omitted, with Heighway's involvement confirmed. The others are Preston full-back John Anderson, Fulham keeper Gerry Peyton and QPR midfielder

Gary Waddock. Peyton's omission would now seem to underline that going forward, Jim McDonagh and Packie Bonner will fill Eoin Hand's keeper berths.

There is a slight question mark over the fitness of Chris Hughton. The Spurs full-back misses his club's defeat to West Ham on the night Hand cuts his squad. Spurs manager Keith Burkinshaw says the player has a thigh muscle injury and it'll be touch and go as to whether he'll play at the weekend against Aston Villa. If he misses that game, his place on the plane to Rotterdam will be in doubt.

Meanwhile, Eoin Hand is travelling back from Zurich where he and assistant Terry Conroy watched the Dutch lose 2-1 to the Swiss in a friendly. Conroy observes that, while the Republic of Ireland are likely to face a largely different line-up when the two sides meet next week, the Dutch pattern of play won't change and, hence, the Zurich trip may prove useful.

On their return, they learn that Ashley Grimes has withdrawn from the squad. The Manchester United player has been suffering from a virus that he hasn't been able to shake. Believing he simply won't be match fit, he pulls out of the squad. John Anderson is recalled in his stead.

\* \* \*

Kees Rijvers, who's taken over from Jan Zwartkruis as full-time Netherlands coach and overseen spring victories against France and Cyprus, will rely on experience and physicality for the clash with the Republic of Ireland. So, Simon Tahamata, who scored the Dutch goal at Lansdowne Road, is left out of his 16-man squad. The Standard Liege winger is not considered suitable for what Rijvers expects to be a rugged affair. Eight of the squad are 29 years old or older. Seven of the squad have experience of either the 1974 or 1978 World Cup finals.

Five players plying their trade outside the Netherlands are chosen. Five players well known to Irish football fans. Five players well known to all football fans. The great sweeper Ruud Krol of Naples, player of the season in Italy. Right-winger Johnny Rep of Saint-Étienne. Defender Michel van de Korput of

Torino. And midfield duo Frans Thijssen and Arnold Mühren of Ipswich Town, two players who have lit up English football in recent times. Indeed, the former was voted Footballer of the Year in England for the 1980/81 season. This is by no means the experimental outfit that lost in Dublin under Jan Zwartkruis a year previously.

The match at Feyenoord's imposing De Kuip stadium is expected to be a 50,000 sell-out. The Dutch have dragged themselves back into contention in the group but their hopes of qualification, like those of their opponents, remain on a knife edge. That said, if they win their remaining three group games, they can finish on 12 points, which would surely see them on the plane to Spain. But these are three tough games. Eoin Hand's Republic of Ireland at home. Guys Thys's Belgium at home. Michel Hidalgo's France away. On the evidence of the group so far, taking all six points looks unlikely. But not impossible. What is certain, however, is that a win over the Irish will put Eoin Hand's men out of the picture. And a defeat for the Dutch will likely end their own interest. A draw? Well, a draw will leave the Dutch needing to beat both the Belgians and the French to book their tickets. Any margin for error will have evaporated.

The Dutch squad will not gather in their training camp in Zeist, around 50 miles from Rotterdam, until the day before the game. They plan to train behind closed doors. Kees Rijvers, with no injuries to report, will not name his side until just an hour before kick-off to keep his opponents guessing.

* * *

On Sunday, 6 September, 14 of Eoin Hand's Republic of Ireland squad gather in London before flying to the Netherlands. There should've been 15 but Chris Hughton will not be travelling. The Spurs full-back, a fixture in Eoin Hand's side, has been withdrawn by Keith Burkinshaw. Hughton missed the weekend's game with Aston Villa. Burkinshaw waited until the very last minute to see if the full-back's thigh muscle injury might respond to treatment. Clearly, that hasn't been the case.

There's better news of Frank Stapleton. The Manchester United striker took a heavy blow to his ankle shortly after scoring his first goal for the club in their 2-1 home defeat to Ipswich. Stapleton played on but manager Ron Atkinson was sufficiently concerned after the match to suggest that the forward wouldn't make the Rotterdam game.

Frank Stapleton, it appears, had other ideas. And, after consulting the club doctor, he travelled to London to join his Republic of Ireland team-mates. Eoin Hand reports that the diagnosis is of heavy bruising rather than any kind of ligament tear. Frank Stapleton's ankle will be heavily strapped. Frank Stapleton will not take part in the Republic of Ireland's initial training sessions on Monday. But Frank Stapleton should be good for Wednesday night.

Kevin Moran, who hasn't played for a fortnight, will also be on the flight to Amsterdam and the one-hour coach journey to Rotterdam. Kevin Moran broke his nose in a reserve-team game against Blackpool but the teak-tough Moran passes himself fit for action. He has no worries about the injury. If he's selected, then he'll be happy to play, he says.

By Monday afternoon, the rest of the squad have arrived. Liam Brady from Italy. Don Givens from Switzerland. Steve Heighway all the way from the United States. All figured for their clubs at the weekend and none were asked to tog out for training. Brady and Heighway are afforded some extra rest, while Givens sits out training as a precaution over a neck strain.

On the eve of the game, Eoin Hand's Republic of Ireland train away from prying eyes at the cavernous De Kuip. Eoin Hand must replace Chris Hughton and Gerry Daly. Hughton's place is almost certain to go to John Devine, who came back into the fold in the friendlies with Czechoslovakia and West Germany B. Eoin Hand may well consider playing Mark Lawrenson in that position. The defender has been settling in at Liverpool and has figured at left-back in recent games. However, with David O'Leary fit, Hand will surely look to play his best centre-back pairing and, hence, Mark Lawrenson should start at centre-half.

Kevin Moran and Mick Martin would appear to be vying to fill the gap left by Daly. Moran played in that position in the ill-fated summer tour and has played in ten of the Republic of Ireland's last 11 matches. But, despite currently being out of favour at Newcastle, Mick Martin's versatility and experience make him the more likely candidate on the night.

Whatever Eoin Hand's decisions, he's decided to play Kees Rijvers at his own game and won't reveal his hand until just before kick-off. It's not a policy he'd normally favour, Eoin Hand tells the media. But if the manager of one of the strongest footballing countries in the world, playing at home, decides to adopt such a tactic, then Eoin Hand has no intention of facilitating him by announcing his team early. If he can make things awkward for his opposite number, Eoin Hand says, then he certainly will do so.

\* \* \*

Bookings against Cyprus and Belgium mean that Gerry Daly won't be in Rotterdam. He is gutted to miss out on such a huge fixture. Gerry Daly hasn't travelled to the Netherlands to see the game. But Gerry Daly will be travelling – some 60 miles – to hear it! The Republic of Ireland midfielder will drive from his Coventry home to Derby where he'll be able to pick up the RTÉ match broadcast on his car radio. Gerry Daly not only believes that his team-mates can get a good result in Rotterdam (he thinks the Dutch aren't as good as the Belgians) but he also truly believes the Republic of Ireland can qualify for the World Cup.

Without wanting to make excuses, Daly believes that bad refereeing decisions have really impacted the Republic of Ireland's campaign. And not just this campaign, other recent campaigns as well. He admits the Republic's away record has been poor. But he insists that very often good performances haven't been rewarded and that the Republic of Ireland have been very unfortunate with both bad luck and referees who weren't, in his opinion, totally honest. Those decisions have disheartened the team at vital stages in matches. It hurts, Gerry Daly says, when a goal is disallowed and, no matter how professional you are, such a decision is bound to affect you.

Unsurprisingly, the role of the officials is on the minds of those within the Irish camp. David O'Leary is confident the team can handle the occasion. And he's hopeful that the Republic of Ireland will get the rub of the green, something they've not had to date in qualification. It's certain to be one of the toughest and most tension-filled games of his career, the 23-year-old tells reporters, but, for him, this Irish team has matured a lot in the past few years and they can handle themselves quite well in such situations. Remember, he says, that only some bad refereeing prevented the team from shocking both France and Belgium away from home. He believes the competition owes the Republic of Ireland something, so Rotterdam may be where the Irish get some kind of reward.

Eoin Hand confesses to having similar thoughts. He feels his players have proven they can handle themselves abroad but believes they just haven't had a fair crack of the whip. But for controversial refereeing decisions, he says, defeats in France and Belgium might have been wins or draws. All he's asking for from the officials are fair decisions. If we can get that, says Eoin Hand, then that will be half the battle.

The referee for the game is Vojtech Christov from Czechoslovakia. He took charge of the European Cup Winners' Cup Final between Arsenal and Valencia 18 months ago and has a good reputation for even-handedness. Hopefully, this is the case and Vojtech Christov's name won't be on everyone's lips come Thursday morning.

\* \* \*

Matchday comes but Paul has four hours to kill before a ball is kicked in earnest at the De Kuip. Home from school, he grabs a snack and then gets fifth class homework out of the way. Paul's been back in school just over a week, the lazy days of the summer holidays left behind. But it's still decent outside and the light won't fade until after the game kicks off at 7pm, so someone will be out on the green for a kickabout or three-

and-in, a game of kerbs or something at some stage to help pass the time.

First things first, of course. The newspaper. Mam has had a map of the world put up on the breakfast-room wall. She's a firm believer that her kids should know where they and other people are in the world. The map helps bring news, whether it be in the paper, on the radio or on TV, to life. It adds important context.

Today, the biggest news is close to home. The map isn't required. Two young Royal Ulster Constabulary (RUC) men, one 19, the other 20, were killed in a landmine explosion in Co. Tyrone. The mine had been placed by the Provisional IRA in a culvert at the side of the road between the villages of Pomeroy and Cappagh. It detonated, most likely by remote control, as a two-car RUC patrol passed. The two dead policemen, constables John Montgomery and Mark Evans, were hurled, along with their vehicle, more than 50 yards by the bomb. Their violent deaths brought to 20 the number of security forces personnel killed in Northern Ireland since the death of hunger striker Bobby Sands four months earlier.

Cardinal Tomás Ó Fiaich, the Catholic primate of All-Ireland, was unyielding in his condemnation of the attack, a stance that drew the ire of the Provisionals. According to the *The Irish Times*, Cardinal Ó Fiaich said that the killing of the RUC men should be called by its proper name – murder. He went on to say that the thought of the two young men being blown to bits by fellow countrymen, perhaps equally young, would give rise to feelings of revulsion in everyone who has an ounce of decency. Cardinal Ó Fiaich called for an end to the carnage.

The Provisional IRA's leadership in Dublin responded, saying that the cardinal's condemnations of violence always seemed to coincide with IRA actions only.

To the map and Poland. Tensions between the Solidarity movement, the first independent union in the Eastern bloc, and the Polish government continue to simmer. Solidarity is pushing for the right of workers to self-management, the right to manage the state-owned and run enterprises in which they work. And the right to appoint their own managers. Solidarity is calling for a national referendum on the matter. It may read like pretty mundane labour relations stuff from a Dublin suburb but, in reality, the fact that Solidarity exists at all is a crack, albeit small, in the very fabric of the Soviet-controlled edifice behind the Iron Curtain.

The Polish military newspaper publicly accuses Solidarity of using worker self-management as a springboard to a takeover of power. Perhaps more importantly, the TASS news service in Moscow makes the same accusation. The Kremlin is also agitated by Solidarity's call for workers to rise in other Communist bloc countries in similar fashion. Could Moscow seek to intervene with more than words?

Paul's eye catches one more story, again involving the shadowy men in Moscow. The Soviets have sharply rejected suggestions that the KGB, the Soviet security police, was behind the assassination attempt on Pope John Paul II in May. They brand the claims reported in *The Guardian* as disinformation and anti-Soviet slander. The English paper reported on suspected links between the would-be assassin Mehmet Ali Agca, a Turkish citizen, and Communist agents. The implication seems to be that the Soviet regime was perturbed at the feelings stirred up by the Pope's dramatic visit to his Polish homeland in 1979.

However, according to the report in *The Irish Times*, Western diplomats in Moscow feel that, despite the difficulties the Polish papal visit caused, the Soviets would be highly unlikely to have authorised such an attack.

In the four months since the Pope was shot, many theories, according to *The Irish Times* story, have surfaced about who was ultimately behind the attempt on his life. Aside from the Soviet theory, there's a suggestion by a Soviet magazine distributed in Italy, *USSR Today*, that the US Central Intelligence Agency was behind the attack, given the differences between Washington and the Vatican over America's involvement in troubled El Salvador. And not long after the shooting, the Italian paper *Corriere della Sera* quoted unnamed Moroccan sources as saying that Libya's Colonel Gaddafi had ordered the shooting to destabilise the international order.

Ultimately, according to *The Irish Times*, what's generally accepted is that the Turkish gunman wasn't a lone wolf attacker. Someone helped him escape jail in Turkey, where he was in detention for the murder of a journalist. And, following his escape, someone paid for his luxurious travels through North Africa and Europe before the assassination attempt. But police and prosecutors didn't, as yet, know who or why.

* * *

Leaving the world of espionage and international intrigue behind, Paul heads outside after tea for a few games of kerbs with John from up the road before match coverage begins at 6.50pm. John is a quality kerbs practitioner. Paul feels that if there were a professional circuit, John, even though aged only ten, could make an impression. He may well be world class. Meanwhile, in the bowels of the De Kuip stadium in Rotterdam, Kees Rijvers and Eoin Hand reveal their hands.

For all the smoke and mirrors, Eoin Hand's team lines up very much as expected. John Devine will fill in for Chris Hughton at left-back. Mark Lawrenson and David O'Leary will play in central defence. It's the first time the two have played there together since Nicosia and the first time Eoin Hand has been able to pair them. Perhaps unsurprisingly, Mick Martin gets the nod over Kevin Moran in midfield.

Eoin Hand's decisions probably were never going to influence the XI chosen by Rijvers. By the same token, given Eoin Hand had relatively little room for manoeuvre, the selection made by Kees Rijvers probably wasn't going to force the Republic of Ireland manager into any kind of rethink. The phoney war was probably all a little pointless. But it added to the drama and tension all the same.

That said, while Kees Rijvers was expected to pick an attacking line-up, his decision to select two central strikers, in Cees van Kooten of Go Ahead Eagles and Ruud Geels of PSV Eindhoven, at the expense of a defensive player raises eyebrows. But just how the Dutch will shape up won't really become apparent until after kick-off. Clearly, Krol will sweep and Ben Wijnstekers will go man-to-man on Liam Brady, as he did at Lansdowne Road. Brandts and Van de Korput will likely pick up Stapleton and Robinson between them. But how will the rest of the side line up? And if they do all go man-to-man, bar Krol, will the Dutch be a little light in wide defensive positions, as Kees Rijvers hasn't selected any orthodox full-backs?

All will be revealed in the ensuing 90-odd minutes. At 7pm Irish time, 8pm local time, Frank Stapleton stands over the ball with Michael Robinson, awaiting Mr Christov's signal to begin the game. The noise inside the De Kuip is thunderous. The atmosphere electric. A shrill blast of the whistle and the Republic of Ireland kick off.

Stapleton bypasses Brady and rolls the ball back to Mick Martin in the centre of Irish territory from the kick-off. Martin controls and plays it directly back to Stapleton in the centre circle. The Arsenal striker moves left and knocks the ball into the path of the galloping John Devine. Bizarrely, the Arsenal full-back has acres of space to attack. In fact, the Dutch are all at sea, perhaps looking to pick up those they are to mark and seemingly unaware of the immediate danger of the overlapping Irish left-back. John Devine charges, unchallenged, to the edge of the Dutch penalty box before curling a delicious low cross behind the home defence as Michael Robinson arrives, unmarked, at the penalty spot. The Brighton striker, perhaps as surprised as his opponents, lunges for the ball and connects but can only steer it past Piet Schrijvers's right-hand post.

The De Kuip gasps. The home side may need a win. They may be set up to get a win. But Eoin Hand's Republic of Ireland are here on business. Right from the off, the Irish intent is clear and the Netherlands will have to fight for anything they get in this game.

The Dutch are jolted into action. A minute later, Johnny Rep collects the ball from a throw, ten yards in from the left touchline. The Saint-Étienne winger skips past Dave Langan and whips a dangerous cross toward the penalty spot. But Mark Lawrenson holds off the muscular Geels and Jim McDonagh claims.

The opening exchanges are played at high intensity. The Dutch shape starts to become clear. They appear to be playing four in attack! Rep on the left and Ajax's quick and elegant Tschen La Ling on the right are pushed up almost as high as the two forwards. Kees Rijvers is looking to occupy all four Irish defenders at once. It's a bold ploy. Elsewhere, Krol, as expected, is the free man at the back. Ernie Brandts is picking up Stapleton, while Van de Korput is clearly assigned to shadow Robinson. Wijnstekers will look to nullify the threat of Liam Brady, while also looking to patrol the centre of the park when the Dutch are in possession.

The Ipswich Town duo of Mühren and Thijssen sit either side. A bold formation indeed, but a risky one. One that leaves space on the flanks for Eoin Hand's Republic of Ireland to exploit.

Four minutes in, Krol receives a pass from La Ling just inside the Irish half and swings the ball left to Rep. The winger runs at Langan again but this time the Irish full-back comes out on top, before sending the ball down the Irish right to Robinson, just short of halfway with Van de Korput in attendance. The burly Irish striker takes the ball into his body, then surprises his marker by spinning away and accelerating into the Dutch half. Krol covers and Van de Korput recovers to nick the ball away from Robinson – only for the Dutch to play a loose ball into the middle of the park that's snapped up in centre field by Heighway. Heighway quickly transfers the ball left to Devine, who's once again in acres of space. Devine drives at Ernie Brandts and for the byline and whips over another dangerous cross that Schrijvers bats away to safety.

Three minutes later, in what is a breathless opening, La Ling picks up possession inside his own half before dribbling 20 yards and finding Van Kooten, who has drifted to the right touchline. The Go Ahead Eagles man finds the sweeper Krol, who has advanced to the edge of the centre circle in the Irish half. Krol carries the ball ten yards, then unleashes a long-range strike that flashes past McDonagh's left-hand post. The Dutch are finding their rhythm.

Having settled, their players now drift and float, the fluidity of their play and movement making life uncomfortable for the visitors.

Ten minutes on the clock and Michael Robinson fouls Van de Korput, who has switched to the right flank. Krol takes the free kick, finding Thijssen in centre field. Thijssen strikes from 30 yards and the ball whistles just over Jim McDonagh's crossbar. More of the game is being played in Irish territory, although the Dutch only have two long-range attempts on goal to show for it and Jim McDonagh is yet to make a save of note.

The Irish keeper retrieves the ball from the ball boy and kicks long upfield. Van de Korput beats Robinson in the air. The ball drops to La Ling on the right side of the field, ten yards inside the Irish half. But before he can skip away, he's fouled by Devine.

Ruud Krol, the Dutch captain, takes the free kick short to La Ling, who takes off on another run across the Irish midfield with Devine in tow. La Ling plays the ball to Rep on the Dutch left and he steps inside Langan and crosses but David O'Leary clears. Rep picks up the ball once more and chips it toward the penalty spot – but McDonagh is there to grab the ball and relieve the building pressure.

The Irish keeper sees Heighway just to his left and rolls it to the winger. Space in front of him, Heighway advances ten yards, then plays the ball infield, looking for Brady. But the alert Frans Thijssen intercepts and immediately plays Van Kooten into the right side of the 18-yard box before continuing his run. Van Kooten controls, then reverses the pass inside to the unmarked Ipswich man, who connects before an Irish player can get close, and steers the ball past McDonagh and into the back of the net. The Netherlands one, the Republic of Ireland nil. Eleven minutes gone. Steve Heighway hangs his head. A risky ball has turned into a disastrous ball. A dreadful goal for the visitors to concede.

The roar is deafening. The roof is raised. The home fans believe. The home players believe. And now the Dutch dominate. Dominate the ball. Dominate territory.

On 17 minutes, the Dutch win a free kick down their right, some 35 yards from goal. Mühren and Brandts stand over it. A cross to the big men surely? No, Mühren knocks it 15 yards to his left to Wijnstekers, who drives it from distance. McDonagh is beaten all ends up but the ball whizzes just over the angle of post and bar. Wijnstekers is not just a man-marker. He isn't just the smotherer of Liam Brady. Wijnstekers can play. And when the Dutch have the ball, he does play.

Three minutes later, Johnny Rep stands up Dave Langan once more and Johnny Rep beats Dave Langan once more. And Johnny Rep crosses to the penalty spot, where Geels controls and lays it off for the charging Wijnstekers. And Wijnstekers drives for goal once more but drives the ball over the top once more. Relief for the Republic of Ireland but the Dutch onslaught continues.

La Ling dances down the right. Balletic and powerful, he beats Brady and then Devine before squaring to Wijnstekers. Wijnstekers rolls it to Mühren, who shuttles it on to Rep on the left wing. Rep, who has tormented Dave Langan in the opening quarter, beats the Irish right-back yet again and then he beats the covering Mick Martin before pulling the ball back from the byline to Mühren 12 yards out. Mühren shoots past McDonagh – but Mark Lawrenson is there to clear brilliantly off the line.

Eoin Hand's Republic of Ireland can't breathe. They're being smothered, overrun. The midfield four struggle to cope. O'Leary, Lawrenson, Devine and Langan at the back are overworked, as Rijvers's front four stretch them, occupying them all across the pitch.

But Eoin Hand's Republic of Ireland have been here before. And Eoin Hand's Republic of Ireland can fight and they do fight. And Eoin Hand's team can play and play they do. Brady, for once finding space, plays a long diagonal pass from left to right that Stapleton chases and catches close to the Dutch corner flag. Stapleton turns to face Brandts, then plays a wonderful ball with the outside of his right boot to Heighway, who is attacking the near post. Heighway connects but can only find the side netting. A warning for the home side.

And then something of a lull as both side draw breath. The Dutch have put in a massive opening 25 minutes and now they must rest a little. The drop in intensity allows the visitors to get back into the game. Mark Lawrenson gets more involved in the play, carrying the ball through midfield and into Dutch territory. Tony Grealish drops deep to pick up possession, while Liam Brady plays further forward, trying to free himself from the attentions of Wijnstekers and create space for others in the middle of the park.

Good combination play out from the back sees Grealish advance towards the Dutch goal. He's bundled over as he finds Stapleton. The Arsenal man lets fly from 25 yards but it is comfortably held by Schrijvers. However, the pattern of the game is changing. The Republic of Ireland are getting more of the ball – getting a proper foothold. Pressing higher as the Dutch retreat.

Devine steals possession off La Ling in the 38th minute and finds Heighway in the middle of the Irish half. The winger is allowed to advance ten yards into Dutch territory before finding Langan wide on the right. Langan, in turn, finds Stapleton just inside the penalty area with a lovely chipped ball. Stapleton holds off Brandts and lays it off to the advancing Martin, whose shot is blocked. The ball is only cleared as far as O'Leary, 15 yards inside the Dutch half. O'Leary picks out Heighway on the right side again. Heighway to Langan, the full-back slipping it inside to Grealish, who fires a rocket from 30 yards. Scrambling across his goal, Schrijvers is relieved to see it fizz only inches past his right-hand post.

Eoin Hand's Republic of Ireland are on top now. Now, the Dutch find it hard to breathe. Now, it's the Dutch who are struggling to deal with the fluid movement of their opposition.

Five minutes before half-time, the home side break out. Rep switches wings and picks up a ball from La Ling. The Ajax man crosses deep for Geels but McDonagh fields and immediately releases Langan on the right. The Netherlands are momentarily out of shape, with both wingers still on the Irish left, so Langan has open water in front of him, which he quickly exploits. The

Birmingham player crosses halfway, considers a pass to Brady, but the Juve man is closely marked by Wijnstekers, so Langan finds Martin in the centre circle instead. Mick Martin swiftly transfers the ball to Brady, who has stolen a yard on his marker, and Brady plays a lovely weighted pass down the right wing to Heighway. The Minnesota Kicks man cruises down the flank, surveying his options. He has time, as no Dutch player seems willing or able to close him down. Mick Martin makes a run to the near post, drawing the attention of the home defence, while Heighway swings over a wonderful cross to the penalty spot for Michael Robinson to attack. The Brighton forward catches the volley perfectly and its 1-1!

'Oh, a super goal!' roars RTÉ commentator Jimmy Magee as Robinson dashes away in ecstatic celebration. And it is a super goal. Pandemonium amongst the 5,000 travelling supporters. Pandemonium in Templeogue. Pandemonium in Paul's sitting room. Oh, a super goal!

Eoin Hand's Republic of Ireland are inspired. 'This is a display of real courage,' says Jimmy Magee. And it is, it is. And it's a display of craft and know-how and of no little skill. Eoin Hand's Republic of Ireland see out the last few minutes of the first half in the ascendancy, the Dutch in shock and left chasing shadows.

The home crowd is similarly rocked, reduced to discontented muttering as Mr Christov blows for half-time. As the teams head for the dressing rooms, the Republic of Ireland players do so to strains of 'You'll Never Walk Alone' from the ebullient travelling support. This is a game that can be won if the men in green hold their nerve and continue to do the right things.

\* \* \*

While kettles are boiled up and down the land at half-time, there's consternation in Paul's house. The Nordmende nine-button touch TV his dad received for long service at work has decided that it would prefer them to watch only the channel, RTÉ2 as it happened, on button two. It does this of its own volition at the time of its choosing, suddenly switching to that channel at the most inopportune of moments.

It had been on its best behaviour in recent days but, at half-time, it decides it has seen enough of events in Rotterdam and clearly feels – no, insists – that *Taxi* on RTÉ2 is preferable. Now, *Taxi* was enjoyed in Paul's house, as it was in many others. But tonight was not the night. But try as they might, switching to button one would see the Nordmende revert to button two before you could even sit down.

The short-term, needs-must solution, as directed by Paul's dad, was to whip open the little door below the buttons and manually retune the TV so that RTÉ1 was now on button two. Crisis averted; the second half is ready to begin.

\* \* \*

Eoin Hand's Republic of Ireland begin the second half as they finished the first, keeping the ball, pushing numbers forward, probing the spaces afforded out wide. But Kees Rijvers has made a change at the interval, bringing on midfielder Jan Peters for striker Geels in a bid to wrest back control in midfield. And the change seems to make a difference after the Republic's confident start.

Krol dispossesses Stapleton and swings it left to Rep. Rep, on halfway, attacks Martin and then Langan before moving the ball through midfield to Van Kooten. The forward holds it up, then finds Krol again. He drives towards the right side of the penalty area and releases the ball to Mühren, who pushes it left before dinking it back toward goal. A cross? An attempted lob from an acute angle? It doesn't really matter, as the ball floats delicately over the desperate McDonagh. Thankfully, for the visitors, it lands gently on the top of the net. RTÉ commentator Jimmy Magee and the De Kuip crowd think it's a goal and react accordingly. But it isn't and the Republic of Ireland survive.

The Dutch pick up the pace. Grealish loses the ball 40 yards from McDonagh's goal. Jan Peters finds Van Kooten on the edge of the 'D'. Van Kooten initially drifts away from the penalty area, then turns and feeds La Ling, who is free down the Dutch right. The winger takes a touch, then stands one up into the penalty area, where Van Kooten has continued his run. The striker is first to the ball, heading down and hard in textbook fashion, but McDonagh blocks with his legs and then grabs the ball at the second attempt.

The Dutch have their dander up. The Irish struggle to keep possession. They dig in, try to stay with their opponents. But it's hard.

On 58 minutes, Rep charges down an attempted pass from Langan 40 yards out on the Republic of Ireland right. Van Kooten, increasingly influential, controls the loose ball in centre field, turns gracefully and flicks it right to Mühren, who launches a cross into the Irish box. Van Kooten wins the ball and, as it drops to his feet, he gently slips it to his right for La Ling, who is arriving and has the goal at his mercy. But the winger can't keep his feet and slices the ball horribly wide.

Kees Rijvers rolls the dice once more on the hour mark, replacing La Ling with the speed, power and experience of René van der Kerkhof. Eoin Hand makes a change, too, as Brighton's Gerry Ryan comes on for the tiring Steve Heighway.

Sixty-five minutes on the clock and the Dutch build once more. Van de Korput drives a long ball from centre field to the right wing and Van der Kerkhof, who is fouled by Devine. The big winger takes the free kick quickly to Peters, who sets off infield, switching the play to Rep on the left. Rep ducks inside Langan and turns him. Langan, in desperation, lunges from behind and brings down Rep just inside the area. Mr Christov blows his whistle and points to the spot. There can be no complaints.

The Dutch No.10, Arnold Mühren, stands over the ball. He takes a couple of steps back and then drives it low to McDonagh's left. The Bolton keeper gets fingertips to the ball but can't keep it out and it's 2-1 to the Netherlands. A punch in the guts for Eoin Hand's Republic of Ireland. A punch in the guts for the travelling 5,000. And a punch in the guts for all watching at home.

But there's still lots of time. There's still hope. This Irish team came back before. They can come back again.

A minute later, they win a free kick 25 yards out and in the centre of the park. Liam Brady shapes to hit it, then shifts it to his right for David O'Leary, who strikes powerfully but wide.

With 18 minutes left, Ronnie Whelan warms up on the touchline as physio Trevor Enderson checks on Mick Martin's well-being. Martin waves Enderson away for now, as McDonagh rolls a ball to Langan on the right. Langan shifts it 20 yards to Martin in the middle of the Irish half. Martin turns and strokes the ball to John Devine. Devine trades passes on the left with Ryan, then returns the ball to the middle of the field, where Mark Lawrenson has advanced. Lawrenson's ability and willingness to carry the ball from deep into opposition territory has become a feature of the game and one the home side have struggled to counter.

The Liverpool man sees space ahead and drives into it – then plays the ball again to Martin, who has drifted all the way across the Dutch back line. Lawrenson continues his run down the right flank and Martin rolls a pass into his path. Lawrenson accelerates, shoulders Krol out of the way, reaches the byline and whips in a cross. Dutch keeper Schrijvers can't reach it and the ball zooms over his head across the six-yard box, where Frank Stapleton dives ahead of a Dutch defender to divert it brilliantly into the net. What a header! And we're all square again! Two-two!

The home side respond. They need a win here. Mühren releases Rep down the left and he pulls the ball back to Peters 25 yards out. Peters strikes but the ball flashes past McDonagh's right-hand post.

Mick Martin's race is run – his legs reduced to stumps. On comes young Ronnie Whelan of Liverpool for his first competitive fixture. What a moment for him and his watching parents, who have travelled to the game! And what a game to be introduced into!

Thirteen minutes left and Jim McDonagh easily fields a cross from Krol before throwing the ball quickly to Liam Brady,

30 yards from the Irish goal on the right. For once, Brady has a little space and time. Whelan darts forward, while Stapleton drops close to halfway on the touchline. Stapleton is Brady's choice and the Manchester United man controls the ball before pushing it past Van de Korput to Whelan. The youngster strides confidently infield, then checks, turns and plays a lovely ball into the path of the indefatigable Langan down the right. He crosses beautifully from near the corner flag. Michael Robinson arrives, soars but just can't get over the ball – and it sails over the Dutch crossbar to the relief of the 45,000 Dutch men and women present.

Desperation sets in as both sides search for openings and a winner. A win would be massive. A defeat a death knell. Ruud Krol pushes further and further forward. Wijnstekers pays less attention to his man-marking duties and pushes on also. Rep picks up the ball on halfway. Does this man never tire? The Dutch winger drives past Whelan and, suddenly, there's no midfield cover. So, he races to the penalty area, Langan now in his wake. But, as Rep prepares to pull the trigger, Mark Lawrenson steams in with a superbly timed challenge, blocking the ball behind for a corner. A moment of defensive brilliance. World class.

Four minutes left. A short period of incessant pressure sees the visitors force three consecutive corners. But Eoin Hand's men fail to take advantage. The Dutch sigh with relief and regather themselves. The game is attack and counter-attack. Burst and counter-burst. A breathless end to the game!

Ryan loses possession and René van der Kerkhof powers down the Dutch right for one final attack – but the extraordinary Mark Lawrenson is covering across. He matches Van der Kerkhof's pace, then executes the most wonderful of sliding tackles on the edge of the Irish area, sending the Dutch winger sprawling and coming up and away with the ball.

Mr Christov blows for a foul – but before Eoin Hand's Republic of Ireland can complain, he checks his watch and blows the final whistle. And that's that. Two-two in Rotterdam. Neither side wanted a draw and both played to win. But, as is often the case in such circumstances, a draw is the result. News, however, of France's 2-0 defeat in Brussels offers crumbs of comfort. The dreams of both sides are still alive, if only just.

* * *

Pride and regret, the overwhelming feelings after an enthralling night in Rotterdam. Pride and regret, not just about this game but pride and regret over the campaign. The Republic of Ireland's hopes of travelling to Spain now hang by the slenderest of threads. Their destiny no longer in their own hands. But there is massive pride in how Eoin Hand's Republic of Ireland have stood toe-to-toe with three of Europe's most powerful football nations. However, there's also regret at mistakes made on this night when a draw doesn't really help the cause. And regret at the mistakes of others, of officials in Paris and officials in Brussels.

Football is a cruel business, Eoin Hand tells the press after the game. But he believes that no one can deny that if his team do qualify for Spain, they'll have done so very much on merit. Tonight we made mistakes, Eoin Hand says, mistakes that might have shattered any team. Yet the strength of the team, he continues, was such that, in the end, they may well have won. Eoin Hand believes that his charges showed huge character in finding a way back into the game and he's very proud that his players were equal to that demand.

Eoin Hand feels his side have played enough good football across the competition to more than merit a place in the finals. And he argues that, when you consider how bad refereeing decisions away to France and Belgium robbed the team of points, you realise how unlucky the Republic of Ireland have been in this group.

Kees Rijvers feels his team could've won the game, bemoaning their inability to take the chances they created. But, at the same time, the Dutch manager is full of praise for his team's opponents. It was a fair result, he tells the media, for if his team should've scored more goals after taking that early lead, then it'd also be fair to say that the Irish team played some excellent football subsequently. Kees Rijvers tells the press that he watched Eoin Hand's Republic of Ireland perform exceptionally well without getting the reward they deserved in Paris and Brussels and that now people will realise just how good a side they are.

Kees Rijvers finishes by saying that it's a pity that so many good teams should be drawn together in the same group. With only two to qualify, the finals in Spain will be the poorer for the absence of the others.

The day after the match, the Irish football press reflect that sense of pride and regret, with the pride being very much to the fore. For Peter Byrne in *The Irish Times*, it was one of the Republic of Ireland's best performances in years, an outstanding night in the annals of Irish sport, flawed only by two lapses in concentration.

For Mel Moffat in the *Evening Press*, it was a 'wonder display', while Con Houlihan of the same parish was most taken by the front-foot manner of the Republic's performance, having endured so many sieges on foreign soil in the past. For him, it was probably the senior international side's best display away from home since the 2-0 victory over England at Goodison Park in 1949! And no matter what the future holds in relation to qualification, Con Houlihan believes that the Irish football public will remember the game as one of the greatest occasions in the history of football on this island.

So, the Republic of Ireland have just one game left to play and there's still hope, albeit slim, of qualification. Given the very unpromising nature of the draw, to be in with a shout as the final hurdle approaches is worthy of high praise. But to qualify, a series of unlikely results and most probably a long wait are required.

After Rotterdam and France's defeat in Brussels, the qualification table looks like this:

## 1982 FIFA World Cup qualification: UEFA Group Two

|  | P | W | D | L | F | A | Pts |
|---|---|---|---|---|---|---|---|
| Belgium | 7 | 5 | 1 | 1 | 12 | 6 | 11 |
| Republic of Ireland | 7 | 3 | 2 | 2 | 14 | 9 | 8 |
| Netherlands | 6 | 3 | 1 | 2 | 8 | 5 | 7 |
| France | 5 | 3 | 0 | 2 | 12 | 5 | 6 |
| Cyprus | 7 | 0 | 0 | 7 | 4 | 25 | 0 |

At best, Eoin Hand's Republic of Ireland can finish on ten points. To do so, they'll need to beat France at Lansdowne Road on 14 October. Even then, however, Michel Hidalgo's men could still pip them to qualification on goal difference if they beat the Dutch in Paris on 18 November and Cyprus at home in the group's final game on 5 December.

The Dutch can finish on 11 points, the same as Belgium's current tally. But that will require a win over the Belgians on the same day as the Irish welcome Platini and Co. to Dublin and another away to France in Paris.

Ultimately, for the Republic of Ireland's World Cup dream to become reality, they need to beat France and hope for a draw between France and the Netherlands or for the Dutch to lose or draw at home to Belgium and beat the French.

Unlikely, improbable, but not impossible. And that slim hope and the desire to support a team that has impressed and inspired throughout the campaign will mean that Lansdowne Road will be bursting at the seams in just over a month's time when Les Bleus come to town.

# 11.

# Hope Springs

A WEEK and a half out from the crucial visit of Michel Hidalgo's France to Dublin on Wednesday, 14 October, one news story dominates in Paul's household. News has broken that tickets have been secured for the big game. Paul and two of his older brothers, plus two next-door neighbours, will be at Lansdowne Road for the occasion. This'll be Paul's first ever international match. Indeed, it'll be his first ever game in which match tickets are required.

The fact that Eoin Hand's Republic of Ireland team can still squeeze on to a flight to Spain – even if it requires an unlikely set of results – means that the old ground will see a jam-packed sell-out on the day. A record attendance for a football match in the country is expected. The manner in which this Irish side have played and competed is surely deserving of such an audience.

The FAI are keen to squeeze every last financial drop from the final home qualifying game of the campaign. Indeed, they're considering following the approach of the IRFU and installing an extra 2,000 seats at pitchside, inside the fencing, behind both goal to add even more to the coffers. There are no rules that compel the FAI or any association to cage or pen fans behind barriers, fences or wire. Moreover, FIFA and UEFA leave any such matters of security to the host association. However, there are heavy penalties, such as fines or possible match bans, if there's any encroachment on to the pitch by fans. One option being considered by the FAI if they are to go ahead with the 'ringside' seats, according to a report in the *Irish Press*, is to thoroughly screen the ticket holders in a bid to keep out troublemakers.

The pitchside ticket machinations of the FAI aren't of concern for Paul, his brothers and two friends, as they'll be standing on the East Terrace, under the seated upper East Stand. Excitement is building as matchday approaches and Eoin Hand names his provisional 22-man squad on Monday, 5 October.

The squad is much as expected, with two talking points – the omission of Steve Heighway and the inclusion of Aston Villa forward Terry Donovan. Heighway, who played his part in Rotterdam's drama, hasn't kicked a ball in anger in the intervening month. The NASL is between seasons and the winger doesn't return to training until 11 November.

Speaking from his Minnesota base to the *Evening Herald*, Heighway explains that he has withdrawn from the party because he knows from experience that he simply wouldn't be fit enough to do himself or, more importantly, the Republic of Ireland justice if he were to play against France. Even if the Kicks were in pre-season training, Steve Heighway doesn't believe he'd have the match sharpness required for such a big game. Pre-season can get you fit, he says, but you need at least four competitive games to be match fit.

Heighway explains that he made the decision after consulting with Eoin Hand and Terry Conroy. And while he's been with the squad all the way through from Nicosia, he'd hate to run the risk of somehow undermining their chances at this late stage.

Yes, he'd absolutely love to figure in the Lansdowne game but Steve Heighway didn't want to put the manager in a difficult position. He thinks that if he'd declared himself available, Eoin Hand would likely have selected him for duty. But he told Eoin Hand that the Republic of Ireland must match France for fitness, 11 against 11, and that this wouldn't be the case if the manager were to select him.

Steve Heighway believes the team can succeed without him. Indeed, he believes the Republic of Ireland team have made huge progress and may be close to a serious breakthrough. The Republic of Ireland now has the best set-up in his 11 years on the international scene, he tells the *Evening Herald*. The side can play superb football and the squad consists of the most dedicated, level-headed bunch of players he's ever been associated with. Steve Heighway tells the paper that the influence of Liam Brady and Frank Stapleton has been key and that, in his opinion, the Republic of Ireland deserve to qualify for the World Cup in Spain.

Aston Villa striker Terry Donovan has been in good form. In the absence of the English champions' top marksman, Gary Shaw, due to an early season injury, Donovan has scored five times; twice in the European Cup against Iceland's Valur, plus goals against Sunderland and Tottenham Hotspur in the league. The 23-year-old was capped once under John Giles against the Czechs in Prague two years ago but he hasn't figured since.

Ashley Grimes misses out again, having only just recovered from the viral infection that saw him miss the Dutch trip. Mick Walsh is also left out. He'll not be sufficiently fit after a September cartilage operation.

Gerry Daly and Tony Grealish are named in the squad but both suffered injuries at the weekend. Tony Grealish was substituted after suffering a groin strain. However, the move was precautionary. The midfielder trained with his Brighton team-mates on Monday and may be considered for Tuesday night's League Cup tie with Huddersfield. Gerry Daly is doubtful for Coventry's cup clash with Everton after bruising his ribs in a coming together with Sunderland keeper Barry Siddall at the weekend.

When Eoin Hand and Terry Conroy announce, as arranged, their trimmed-down 18-man squad on the Thursday after the midweek English League Cup fixtures, the news on Gerry Daly is bad. Gerry Daly hasn't figured for his club in the Everton game. Instead, Gerry Daly had an X-ray at a Coventry hospital that showed that, rather than just bruising his ribs in the clash with Barry Siddall, he has suffered a fracture to his breastbone. Gerry Daly will be out for at least a month. It's a major blow to Eoin Hand's plans.

The news on Tony Grealish is better. The midfielder passed a fitness test before Brighton's League Cup game on Tuesday, although manager Mike Bailey decided not to risk him. A club spokesman reports that Tony Grealish is perfectly fine, the club has been in contact with Eoin Hand to allay any fears and Tony Grealish will be available for the game with West Brom at the weekend.

On Thursday, Eoin Hand announces a 17-man, rather than an 18-man, squad for the visit of France. Gerry Peyton, Terry Donovan, John Anderson and Kevin O'Callaghan are left out. Of Terry Donovan, Eoin Hand says that he is a player for the future and is in his plans but, as he would be very unlikely to play, his omission is a matter of economics. Essentially, the FAI don't really want to pay for him to travel to Dublin.

Kevin O'Callaghan's omission is slightly more surprising, given Steve Heighway's absence. But Eoin Hand feels that the Ipswich winger is still not quite ready for a fixture of this nature. He notes that, despite the youngster's obvious quality, Ipswich Town manager Bobby Robson is also blooding him carefully.

With only four frontmen chosen – Stapleton, Ryan, Givens and Robinson – the feeling is that Liam Brady will be deployed in a more attacking role than he has been to date. A role more akin to the one he fulfils at Juventus. Mick Martin may get the nod in midfield in place of Daly, as he did in Rotterdam. However, the form of former Home Farm player Ronnie Whelan, who deputised for Ray Kennedy and scored in Liverpool's 5-0 League Cup win over Exeter on Wednesday night, is pushing his claims for a first start in green. Whelan was described as the outstanding player on the field in the cup tie and performed very capably in the league against Swansea on the previous Saturday.

Moving Mark Lawrenson into midfield, an option used in the win over the Dutch early in the campaign, with Kevin Moran filling in at centre-half, is another possibility. However, such was the quality of Mark Lawrenson's performance at centre-back in Rotterdam that Eoin Hand is unlikely to deploy the Liverpool player anywhere else. The more so given the encouraging nature of his partnership with David O'Leary and the pace the French have in attack.

*Soviet military hardware on the outskirts of Kabul, Afghanistan, in the winter of 1980 as the Cold War threatens to heat up.*

*Wreckage of a US aircraft 300 miles south of Tehran, part of the abortive April 1980 mission to rescue American hostages held in the Iranian capital.*

*Terror in London: BBC sound recordist Sim Harris makes his escape as the SAS storm the Iranian Embassy in London on 5 May 1980.*

*Mark Lawrenson scores the winner against the Dutch at Lansdowne Road on 10 September 1980.*

*Crisis in the Middle East: Oil refineries burn near the Iranian city of Abadan in September 1980 in the early days of the Iran–Iraq War.*

*A pensive Eoin Hand as the Irish prepare to take on Belgium at Lansdowne Road on 15 October 1980.*

*Tony Grealish celebrates his equaliser against Guy Thys's men.*

*Different class – Michel Platini and Liam Brady exchange pennants before the qualifier in Paris on 28 October 1980.*

*Troubling times: Irish fans draw attention to the hunger strikes in the Maze Prison during the Republic of Ireland's clash with Belgium on 25 March 1981.*

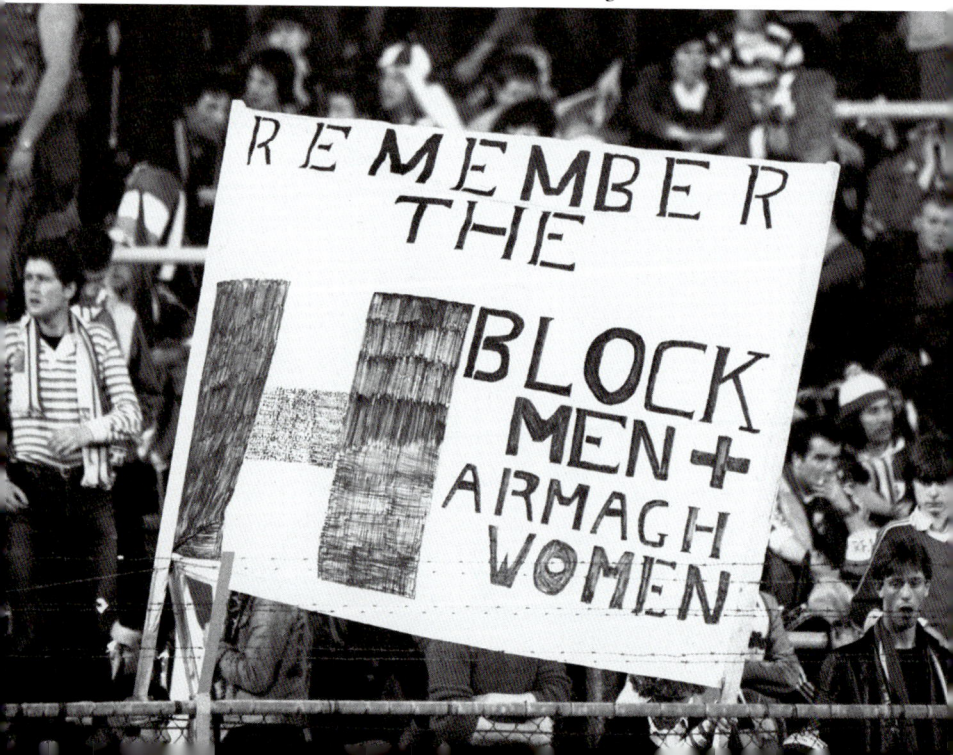

REMEMBER THE

BLOCK MEN + ARMAGH WOMEN

*Frank Stapleton celebrates his 'goal' against the Belgians at the Heysel Stadium, but Liam Brady is already looking to the referee.*

*Gerry Daly and Tony Grealish challenge Raul Nazare's decision to disallow Stapleton's strike.*

*Jan Ceulemans's 88th-minute header breaks Irish hearts.*

*Nothing is sacred: Pope John Paul II is shot in the Vatican City on 13 May 1981.*

*Liam Brady acknowledges the travelling Irish support at the De Kuip after the pulsating 2-2 draw in Rotterdam on 9 September 1981.*

*The Irish team to face France on 14 October 1981. T. Ten-year-old Paul is somewhere between the heads of Mark Lawrenson and Seamus McDonagh.*

*A delighted Frank Stapleton celebrates as the Republic of Ireland take an early lead in their stunning 3-2 win over France at Lansdowne Road.*

\* \* \*

Meanwhile, Michel Hidalgo has named his squad for the game. But France have not been in good form. They have lost five of their last six games and Michel Hidalgo is worried. Getting the four points they need from their last three games – away to the Republic of Ireland and home to the Netherlands and Cyprus – can't be taken for granted.

And Michel Hidalgo's job has been made more difficult with the news that Liam Brady's shadow and tormentor in Paris, Jean Tigana, will miss the game in Dublin through injury. Moreover, the French golden boy, Dominique Rocheteau, suffering from an Achilles problem, will also miss the fixture.

Michel Hidalgo has struggled to find a settled team. He has used 25 players across the qualifying campaign, perhaps a factor in their struggles for consistency. The French have tremendous ingredients but are yet to find the right recipe. They've lost away to both the Netherlands and Belgium and the trip to Dublin, given their current run of form, is clearly a concern.

Several of his players have lost confidence, Michel Hidalgo tells the French media, and even richly talented players, men like Didier Six, are simply disappearing during matches.

Midfield star Michel Platini also sounds somewhat pessimistic. A defeat wouldn't be a disaster, he says, because France will still have two games to play in which to get the points they need. But the French skipper admits that a number of players didn't seem motivated or up for it in Brussels, which, for him, is inexcusable in a World Cup tie. We must not show this attitude against the Irish, he insists. He and his team-mates know that it'll be difficult to get a result in Dublin but if they are to lose, they must at least do so playing well.

Michel Hidalgo's preparations should be a little smoother than those of his counterpart, Eoin Hand, however. The French FA have postponed league matches on the weekend before the Dublin trip. The last round of fixtures before the Lansdowne match are played on Wednesday, 7 October – a full week before the World Cup clash. So, when Michel Hidalgo trims his squad to 16 after the midweek league fixtures, he does so in the knowledge that all have come through the games unscathed and will convene for their training camp in Le Touquet on Friday, before travelling to Dublin on Monday.

Eoin Hand has no such comfort. With a full round of English fixtures on the Saturday before the game and then Liam Brady and Don Givens in action on Sunday, he'll have an anxious wait by the phone over the weekend.

\* \* \*

While Michel Hidalgo's France make their preparations, including a practice match against Lens at their Le Touquet base, Eoin Hand's Republic of Ireland squad begin to gather in Dublin on Sunday. While Michel Hidalgo's French squad have had the weekend off from competitive action, Eoin Hand's men have played league matches in England, Scotland, Italy and Switzerland. While Michel Hidalgo has been able to work with his squad without distraction, Eoin Hand has been sat by the phone waiting for news on the fitness of his players.

And the news is not good. Tony Grealish, the tiger in the Republic of Ireland's tank, will not play against France. Tony Grealish, who a week earlier had a groin problem, was deemed fit to play at the weekend against West Brom. But Tony Grealish does not finish the game. Tony Grealish limps from the field with a calf-muscle problem. Despite intensive treatment in Brighton after the game on Saturday and intensive treatment on his calf muscle on Sunday, the injury doesn't respond. Brighton inform Eoin Hand on Sunday afternoon that Tony Grealish cannot play.

It's a serious blow. Eoin Hand has now lost two of his first-choice midfield players in Grealish and Gerry Daly. To lose two of our regular players is a sickener, Eoin Hand tells the press after training on Monday. And it is a sickener. Tony Grealish and Gerry Daly have been two of the brightest sparks in the campaign thus far. They bring energy, guile and goals to the team. And the Republic of Ireland will need energy, guile and goals if they are to defeat Michel Hidalgo's France on Wednesday.

There's also concern over the fitness of Kevin Moran. The Dubliner clashed with Asa Hartford in the weekend's Manchester derby. Kevin Moran received a blow to his calf, which has swollen badly. The diagnosis is a small blood clot that may take a little time to clear. The former GAA star is a doubt for the game. But Eoin Hand isn't giving up.

Normally, this type of injury would put a player out for weeks, he explains, as a blood clot is not easily broken up. But, he reminds the assembled reporters, when we talk of Kevin Moran, we are talking of a different species. Because Kevin Moran is one of the most resilient men in football and, given his strength of character, his resolve, there is, says Eoin Hand, a reasonable chance that he'll be available. In the meantime, it's rest and treatment, with a decision likely to be left as late as possible. So, on Monday, while his team-mates trained at the Maccabi grounds in Kimmage, Kevin Moran was resting in bed in his hotel room, his right leg elevated in an effort to reduce the swelling.

Kevin Moran is important and will be given every chance to prove his fitness, because should he be fit, then Eoin Hand will have better options in midfield. If Kevin Moran is fit, then, for instance, Mark Lawrenson can play in the middle of the park in place of Tony Grealish. It may not be the Liverpool defender's favoured position but he's proven himself more than capable in such a role.

Despite the injury concerns and the withdrawals, however, Eoin Hand's assistant, Terry Conroy, is confident that the Republic of Ireland can win. Terry Conroy is very upbeat indeed. In fact, Terry Conroy has never been as confident before an important game. Eoin Hand's assistant rates the French very highly but believes they are very beatable. The Belgians and Dutch have shown that.

Talking to the press, Terry Conroy points to how much more resilient and difficult to beat the Republic of Ireland have become, particularly in Dublin. Terry Conroy points to the fact that the Republic of Ireland now have four or five players who can be considered world class. And Terry Conroy believes that, with the right service to Michael Robinson and Frank Stapleton, especially in the air, the Republic of Ireland can inflict real damage to the hopes of Michel Hidalgo's men.

\* \* \*

Eoin Hand and Michel Hidalgo name their teams on Tuesday afternoon, the day before the match. There's to be no repeat of the phoney war witnessed between Hand and Rijvers before the Rotterdam game. Kevin Moran will start in the centre of defence, subject to a fitness test on matchday. He did some light training on Tuesday morning, his injury finally showing signs of responding to intensive treatment. The Irish camp are hopeful.

Eoin Hand has plumped for a 4-4-2 formation. There are no surprises up front, where Stapleton and Robinson will lead the line. Chris Hughton is restored at left-back. John Devine, who performed admirably against the Dutch, is naturally disappointed. But Chris Hughton is the more experienced player and deserving of his place given the consistent excellence of his performances during the qualifying campaign. David O'Leary will partner Moran, while Dave Langan will once again patrol the right flank.

Midfield had been the area of most conjecture. Perhaps unsurprisingly, Mark Lawrenson will deputise for Tony Grealish, his ability to cover the ground and reclaim possession key weapons in thwarting lightning French counters. Mick Martin, ever dependable, will sit alongside him in the middle of the park, while Ronnie Whelan will be stationed on the right to fill the space vacated by Gerry Daly. Liam Brady will seek to influence the game from the left, although he is likely to have freer rein to his movements than his midfield colleagues. Liam Brady's abilities will be used to the fullest, says Eoin Hand. He will not be restricted in any way.

Having struggled to find a consistent formula across the campaign, despite the many talents available to him, Michel Hidalgo has shuffled his pack once more. Only four players who started in their win over the Irish in Paris are chosen – defenders Maxime Bossis and Christian Lopez and midfielders

Jean-Francois Larios and Michel Platini. Didier Six, who started that game, is demoted to the bench, replaced by the exciting talent of 19-year-old Monaco forward Bruno Bellone, who wins his first cap. Jacques Zimako, who so impressed when coming on as a sub in Paris and scored France's second goal, is also on the bench. Bordeaux's Rene Girard comes into midfield, gaining his first cap at the age of 27.

Michel Hidalgo's formation will ostensibly be a 4-4-2, although, like Liam Brady, Michel Platini is likely to be given licence to roam. The general sense is that Hidalgo has picked a team to contain the Republic of Ireland and to counter swiftly. Given their recent form and the circumstances of the group, the French seem set up to at least earn a point. *France Football*, in a gloomy editorial on the state of French football, argues in favour of such a pragmatic approach if anything is to be taken from Dublin and if the French are to qualify. The attacking intent of Michel Hidalgo's selections has left them far too open at times, as evidenced in their defeats in the Netherlands and Belgium. Some Belgian pragmatism wouldn't go amiss, argues the editorial. The ability to contain dangerous situations and turn them around to the French advantage must be developed by all defenders and attackers on the pitch, the editorial says.

\* \* \*

Matchday dawns in chilly Dublin. The newspapers are full of previews and features around the match. There's also a clarion call from Eoin Hand for the fans on the day to get behind their side and drive them on. Eoin Hand believes the French crowd played their part in the home side's victory when the two sides met at the Parc des Princes and he'd like the Lansdowne Road crowd to repay the compliment and shake the ground to its very foundations.

This is the most important international match we've played in nearly 20 years, says Hand, in his pre-match comments to the press. A win keeps the World Cup dream alive. Eoin Hand believes that the players will need every ounce of encouragement they can get. Eoin Hand wants to hear the fans roaring their approval of every movement and lifting the lads when things may not be going so well. And Eoin Hand will be delighted if he can't hear himself thinking for the noise.

While Kevin Moran undergoes a strenuous fitness test under the watchful gaze of the Republic of Ireland manager and his backroom staff on the morning of the game, Paul is in school imploring the clock to get a move on. It's bad enough when he wants to get out of there on a normal day. Worse when there's a big Ireland game on the telly. But torture today. Torture as the clock is tortuously slow, taunting and tormenting the ten-year-old boy with his first big international football match ahead of him. When it strikes midday, he'll be out the door. Out of there with his older brother from sixth class who is also Lansdowne bound.

And when noon finally slouches lazily around, out they go. Notes to their teachers handed over in the morning carry their release clauses. Out of the class. Out of the gates. And jogging home for grub, to wait on their older brother from fifth year in secondary school – who will lead the expedition – and Gar and Johnny from next door, who attend a different school. When all are convened, Paul's dad drives them to Rathmines before the five disembark and walk the rest of the way, through Ranelagh, down Appian Way, down Waterloo Road amongst the gathering throngs and on to Lansdowne Road.

The match is a 53,000 sell-out. It's been sold out for ages. A record for a football match in Ireland, as was expected, eclipsing the previous record attendance by some 6,000 – a 1-1 draw with England in a World Cup qualifier in 1957. The FAI have asked fans to arrive early, at least an hour, but ideally two, before kick-off at 4pm to avoid congestion through the 59 turnstiles. The Artane Boys Band will be there to entertain although, for some, that might encourage a tardy arrival. Taoiseach Dr Garret FitzGerald will also be in attendance, the first Irish premier to attend an international football game in more than 20 years.

Meanwhile, Kevin Moran proves his fitness and will play. A little later, Paul, his brothers and their two friends arrive at Lansdowne Road, around 90 minutes before the game is due to start. Their tickets are for the East Terrace, the standing area running the length of the Lansdowne pitch on the opposite side to the television cameras, below the seated Upper East Stand. There's massive media interest in the fixture. Unprecedented interest. The Lansdowne Road press box holds 112 people. But, reportedly, the FAI received 220 applications for passes from the written press alone, 54 of them from France! The match will be broadcast across 12 radio stations in Europe and two French TV stations will take the pictures live.

Paul and his brothers position themselves on the south end of the terrace (to the far right as their families will see it on TV), close to the already heaving South Terrace. They're tucked up just under the cover afforded by the seated area above, just in case the weather takes a turn from the current chilly dryness. The initial positioning seems sound, a decent view of the pitch and giving shelter if needed. But gradually, as kick-off approaches, Paul's view of the pitch dwindles until all he can clearly see is a strip of the greensward that essentially contains the 18-yard box and goal at the South Terrace end. Looking north provides glimpses of the other goal through a forest of heads, shoulders, armpits and backs. But, as the tension builds and the atmosphere crackles, in a way, in many ways, it doesn't really matter. Because it's like nothing he's ever witnessed before. He's in a dreamland. And the game hasn't even started yet.

\* \* \*

Eoin Hand's Republic of Ireland will kick off and will be attacking the South Terrace goal. Michael Robinson turns to his team-mates, issues a call to arms with a clenched fist and then, on the referee's whistle, touches the ball to Frank Stapleton, who knocks it back to Liam Brady, who finds Chris Hughton at left-back. Hughton, in turn, rolls it back to keeper Jim McDonagh, who gets an early touch of the ball to ease any nerves. The Bolton keeper launches it forward to a great roar from the home fans. Ronnie Whelan challenges but loses out. The French return the ball long with gusto. David O'Leary mis-heads to Alain Curiol, who runs left before laying the ball off to Jean-François Larios.

Larios returns it to Curiol, who is immediately dispossessed by O'Leary. The rangy Arsenal defender finds Whelan 20 yards inside the Irish half on the right. The young Liverpool man controls with his left then plays a lovely ball inside for Stapleton, before sprinting down the right wing looking for a return pass. Ronnie Whelan shows no sign of nerves. Stapleton advances but is tackled by centre-back Philippe Mahut just as he tries to find Whelan. The ball comes off Stapleton and goes into touch and France have a throw 30 yards from their goal on the left flank. Mahut, his messy mop of blond hair tussled in the breeze, shows for the ball, receives it and is upended by Mick Martin in an early show of force by the Irish midfielder. *Bienvenue à Dublin, Philippe!*

The two sides spar in the early stages in similar fashion. Eoin Hand's Republic of Ireland look to go long to Stapleton and Robinson as they attempt to establish position deep in French territory. The French, a new side in many respects, look to work the ball through playmaker Michel Platini as they try to settle into their passing rhythm.

Four minutes on the clock and France build down their left, 15 yards into the Irish half, with Gérard Janvion finding Larios on the left touchline. Dave Langan steams in, his first chance to leave an impression. Larios, however, deftly evades the right-back's lunge and passes back inside to Janvion. But Ronnie Whelan is there, robbing France's left-back with a brilliantly timed challenge that releases Michael Robinson into the space left behind the marooned French defender. And the Brighton & Hove Albion man is away!

Michael Robinson storms up the inside-right channel, with Langan supporting on the touchline. Stapleton has peeled away, running toward the centre of the 'D', with Mahut in tow. Christian Lopez races across to try and snuff out the danger but Robinson pushes the ball around him and Lopez crashes into the retreating Janvion, with both ending up on the deck as Robinson reaches the byline and whips in a cross. Stapleton and Mahut race for a touch. Both seem to meet it at the same time on the edge of the six-yard box ... and the ball is in the back of the net!

Lansdowne Road erupts. Stapleton runs to Robinson in delight. The place goes mad. Paul, who sees the goal as it occurs in that narrow field of vision available to him, goes mad. The crowd surges forward and back, left and right. Unnerving, yet exciting. Amazing.

Mick Martin congratulates Frank Stapleton and has a word. Is he asking if he touched it? The answer is likely 'no'. The French defender got the crucial last touch. An own goal. But no matter. One-nil. One-nil to Eoin Hand's Republic of Ireland after only five minutes of play.

As the crowd settles, so Paul's big brother suggests they stand in front of the crush barrier they'd been leaning against, to avoid being pinned to it should the Republic of Ireland score again. They duly move. Attempts to sit on the barrier for a better view fail.

Meanwhile, France look to respond. Look to pass their way back into the game. But Eoin Hand's Republic of Ireland strive to keep the heat on them, looking time and again for the runs and hold-up play of Stapleton and Robinson. The passing is crisp but the tackles are crisper. The pace is intense.

Nine minutes in, Jim McDonagh launches a long goal kick right up the centre of the field. Stapleton rises, wins the header and the ball runs to Robinson ten yards closer to goal. Robinson, spotting the run of Whelan to his right, hooks the ball over his shoulder for the Liverpool man to chase deep into the French box. But keeper Castaneda sees it all the way, grabs it and quickly throws the ball to his right to full-back Maxime Bossis.

Bossis plays it in infield to Rene Girard, who has dropped deep. Bordeaux's Girard turns and plays the ball forward to Didier Christophe of Monaco, just short of halfway. The hulking midfielder rolls it to the right again, where Bossis has advanced. Bossis pushes it to the intersection of halfway and the right touchline, where Michel Platini has drifted. Under pressure from two green shirts, the French captain tricks both Liam Brady and Mark Lawrenson and finds Girard crossing halfway, ten yards in from the touchline. Girard strides forward, then returns the ball to Platini, who is now further down the right wing. Platini pauses before playing the ball back to the supporting Girard, who quickly plays it forward to Curiol, 25 yards from the Irish goal, travelling right to left. Curiol controls with his right foot, then flicks it to Bruno Bellone inside the 'D'. The 19-year-old controls, spins and then shoots unerringly past McDonagh for the equaliser. The stadium, bar the distant noise of the 2,000 French supporters, is silenced. Paul sees nothing of the ball once it passed halfway. The wind being sucked out of the stadium is enough to tell him that the news is not good.

The goal is brilliant. The French may have struggled off the ball at times in this campaign but, on it, they can be sublime. Ten passes from keeper to scorer and Eoin Hand's Republic of Ireland are undone.

The home side are rocked. As they try to regather themselves, they struggle to keep the ball. Long balls to the two frontmen, effective in the first few minutes, are picked off by the French, as Lopez and Mahut get on top of Stapleton and Robinson.

The French have a spring in their step. Eoin Hand's men are chasing shadows. Tackles no longer landing. Eleven minutes on the clock, Janvion, who has moved to the right flank, easily intercepts another long ball by O'Leary 30 yards from his own goal. He nods it right to Bossis, ten yards short of halfway. Bossis turns, sees space ahead and drives into it. Brady lets him go and the full-back takes advantage, skipping past Chris Hughton's lunge, inside Lawrenson far too easily, then covers another ten yards before shooting from 25 yards, chest-high to McDonagh's right. The Irish keeper dives but can only bat it down. Platini and Bellone dive for the loose ball but Langan wins it, knocking it back to his grateful keeper.

Good as the French are on the ball, out of possession they are vulnerable. A minute later, Lawrenson finds O'Leary on halfway with a throw. The Arsenal defender launches the ball long to the edge of the French area, where Robinson nods it down to Stapleton to the left of Castaneda's goal. Stapleton holds off the close attention of Mahut, rolls him, then shoots from an acute angle. Castaneda pushes it around the post for an Irish corner. The set piece comes to nothing but France can clearly be got at.

That said, the visitors consistently create dangerous moments in possession. Langan does brilliantly to track and get ahead of Curiol, who looks to connect to a wonderful Bellone cross from the French right. The Birmingham man arrives just in time to head clear as the Monaco player is set to strike.

The Irish continue to work the channels and force a couple of corners. On 19 minutes, O'Leary flicks one on at the near post, Kevin Moran hooks an effort over his shoulder at goal from eight yards out but Castaneda gathers safely.

Captains Platini and Brady are more in the game now. But it's Platini who's catching the eye. Deep in the French half, he robs Hughton to break up an Irish attack. Michel Platini advances and mulls over his options before rolling a clever ball that cuts out the recovering Whelan to find Larios powering over halfway. Larios, 30 yards from the Irish goal, checks, looks right and then plays in his captain, who has followed the play, to the right of the 'D'. Platini touches, then strikes from just inside the area but the ball flashes just wide of McDonagh's right-hand post. Magic from Platini. A warning for those in green.

The styles of the two teams contrast. Eoin Hand's are the more direct, the French easier on the eye. But in a sudden change of approach, rather than kicking long, Jim McDonagh bowls a quick ball to Whelan on the right. The young midfielder controls and plays a delicious ball up the inside-right channel, where Mick Martin has made a break into a pocket of space. Martin carries the ball forward then plays a pass for Robinson, who is running left to right and into the French box. The run unsettles the pursuing Janvion, who puts the ball behind for a corner.

Liam Brady stands over it, then curls an inswinger into the box. Stapleton rises with Christophe, who gets a touch that sees the ball drop just outside the six-yard box. A scramble ensues, the ball smuggled away to the left side of the area, where Mick Martin retrieves and returns it into the mixer. Castaneda comes to claim in a ruck of players but misses entirely. O'Leary, lurking at the far post, turns the ball back across the six-yard area and Frank Stapleton is there to delightedly smash it home. Two-one Ireland!

Paul sees this one, too, amongst the heads and shoulders of those in front of him. The roar shakes Lansdowne Road and the barrier behind him does its job, the boys able to maintain their position on the terrace as the joyous crowd heaves and surges around them.

Michel Hidalgo's France may have played the more impressive football but Eoin Hand's Republic of Ireland, with a quarter of the game gone, have the lead once more. Eoin Hand's tactics, using the high ball and running the channels, has worked, even if the approach hasn't been especially pretty. Frank Stapleton has been immense. And in Ronnie Whelan of Liverpool, aggressive in the tackle and oh-so assured in possession, the Republic of Ireland look to have a young player of serious calibre.

France restart, but Frank Stapleton, working back deep on the left side of the Irish defence, dispossesses Girard, shields the ball, then rolls it to Liam Brady on the touchline, just a yard away. Brady quickly transfers it back towards the Irish goal, where Mark Lawrenson is waiting. Lawrenson shifts it right as Christophe closes him down, then sweeps it to his clubmate Whelan ten yards short of halfway on the right-hand side of the pitch. Ronnie Whelan has space in front of him and accelerates into it, covering 30 yards unmolested, before cutting inside on to his left foot. Janvion can't get to him. Lopez and Mahut back off. So Ronnie Whelan lets fly. The ball boys behind the goal leap in excitement as the ball beats the flailing Castaneda but Whelan's effort just clips the top of the crossbar, much to the relief of the visiting keeper. What a run and effort by the youngster! France may have Bellone but the Republic of Ireland have Ronnie Whelan.

Up goes the chant – 'IRELAND, IRELAND, IRELAND' – and the noise is deafening, just as Eoin Hand wished. Michel Hidalgo's France look rattled, unable to regain their rhythm. Eoin Hand's Republic of Ireland have upped the tempo noticeably. There's no peace for the French players. Nowhere to go as the Irish press higher and hungrily for every ball. Even when they have a throw-in, the Irish give no quarter. Bossis tries to steal a few yards with ball in hand but Robinson says 'no' and pushes him back. Referee Rolf Eriksson of Stockholm rushes over to intervene. No quarter is to be granted. The French are having to fight for every yard as the Republic of Ireland sense blood.

Robinson is a man possessed. Not a dog with a bone, more a dog without a bone, the bone of his dreams, a bone he very much wants back. Michael Robinson hounds the visiting defence when they have the ball. Stapleton is of like mind. And the two are now dominating their markers, Lopez and Mahut. The ball is sticking whenever it's played forward, allowing Eoin Hand's men to play more and more of the game in the French half. Curiol and Bellone have only observer status. Michel Platini is starved of service. Liam Brady is now painting the pictures. France are uncomfortable, squirming like men in hair shirts and ill-fitting trousers.

Thirty-nine minutes on the clock, Hughton wins the ball off Curiol and plays it back to McDonagh. The keeper thinks about releasing Langan on the right but then decides, instead, on a long punt. He launches it, right down the centre of the pitch. Robinson runs to get a head to it, closely followed and then challenged by Lopez. The Brighton forward gets there first but his flicked header only drops to Janvion, facing his own goal 35 yards out. Stapleton rushes him and Janvion panics, rolling the ball into the path of the onrushing Robinson, who has anticipated the defender's next move. Head in hands, Janvion watches in despair as Robinson intercepts his errant pass just inside the 'D' and then thrashes the ball past the French keeper and into the back of the net. Lopez turns and berates his colleague as Robinson turns and runs toward the East Stand, directly in Paul's line of sight, arms raised in celebration.

Three-one to Eoin Hand's Republic of Ireland! IRELAND, IRELAND, IRELAND. Daylight between the sides, uproar in the stands and on the terraces.

Michel Platini drops deeper, seeking to wrest some control. But the Republic of Ireland are in no mood to give ground. Their energy levels and intensity are off the scale. And those energy levels and that intensity carry the men in green to half-time, two goals to the good.

\* \* \*

As the two sides return to the field for the second period, the Artane Boys Band refuse to yield. Marching in step and elaborate formations, belting out their tunes, intent on finishing, no matter what the players or the crowd think. Eoin Hand, standing beside his assistant, Terry Conroy, turns to sign autographs while they wait. And, finally, the Artane Boys Band, sated, retreat from whence they came and Mr Eriksson blows for battle to resume.

The half begins poorly for France. Janvion, Platini and Christophe try to build down their left but the hulking Christophe's attempt at a first-time pass to Janvion on the wing sails high over the full-back's head and into the laughing crowd behind. Whelan takes the throw quickly, finds Langan. Langan plays that channel ball once more to the ever-willing Stapleton, who turns, takes on Mahut and wins a corner kick.

Liam Brady saunters over to take it at the Havelock Square End and is confronted by the sight of fans sitting on the ground very near the corner flag. Clearly, the pitchside seats are overflowing in some way. The fans back off and scatter to give the captain room. Brady takes, Castaneda flaps, O'Leary returns it into the area but Lawrenson is offside.

France build, this time managing to hold possession as Platini takes control deep in his half. He finds Lopez to his right. Lopez forward to Curiol on halfway. Curiol moves infield and finds Platini once more, now inside the Irish half of the centre circle. Platini checks then switches the ball right to Larios. Larios to Girard, who finds Christophe, who is now on the right flank. Platini breaks forward as Christophe gathers himself, then crosses long and high into the Irish penalty area, where Platini arrives untracked to head at goal. But McDonagh gathers comfortably.

Minutes later, Bellone almost intercepts a back pass to McDonagh as Langan and O'Leary get their wires crossed. The ball is hastily kicked to touch. Janvion takes the throw, to Platini. Back to Janvion and then infield to Christophe, 30 yards from goal. Christophe picks out Curiol, running right to left across the edge of the area. Curiol controls, then turns sharply, laying off the ball to Platini once more. Platini shoots but McDonagh dives to his right and makes another comfortable save.

Two attempts on target from Platini in the opening minutes of the half; a warning for Eoin Hand's Republic of Ireland.

Having distributed short so far in the second period, Jim McDonagh returns to the high, long punt. Christophe misreads the flight of the ball and can only find Lawrenson in the middle of the park, 15 yards inside French territory. Mark Lawrenson clips a high ball 20 yards forward in search of Robinson. Robinson, just to the left of the 'D', beats Lopez in the air and directs his header to Frank Stapleton 20 yards out. Stapleton kills it, then chips Castaneda, who is frozen to the spot! Lansdowne gasps at the Manchester United striker's audacity but the ball sails inches wide. Brilliant from Stapleton. What a game he's having!

Paul sees nothing of it after the ball leaves McDonagh's boot. But the reaction of the crowd tells him all he needs to know. So close!

On the hour mark, McDonagh goes short after another French attack fails to threaten, bowling it out to Dave Langan. Langan pushes the ball inside to Mick Martin and continues his run. Martin finds Brady, who's travelled in from the left. Brady to Langan once more, then Martin again and then Brady leaves the bewildered Christophe on his backside with a delightful feint and change of direction. Liam Brady quickly passes to Martin, now on the right, and the Newcastle player swings over an early cross. Michael Robinson rises with Castaneda. The French keeper gathers but winces in pain as the Irish forward leaves a little on him. Castaneda is furious. Mr Eriksson wags a finger at Michael Robinson. Michael Robinson smiles sheepishly.

Castaneda launches a long, deep punt from the goal kick and the ball is worked to Bellone on the right touchline, where the youngster is met with a crunching tackle by Dave Langan, much to the delight of the home crowd. Affronted, Bellone kicks out in annoyance, then shoves Langan, who is more than happy to see the French youngster's frustration. Fifteen minutes into the second half, Michel Hidalgo's men haven't really landed a blow of any consequence on the home side as they try to get back into the game. The physicality of the Irish is a problem for the visitors.

Five minutes later, Bruno Bellone is withdrawn. Hidalgo needs something to change, so he makes a change. The experienced Didier Six enters the fray. Perhaps in a sign that the Irish legs are beginning to tire, Liam Brady, losing out in a challenge in the centre circle to Larios, hacks down the French midfielder from behind before he can do any damage, and is booked.

Perhaps sensing a waning of the Irish intensity, the 51,000 home fans seek to lift their heroes. Another long clearance from McDonagh sees Robinson and Mahut clash, then fall to the ground. A lengthy stoppage ensues as both receive treatment. The rest is welcome. Robinson recovers but Mahut does not. There's polite applause as the blond centre-half, who has had a torrid afternoon, is helped from the field by the French medical staff and replaced by Francois Bracci of Bordeaux. And there's a great roar of adulation as Michael Robinson rises to his feet and returns to the game.

The match resumes with a French throw 20 yards from the Irish byline on the right. Six throws it backwards to Larios, who shifts it inside to Girard. Girard knocks it back to the right for Bracci, giving him his first touch. The defender launches it into the Republic of Ireland box but O'Leary heads it away to the edge of the area, where Mark Lawrenson plays a first-time pass to set Ronnie Whelan galloping away into space on the right. Whelan slips a pass up the right channel to Stapleton, who returns it to Whelan with the sweetest of backheels. The Liverpool man shrugs off the attentions of the backtracking

Janvion and closes in on the French defensive third but his charge is halted by an agricultural challenge by the sliding Lopez. Free kick Ireland. Pressure relieved. A wonderful passage of play by the men in green.

As the game enters its final 15 minutes, French urgency increases. A strong tackle by Martin on Janvion ten yards inside the Irish half sees the ball travel a further 40 yards back towards the Irish end and out for a corner. Janvion takes it himself. Kevin Moran rises highest to clear. But the danger is only temporarily averted, as the ball falls to Lopez, whose strike from the edge of the area is deflected behind for another corner over on the French left. Platini wastes little time in swinging it in the direction of the giant Christophe. The shaggy-haired midfielder heads down towards the six-yard box and Larios connects but McDonagh, in close attendance, brilliantly blocks the effort and Whelan clears it once more for another corner.

This time, France go short. Christophe wins the ball from the ensuing cross but it floats away to the left side of the area where Brady, socks now round his ankles, retrieves and finds Langan. Langan picks out Whelan in midfield. Ronnie Whelan looks to break quickly, realises he has no support, so goes back to Martin, who turns it back to McDonagh and safety, and perhaps a moment or two to draw breath.

Eoin Hand's Republic of Ireland are treading water now. Running on fumes. They delay over throws. They delay over free kicks. They delay over goal kicks. The ball no longer sticking up front with Stapleton and Robinson. The two forwards are no longer making as many runs into the channels. Their legs worn to stumps, the crucial out-ball options are reduced as France dominate.

The Lansdowne Road crowd urge on their heroes but France sense the drop in tempo. Michel Platini is directing affairs, increasingly influential, increasingly elusive.

Eighty-three minutes gone and Moran's long ball has no takers in green. Didier Christophe brings it down 40 yards from his own goal and ploughs forward. Whelan is unable to go with him. Crossing halfway, the Monaco midfielder finds

Larios and then Janvion picks up the play on the left wing. Janvion rolls it down the line, level with the Irish penalty area, for Six. Six turns, then flicks a cute ball past Langan to find Janvion once more, free and close to the byline inside the area. The Saint-Étienne full-back pulls the ball back low and hard. It clips Whelan, evades McDonagh and is goalbound until the off-balance Chris Hughton blocks its path. But Hughton cannot clear the danger and Michel Platini, six yards out, crashes the ball into the roof of the net. The deficit is halved. The goal was coming. You could smell it.

Paul sees Michel Platini thrash the ball high into the Irish rigging. Paul hears the silence. Paul feels the silence more. The clock. Everyone looks to the clock. How long is left? Seven minutes. Not long. Too long. IRELAND, IRELAND, IRELAND.

Eoin Hand's Republic of Ireland dig deep. Mick Martin fires one in from distance and is delighted to see it deflected for a corner kick. Tick, tock, tick, tock. Liam Brady saunters over to the corner flag on the French left. The fans on the grass shuffle on their backsides once more to make way. Liam Brady goes short to Ronnie Whelan, they trade passes and then Liam Brady floats the ball right-footed across the French penalty area. The visitors are caught napping. Lawrenson, unmarked at the far post, heads down and Robinson, ten yards out just left of the penalty spot, strikes! But the ball hits Christophe and skims the outside of Castaneda's left post and goes out for another corner. Michael Robinson holds his head in disbelief.

France clear the resulting set piece, Irish hearts in mouths as they break. But Mick Martin intercepts Christophe's ball for Janvion and Hughton clears up the left touchline, where Lopez heads it out for an Irish throw deep in French territory. Brady takes his time once more. The hobbling Stapleton takes his time too. Brady throws it to his former Arsenal colleague, who cleverly draws a foul from Bracci and the Republic of Ireland have a precious free kick level with the French area on the left.

Four minutes left on the clock. Liam Brady would use all of them but Mr Eriksson says 'no', urging the Juventus man to get on with it. Brady does as he's told and plays the ball in head-height to the near post. Frank Stapleton flicks on, Michael Robinson challenges and the ball falls to Ronnie Whelan but he can't control his volley as the ball bounces awkwardly and his effort sails high and wide and into the pitchside seats behind the French goal. Tick. Tock. Tick. Tock. Three minutes on the clock.

Girard tries to find the lesser-spotted Curiol down the right wing but Kevin Moran shepherds the ball over the touchline. Eoin Hand uses the break in play to withdraw the redoubtable Frank Stapleton, who's given one of the greatest displays of centre-forward play ever witnessed at Lansdowne Road. Seldom was a standing ovation more deserved. Don Givens trots on. Tick. Tock. Tick. Tock. Two minutes left.

Paul can see very little. But that's a good thing. It means the football is not in the Republic of Ireland penalty area. Bracci plays it to Girard in midfield. Liam Brady robs him and the ball breaks between Larios and Moran. Moran is the quicker and, boom, he launches it long down toward the far-left corner, Michael Robinson in chase.

Robinson gets there, Bracci arriving just behind him. The Brighton striker takes it to the corner flag, trying to kill the clock. Bracci shoves him in the back in a fit of pique and Mr Eriksson awards Eoin Hand's Republic of Ireland another precious free kick.

Mark Lawrenson takes. Surprisingly, rather than keep the ball in the corner, he fires it across the box. Moran rises and ships a heavy blow from Christophe, leaving him a crumpled figure on the turf just outside the French area. The game continues. Brady retrieves and then looks to Moran but, with the Mr Eriksson waving him on, he finds Whelan on the right. Whelan, faced by French numbers, turns it back to Dave Langan, who plays it infield to Mick Martin. The Newcastle midfielder flicks it back toward the French penalty area, over the crumpled Moran. Still no whistle. Janvion heads clear and Larios picks it up just short of halfway on the right.

Larios looks up, turns inside and picks out Didier Christophe ten yards into the Irish half on the edge of the centre circle. *Why didn't Mark Lawrenson just keep the ball in the corner? What on earth was he thinking?* Christophe plays the ball 30 yards to the French right, where Maxime Bossis waits on the corner of the Irish area. *Oh, why didn't Mark Lawrenson keep the bloody ball in the corner?* Bossis rolls it back to Bracci ten yards behind him. The substitute swings a high ball deep into the 18-yard box. Panic ensues. *What was Mark Lawrenson thinking?*

Curiol jumps for it but Mick Martin heads clear to the edge of the area, where Brady whacks it back to halfway and out for a French throw. Tick. Tock. Tick. Tock. Relief. The pressure relieved. Mark Lawrenson is off the hook. Kevin Moran returns to man the barricades. One minute left.

Bracci throws up the right touchline to Bossis once more. Then back to Bracci and another long cross into the box. Moran meets it, slicing his clearance over to the left of the field, where Janvion controls, beats Ronnie Whelan, then stands up Langan before beating him too. Fifty-one thousand hearts in mouths. Fifty-one thousand people cannot breathe.

Langan chases back but is powerless to stop Janvion cutting right and crossing. One hundred and two thousand hands are on heads! Curiol arrives, controls and pokes an effort that's heading off target to the left of goal but Six is there and Didier Six redirects the ball toward the goal from six yards out!

Oh no! But oh yes, Jim McDonagh! Jim McDonagh dives to his right to push the ball away, making the save of his life. Six lunges for the loose ball and dives over Irish legs in the hope of earning a penalty. But the football rolls over the byline and Mr Rolf Eriksson of Stockholm is unmoved.

Jim McDonagh. Heroic Jim McDonagh places the ball for the restart. Paul can see Jim McDonagh placing the ball for the restart. Deliberately, carefully, he places it. Then he kicks it and that's that! Mr Eriksson calls time and there's time for no more!

Eoin Hand's Republic of Ireland have beaten Michel Hidalgo's France by three goals to two. Fans storm on to the pitch in exuberant celebration as the players dash for the dressing rooms. What a win! What a moment! What a game for your first game! What a way to keep the World Cup dream alive!

As they leave for home, Paul feels as if he's floating on air. And he's nearly right, as his feet, indeed, aren't touching the ground! Inexperience has seen the boys leave the stadium just after the full-time whistle. Paul's feet aren't touching the ground – not because of transcendent joy – his feet aren't touching the ground because of the crush of fans trying to get out of the gate at the South Terrace end of Lansdowne Road. But Paul doesn't care. Paul doesn't know any better. And Paul doesn't care because he's lived football's majesty. And Paul doesn't care because the Republic of Ireland have beaten France. And Paul doesn't care because the Republic of Ireland can still go to the World Cup in Spain.

* * *

Eoin Hand has been off cigarettes for six months. Having survived the last seven minutes of the game without resorting to a smoke after Michel Platini cut the Irish lead in half, Eoin Hand tells the press that he believes he'll surely never smoke again. And if he can survive his post-match media duties in the smoke-filled press room in the bowels of Lansdowne Road, then his resolve to beat the habit will surely prove unshakeable.

Eoin Hand is thrilled with the result. But he's less thrilled with a line of questioning that appears, in his mind, far too critical, with too much focus on how his Republic of Ireland team struggled in phases throughout the second half. Eoin Hand reminds those assembled that his Republic of Ireland have just won a World Cup match against a very good French side. So, how about that?

The contrast between his side's barnstorming opening 45 minutes and a second half where the French were often in the ascendancy was down to the French needing to throw caution to the wind, he explains. It wasn't his intention to simply contain the opposition in that second period. Eoin Hand told his lads to play the second half as if it was a scoreless draw. But a quality French side was always going to ask questions, so his charges had little option but to dig in at times. Perhaps they should be given greater praise for that? More praise for holding out? And more praise given they had to play the game without Gerry Daly, Tony Grealish and Steve Heighway?

Reflecting on a qualifying campaign that has seen his Republic of Ireland team score 17 times, comfortably outscoring the Dutch and the Belgians, Eoin Hand believes it'll be a footballing injustice if his team do not qualify for Spain. He reminds all present that the Republic of Ireland have taken ten points in one of the toughest groups in the qualifying competition. And Eoin Hand is correct. That return against three of European football's powerhouses represents serious progress for the international side, even if qualification isn't to be achieved.

But dreams of Spain, even if unlikely to be realised, have not yet been extinguished. Later that evening in Rotterdam, the Dutch put three past a somewhat disinterested Belgium, who have already qualified. The win gives the Dutch serious cause for hope. A victory in their last game against the French in Paris will see them take second place in the group on 11 points.

But should the French win that clash on 18 November, then Michel Hidalgo's men will just need to dispose of Cyprus in early December to edge out Eoin Hand's men on goal difference. However, should France and the Netherlands draw, then the Republic of Ireland will face a play-off at a neutral venue against Kees Rijvers's men – a one-off qualification shoot-out.

So all eyes will turn to Paris on 18 November. Eoin Hand's team have no control over events. There'll be nothing they can do but watch. But a draw isn't impossible under the circumstances. Both sides need to win. And as the Republic of Ireland's trip to Rotterdam back in September under similar circumstances proved, a draw can very easily be the outcome when two sides go hammer and tongs for victory.

## 1982 FIFA World Cup qualification: UEFA Group Two

|  | P | W | D | L | F | A | Pts |
|---|---|---|---|---|---|---|---|
| Belgium | 8 | 5 | 1 | 2 | 12 | 9 | 11 |
| Republic of Ireland | 8 | 4 | 2 | 2 | 17 | 11 | 10 |
| Netherlands | 7 | 4 | 1 | 2 | 11 | 5 | 9 |
| France | 6 | 3 | 0 | 3 | 14 | 8 | 6 |
| Cyprus | 7 | 0 | 0 | 7 | 4 | 25 | 0 |

# 12.

# Death of a Dream

AT HALF-TIME in the Parc des Princes on the night of 18 November 1981, the Irish dream of World Cup qualification is still very much alive. The French and Dutch, consumed by nerves and tension, are deadlocked. It's nil-nil. As it stands, France will bow out, even with a game against Cyprus to play, the Dutch will live to fight another day and that other day will be against Eoin Hand's Republic of Ireland in a World Cup qualification play-off, likely early in the new year.

Eoin Hand and his assistant, Terry Conroy, have led an FAI delegation to Paris hoping to witness the stalemate that could potentially open the door to the promised land. Eoin Hand and Terry Conroy believe. Hand tells the media that, having assessed both sides' prospects, a draw could be very much on the cards. The Dutch, knowing a point is enough to keep them in the race, will play it safe and seek to frustrate the French. The experienced side selected by Kees Rijvers for the game – including greats Ruud Krol, Johnny Rep and Johan Neeskens – has the wherewithal to do just that.

Assistant Terry Conroy believes that when playing at home, France have the beating of any side but that, at some stage, the luck of the Irish must surely hold true and this could be just the occasion. Given the controversially disallowed goals in Paris and Brussels, a change of fortune for the Irish is surely overdue.

Back home in Ireland, the match is screened live, the hopes of the football nation hanging on a game that Ireland cannot influence. Paul, like so many others, is glued to the TV – hope still in his heart. He's dragged himself through another school day, the match a beacon in a gloomy winter week, Christmas looking so terribly far away. He could do with a lift. Live football, any live football, is to be cherished. And here's a game, if the result is right, that could lift not just this ten-year-old but the whole country.

It'd been a dreadful few days on the island of Ireland. Performing his routine inspection of the newspaper, this time the *Irish Press* on matchday, Paul was faced once more with the mounting tale of terror and murder north of the border. It made for the grimmest of reading. Four days previous, the Reverend Robert Jonathan Bradford, the Ulster Unionist MP for Belfast South, had been assassinated by the Provisional IRA while holding a political clinic in a community centre. The caretaker of the building, Kenneth Campbell, was also murdered in the attack.

Bradford's funeral took place the day before the match in Paris and so it and the fallout from his murder dominate the newspapers. In the days since his death, tit-for-tat sectarian murders have seen the lives of two young Catholic men, 18-year-old Thomas McNulty and 21-year-old Peadar Fagan, as well as that of 42-year-old RUC man Albert Beacon, cruelly taken.

At Bradford's funeral, the celebrant, the Reverend Roy Magee, called for the reinstatement of the death penalty. A plea met with a round of applause amongst those gathered. Across the North, memorial services were held for the MP – with an estimated crowd of 10,000 gathering at Belfast City Hall.

In response to the wave of killings and the acute sectarian tensions, all police leave has been cancelled and 600 British troops moved in from the British mainland. The Reverend Ian Paisley, firebrand leader of the Democratic Unionist Party, has called for an all-out strike on Monday and, reportedly, has met with representatives of main loyalist paramilitary groups to discuss strategy.

Dáil Éireann (the Irish parliament) took the unprecedented step of passing a vote of sympathy with the widow and family of the Reverend Bradford while condemning his killing. Such votes would normally be reserved for the deaths of members of the Dáil itself or for international leaders. Dáil members stood in silence on Tuesday after Taoiseach Dr Garret FitzGerald and the leader of the opposition, Charles Haughey, condemned the spate of murders.

Dr FitzGerald said that the killing of an elected representative calls for particular condemnation. The assassination also served to remind everyone of the real objectives of the organisation responsible. He added that the IRA had once again shown its utter contempt for human life and for the democratic process, which it had recently sought to distort for its own ends. The taoiseach noted that the nationalist leader of the Social Democratic Labour Party in Northern Ireland, John Hume, had described the IRA's recent campaign as one of 'sectarian genocide' directed against Protestants. Dr FitzGerald went on to plead with loyalist groups not to respond in kind to the IRA's deliberate sectarian provocation. A call that was tragically falling on too many deaf ears.

Grim days. Dark days. And still only the early days of winter. No wonder Paul and many, many others reached out to the football for distraction, for respite from a troubled world too often filled with menace and tragedy. So, after homework and dinner, then servings of *Grange Hill* and *Life on Earth* on BBC2, Paul switches over to RTÉ One for the Republic of Ireland's, the Netherlands' and France's date with destiny.

And with 45 minutes gone, the match offers hope. The pattern of the game has been as expected. The Dutch have played from the off with a *what we have, we hold* mentality. Despite their many talents, an abundance of caution clearly pervades their thinking. The three corners they won in the first half illustrate the point. On each occasion, the Dutch commit no more than three players into positions inside the French penalty area. Such was their lack of attacking intent that a cockerel thrown on to the field at kick-off by someone in the home support was able to stand his ground largely untroubled just ahead of French left-back Maxim Bossis for the whole of the first period. In fact, the bird was only discommoded by the adventurous runs of the defender in his many forays forward.

France have dominated possession but only have a shot just over the bar by Bernard Lacombe on 24 minutes and a Michel Platini strike, saved by Dutch keeper Hans van Breukelen on the 40-minute mark, to show for their efforts. The Dutch, expertly marshalled by Ruud Krol, have defended stoutly. But there was a growing sense as the half wore on that ceding so much possession to French captain Platini and his midfield colleagues, Alain Giresse and Bernard Genghini, all of whom look sharp and inventive, was to invite trouble.

Kees Rijvers is the first to adjust his side, bringing on Simon Tahamata at half-time to play with three frontmen – the winger joining Johnny Rep and Cees van Kooten in attack. It's the first bold Dutch move of the night.

Michel Hidalgo keeps faith with his initial selection, determined not to panic. Notably, there is one French change – the cockerel will not feature in the second period. And it's just as well because the position he'd occupied is one that Didier Six and Gérard Janvion are very much intent on filling in the second half of the game as France go in search of a goal.

Right from referee Antonio Garrido's opening whistle, Platini assumes control once more, dropping deep to make the play. France resume at a higher tempo, playing more like they did against the Irish a year before, when Eoin Hand's men were almost blown off their feet.

France's first attack is a clear show of intent. Marius Tresor instigates a move that ultimately sees the big defender as one of five French players who attempt to get on the end of a Giresse cross. The home crowd roars approval and encouragement.

But moments later, Arnold Mühren has a clear sight of the French goal. Giresse is robbed in the centre circle and the ball runs to the giant Van Kooten. The Dutch striker runs left, then turns back and finds Tahamata. The winger jinks inside Genghini and spots the run of the Ipswich man, slipping him in behind Lopez, 30 yards from goal. As Bossis struggles to cover from the right, Mühren chips Castaneda but the ball loops high and wide, to the relief of the home crowd, who are silenced just for a second. A big chance for the Dutch.

The opportunity emboldens the men in orange as they enjoy a period of possession in the French half for the first time in the match. The great Neeskens, quiet for 55 minutes, is suddenly to the fore. But this new sense of adventure, the feeling that there may be something more than a draw in this game for them, is a help to Michel Hidalgo's France. Now, there is space for Les Bleus to exploit behind enemy lines as the Dutch commit more men forward and Krol takes a defensive starting position just a little higher up the pitch.

The next French attack is illustrative. A wonderful mazy dribble by Six from deep in his own half draws in three Dutch players. Six slips the ball back to Platini, who immediately sets Tresor free to storm forward through the middle of the park. Tresor finds Genghini, who attacks down the right of the Dutch box before going down under a challenge – but Mr Garrido correctly waves away the penalty appeals to howls from the home fans. A brilliant tackle by Ben Wijnstekers.

The game comes alive. France storm forward again and Genghini finds Giresse, who races towards the Dutch penalty area before slipping it inside to Platini, 25 yards out. Neeskens lunges to prevent the French captain shooting but fouls Platini, and France have a free kick on the edge of the 'D', directly in front of Van Breukelen's goal.

Michel Platini eyes glory. He takes the free kick but disappointingly crashes it into the six-man orange wall. But Gallic groans are silenced almost immediately as the referee blows for another free kick, this time just a yard more to the left and two yards further forward. Jan Peters, who'd been to the right of the wall, is penalised for not being ten yards from Platini's original strike. It seems harsh. No one calls for it. Peters doesn't directly affect Platini's initial effort but when the ball rebounds off the wall, it does come to Peters, so perhaps an advantage was gained.

Platini, like the baying crowd, is visibly delighted with a second opportunity – celebrating the ref's decision with two clenched fists. The Dutch are clearly worried about the French captain's set-piece prowess. Van Breukelen seems unsure where to stand on his goal line, shifting left and right before settling on a position left of centre. As Platini addresses the ball, Ruud Krol moves past his keeper to station himself at the right-hand post, fearing Platini will clip it over the wall. Platini steps up and lashes a curling ball past Van Breukelen just inside the left-hand post. The keeper, seemingly unsighted, barely sees it, barely reacts. A moment of pure brilliance! Platini scores, the Parc des Princes explodes. 'Oui, Michel! Oui, Michel!' they roar.

Michel Platini turns, runs to the halfway line and falls to his knees as his team-mates arrive to celebrate. The heavy tension in the crowd is released. The Paris night is filled with the roar of 50,000 voices and the blasts of nearly as many air horns and klaxons.

As Hans van Breukelen retrieves the ball from the corner of the net, the nature of the game has changed. Kees Rijvers's men can no longer just contain their opponents. They will not go to the World Cup unless they can find a goal. Eoin Hand's Republic of Ireland will not be going to the World Cup either, unless the Dutch can find a goal. On the eve of the match, Eoin Hand told the *Irish Examiner* that even if the Dutch fell behind in the game, he believed they had it in them to strike back. All is not lost. Not yet anyway.

On the field of play, tempers fray as Genghini and Peters clash. The French midfielder slides in to dispossess Peters and the Dutchman makes sure to leave his stud marks on Genghini's thigh in response. Peters is awarded the free kick for Genghini's original challenge. He takes the free kick from wide right. But it's a limp, weak effort that barely makes it to the edge of the French area. It indicates a sense of dejection. A loss of belief.

Celebratory smoke bombs cause Mr Garrido to pause the game for a minute until the air clears. He then penalises Van de Korput for holding Lacombe, before booking the defender for a subsequent show of dissent as the Dutch side begin to lose their composure.

But the visitors push on, as they must, and Platini and Giresse revel in the space afforded. Just past the hour mark,

Platini – sublime in every aspect of midfield play on the night – splits the Dutch rearguard with wonderful awareness and vision to find Lacombe running left to right inside the penalty area. The striker tries a backheel to Six, who is free on the penalty spot and must surely score, but Lacombe gets it all wrong. It should be two for France. But the opening is spurned. The Netherlands, and the Republic of Ireland, breathe again.

And a minute later, the Dutch are almost in. Tresor misjudges the flight of a spinning ball and full-back Poortvliet's acrobatic kick from the byline finds the hulking Van Kooten eight yards out. A chance! Dutch and Irish fans are out of their seats wherever they are watching ... but they slump back down, deflated, as the Go Ahead Eagles forward clumps the ball horribly wide.

France relax. And now France are visibly beginning to enjoy themselves. Six torments Wijnstekers, then tricks Tahamata on the left wing before finding the supporting Maxime Bossis. He plays a one-two with Giresse before picking out Rocheteau on the edge of the Dutch penalty area. Dominique Rocheteau impudently tees up Giresse, whose volley sails just wide of the far post. Brilliant football. Magnifique.

Platini bamboozles Peters deep in the French half, then releases Genghini, who finds Rocheteau wide left. He dances inside the Dutch cover and bears down on the left edge of the penalty area, finding Six along the 'D'. Six turns and shoots but Van Breukelen saves and, though he spills the ball, is quickest to react. The Dutch are barely holding on. Dutch and Irish dreams are slipping away as Kees Rijvers's men struggle for purchase.

Zimako replaces Lacombe, who has run himself to a standstill, on 70 minutes. Winger La Ling replaces defender Van de Korput as Kees Rijvers rolls the dice.

The Netherlands up the intensity but continue to offer no real sense that they can get back on terms. France are defending comfortably, while always seeming to threaten a swift counter.

With 12 minutes left, the brilliant Michel Platini, who has been suffering from cramp, leaves the fray. The French captain wastes as much time as he can, limping after Mr Garrido to shake his hand before departing, looking to upset any Dutch rhythm and run down the clock. It's a blow for the French fans to see him depart but that blow is softened considerably given that his replacement is Jean Tigana!

The tension ratchets up a few more notches and the clock ticks down. France are in control. This result will almost surely secure their qualification. But a goal for the Dutch, no matter how unlikely it seems, would revive the hopes of two nations.

Van Breukelen punts long with a goal kick as the Dutch go direct – the clock demanding that they dispense with any artful building from the back. The results are no better. But they are not beaten yet. Eighty minutes on the clock and Peters drives down the right wing before crossing dangerously into a French penalty box now flooded with Dutch players. But Jean Tigana is there with a wonderful, volleyed clearance that gives the Netherlands their first corner of the second half.

Six players in orange await the set piece – in stark contrast to the three committed forward for corners in the first half. But Janvion easily heads away the ball at the near post. Giresse completes the clearance, releasing the speedy Zimako down the right as France break. Zimako to Six, Six to Zimako and, in a thrice, the substitute is in on goal but Van Breukelen comes out bravely to claim. The Dutch keeper restarts without delay and Tahamata scampers deep into French territory before being fouled by Tigana wide left.

The substitute swings over the kick himself and finds Van Kooten free at the far post. The big striker controls and, with the goal at his mercy, fires over the bar! But it wouldn't have counted, even if he had hit the target. It wouldn't have counted because the big striker had shoved Tresor in the back. No wonder he had so much space.

Eight minutes left. Castaneda takes the resulting free kick and launches it upfield, where Genghini flicks on to Rocheteau. Rocheteau kills it and takes the ball wide left before turning to face the shadowing Ruud Krol. Dominique Rocheteau twists. Dominique Rocheteau turns and then Dominique Rocheteau crosses low, left-footed across the box, where Didier Six arrives from the right wing and directs the ball past Hans van Breukelen and into the Dutch net. Didier Six's goal sends the Parc des Princes into raptures and Didier Six's goal surely sends France to the World Cup in Spain.

Hearts break and dreams are shattered all over the Netherlands. Hearts break and dreams are shattered all over Ireland. And hearts break and dreams are shattered in Paul's sitting room. It was a vain hope. A long shot. The French may not have travelled well. But in Paris, they've often been imperious, untouchable. And, tonight, France have been imperious and untouchable once more.

The Dutch are done. They play on but they are done. Tresor will not yield. Bossis will not yield. Lopez will not yield. Genghini, Giresse, Tigana will not yield. Smoke fills the air once more. Firecrackers explode. Every French touch is greeted with a roar. Photographers surround Michel Hidalgo on his bench. The Netherlands win a free kick 20 yards from goal in the 90th minute. La Ling crosses, Neeskens arrives but heads the ball high and wide and nowhere in particular. A minute later, Tahamata repeats the trick, shooting high and wide when well placed. The Netherlands' night in a nutshell. Kees Rijvers's men have been toothless. Heads hang. The Dutch are done.

Mr Garrido blows his whistle one last time. The Parc des Princes explodes once more. France are surely going to the World Cup. Only Cyprus now stand in their way. Cyprus, who've played seven games and lost seven games. Cyprus, who've scored four times but conceded on 25 occasions. There's still the Cyprus game, Paul says to his dad, his relentless child's positivity about this Ireland team shining through. 'Anything could happen, couldn't it, Dad?' 'Yes,' his dad says, smiling supportively, 'anything could happen.' But that smile says that he really wouldn't bet on it.

## 1982 FIFA World Cup qualification: UEFA Group Two

|                    | P | W | D | L | F  | A  | Pts |
|--------------------|---|---|---|---|----|----|-----|
| Belgium            | 8 | 5 | 1 | 2 | 12 | 9  | 11  |
| Republic of Ireland| 8 | 4 | 2 | 2 | 17 | 11 | 10  |
| Netherlands        | 8 | 4 | 1 | 3 | 11 | 7  | 9   |
| France             | 7 | 4 | 0 | 3 | 16 | 8  | 8   |
| Cyprus             | 7 | 0 | 0 | 7 | 4  | 25 | 0   |

Michel Hidalgo is bullish post-match. We were criticised so much that this was the only way to respond, he tells the assembled media. My happiness is above all for my team, he adds, because it is they who deserve it. Kees Rijvers is both realistic and philosophical. We didn't dare enough, he admits. His team didn't take the play to the French quick enough through midfield. And it wasn't until it was too late in the match that they finally showed themselves. We're eliminated, he says, but life continues.

Eoin Hand says that at half-time he'd had real hope that the Republic of Ireland's luck might be about to change. But, in the end, the home side were worthy winners and Eoin Hand believes, like Paul's dad in Dublin, that it'd be simply too much to expect France to be held to a draw or to lose to Cyprus, especially at the Parc des Princes.

Eoin Hand's Republic of Ireland camp are left to reflect on the iniquities of Paris and, particularly, of Brussels. And their frustration is magnified with news of the qualification of Ron Greenwood's England and Billy Bingham's Northern Ireland from much less testing groups. To make matters worse, both amassed just nine points and yet both will travel to Spain for football's greatest extravaganza, while Eoin Hand and his squad, who earned ten points in the UEFA region's toughest group, will likely watch from afar because, short of a Cypriot miracle, the Republic of Ireland will cruelly miss out on goal difference.

Talking to the *Evening Press* the day after France's big win, the Cyprus manager dismisses any hopes of an upset. We'll go to Paris hoping for a good result, Kostas Talianos tells the paper, but there's no chance that we'll beat France. France are much too good, he explains. All he can promise is that his team will try hard. But the French are world class. It'd be nice if his team could help the Republic of Ireland's cause, he says, but he regrets that, realistically, they'll be unable to do so.

And so it comes to pass. Two winter fixtures in the French capital see the slow lingering death of the Republic of Ireland's dream of qualification for the 1982 World Cup. The final throes play out on Saturday, 5 December, when France, as expected, beat Cyprus easily, winning by four goals to nil in Paris. There has been no live television coverage on RTÉ this time. Precious little is written about the game in the run-up. And precious little is written about it afterwards either. Hope had long departed amongst the realistic.

For the record, Michel Hildago's side dominate from the first whistle and effectively put their meek opponents to bed midway through the first half with goals from Rocheteau and Lacombe. The second half is a procession and the French add two more through Lacombe and Genghini to copper-fasten the result and qualification for Espana 82.

Paul's optimism and belief that anything could happen are flattened. But at least he wasn't the only person who got it wrong. John Giles said that he couldn't see the two places from the group being filled other than on a points basis after his Republic of Ireland side had spurned chance after chance in Nicosia on the way to a 3-2 win in their first qualifier. And yet, 21 months later, the cold hard facts of the matter show that France, and not the Republic of Ireland, will go to Spain by virtue of a superior goal difference.

Eoin Hand's Republic of Ireland have come so close, so agonisingly close to the dream of a first World Cup qualification. They've made the country proud. They've played brilliantly at times. They've created many great moments and memories. But this is of little consolation to Eoin Hand and his Republic of Ireland team. It's of little consolation to the Irish football public. And it's of little consolation to a ten-year-old boy who lives for football. In fact, it's of no consolation at all. The dream is shattered. And despite all that they did so well, all of the positives, it's hard, so very hard, not to look back in anger and regret Paris and, especially, Brussels. And so hard not to wonder … what if?

## 1982 FIFA World Cup qualification: UEFA Group Two final standings

|  | P | W | D | L | F | A | Pts |
|---|---|---|---|---|---|---|---|
| Belgium | 8 | 5 | 1 | 2 | 12 | 9 | 11 |
| France | 8 | 5 | 0 | 3 | 20 | 8 | 10 |
| Republic of Ireland | 8 | 4 | 2 | 2 | 17 | 11 | 10 |
| Netherlands | 8 | 4 | 1 | 3 | 11 | 7 | 9 |
| Cyprus | 8 | 0 | 0 | 8 | 4 | 29 | 0 |

# 13.

# Sliding Doors

IMAGINE RAUL FERNANDES NAZARÉ saw what we all saw? Imagine he made the right decision? Imagine Eoin Hand and his team had gotten that little bit of luck that others seemed to get? Imagine they'd gotten that little bit of justice on a miserable, rain-sodden night in Brussels? Just imagine …

*… Eoin Hand is out for a quiet meal with his family on a February night in 1982. Or it would be quiet, if people didn't keep interrupting to give their thoughts on his Republic of Ireland football team and their thoughts on the job he was doing as manager. People feel he's public property. People feel they can say what they like. And they do. Over and over. But that's okay. Eoin Hand is getting used to it. Eoin Hand knows people are excited. Eoin Hand knows that the World Cup in Spain is only months away. And Eoin Hand knows that, in the dark of winter and in grim political, economic and social days, people need to look forward to something good, to grab hold of something good.*

*'Excuse me, Mr Hand,' says a man in his early 40s, who has apologetically approached the table. 'Very sorry to interrupt but I just wanted to wish you and the lads all the very best in Spain. You've done an extraordinary thing.'*

*Eoin Hand thanks the man, shakes his hand and chats amiably and briefly about the adventure to come. Eoin Hand understands. Eoin Hand knows the score. After the man has left, Eoin Hand turns to his wife and says: 'In football, you're either a hero or a bollocks, there's no in between. At the moment, I'm a hero. So we'd better enjoy it.'*

*Eoin Hand is a man in demand. The public and the media would all like a word. Big clubs are watching closely. After all, Eoin Hand, at 36, is set to be the youngest manager ever to lead a team to a World Cup finals. And Eoin Hand will be doing the heretofore undoable – he'll be leading the Republic of Ireland senior international side to its first major tournament. No wonder everyone wants a piece of Eoin Hand. No wonder they hang on Eoin Hand's every word. And no wonder Eoin Hand is a person of interest across the game, amongst its legion media and amongst its many clubs.*

*Four months out, the excitement is building. Four months out, the World Cup is seemingly on everyone's mind. Four months out and plans are being made. Plans never made before. Plans never made before by the FAI. Plans never made before by the Republic of Ireland football team. Plans never made before by Irish football fans. Plans for transport. Plans for places to stay. Plans to save, beg and borrow. Plans for time off. Plans for passports. Plans for a training camp. Plans for the world champions, Argentina, and the opening game of the World Cup itself at the Camp Nou in Barcelona on 13 June. And plans, too, for group matches with Hungary and the exotic, unknown El Salvador.*

*Reflecting on the qualification campaign, which featured three European football heavyweights – Belgium, France and the Netherlands – Eoin Hand will point to Frank Stapleton's goal in Brussels in March 1981 as the pivotal moment, the moment where his team's fortunes turned. Having dropped a point at home to Guy Thys's men in their third qualification game, it was vital the Republic of Ireland get something from the return fixture.*

*The goal was somewhat controversial. The Belgians were incensed, believing that referee Raul Fernandes Nazaré should've chalked it off. For the Belgians, the Portuguese official had wandered into the path of Liam Brady's free kick, impeded a Belgian defender and inadvertently helped Frank Stapleton to score. As Mr Nazaré looked to his linesman, Eoin Hand believed the goal would be disallowed. Eoin Hand believed that, like in Paris earlier in the campaign, like in Sofia under John Giles and like in Paris before that, the officials were looking for a reason to disallow the goal.*

*The Republic of Ireland management and players had become accustomed to seeing goals in foreign climes inexplicably chalked off. But not this time. Not this time. For this time, Mr Nazaré pointed to halfway and the Republic of Ireland led 1-0.*

*That Belgium replied late on made no matter – the point secured in Brussels ultimately sending the Republic of Ireland to Spain in their stead. As Eoin Hand's assistant, Terry Conroy, wryly observed, the luck of the Irish had finally held through …*

\* \* \*

Of course, the concept of the sliding doors moment – a pivotal juncture in life where a decision or event can lead to significantly different outcomes – offers no certainty that said outcomes will be any more favourable. Had Raul Fernandes Nazaré awarded Frank Stapleton what appeared a perfectly good goal all those years ago, it's possible that Belgium, who were a strong, resilient football team, could still have run out as winners in Brussels.

But for me, the ten-year-old Paul, now 53, it's much more fun to imagine the best-possible result or at least one that would have tilted the balance of the group in the Republic of Ireland's favour. A result sending the Irish to a first major tournament well before that eventuality six years later. And it's an idea that spawned a book, this book, in homage to the first Republic of Ireland team I ever went to see and, arguably, the most accomplished, in both ability and approach, the country has ever fielded.

When the Republic of Ireland finally did make it to the top table, the 1988 European Championship, qualification famously revolved around Jack Charlton's own sliding doors moment. A moment in which he and his team had no hand, act or part. Gary Mackay of Hearts and Scotland's 86th-minute winner in the Sofia rain in a game that meant little or nothing to the Scots is possibly the most famous goal in Irish football history.

Had Mackay not scored, Bulgaria would've gone to West Germany and it's entirely possible that the glory years that Irish fans enjoyed under Big Jack may never have materialised. Failure to qualify, allied with poor attendances and a brand of football that many found hard to stomach, would likely have seen the Englishman lose his job after just one qualifying campaign. But on such moments, worlds turn and lives change.

Raul Fernandes Nazaré's infamous decision has haunted a generation of Irish football fans. And while Michael Robinson also saw a goal disallowed in Paris in controversial circumstances during the same campaign, the Portuguese official's ruling at the Heysel Stadium was seen as the more pivotal. It has certainly lived longer in the memory.

Eoin Hand's side had performed admirably in the Parc des Princes. Despite the concession of an early goal, they'd hung on grimly while being entirely outplayed by the Platini and Tigana-inspired French for the first 35 minutes, before working their way back into the match. Had Robinson's effort counted, there was still a sense on the night that the French had more class, more gears to run through and that, ultimately, their victory was a deserved one.

Brussels was an entirely different affair. Robinson, Stapleton, Langan and Co. gave as good as they got. A point from the night certainly wouldn't have flattered Eoin Hand's team. For a younger audience, it's worth pointing out that Raul Fernandes Nazaré's decision to disallow the goal was, for an earlier generation, the same as the *Thierry Henry handball* moment. The same heartbreak. The same disgust. But it was made all the more painful because the Irish had hopes similarly and familiarly derailed in recent memory. And because the Republic of Ireland had never got so close to qualification.

The depth of feeling around Brussels was illustrated 20 years later when author Paul Howard, then a journalist with the *Sunday Tribune*, travelled to Lisbon to challenge Raul Fernandes Nazaré as to his thinking on the night. Armed with Eoin Hand's video copy of the game, Howard came away none the wiser.

Nazaré, then 64, told Howard how he was well aware of how important the game was to the Irish and recalled the sadness in their eyes at the final whistle. Misremembering the anger of the

Irish camp for sadness may have been understandable so long after the fact. But Nazaré's inability to convincingly explain his decision only served to reignite the frustration of readers who witnessed the events of that infamous occasion.

His initial recollection was that Frank Stapleton was offside. Nazaré then explained to Howard that it really wasn't his decision to make because his linesman had raised his flag to alert him to the infringement. Then, on thinking a little deeper, Raul Fernandes Nazaré claimed he'd actually blown for offside before Stapleton tucked the ball away; so, indeed, there never really had been any goal to disallow!

Paul Howard suggested they look at the video evidence. RTÉ commentator Jimmy Magee's voice filled the living room in Nazaré's Lisbon apartment. 'Kevin Moran has come forward for it. Ireland have positioned Moran, No.5, Stapleton, No.8, and Robinson, No.11. They're the only three. There's nobody out of shot ... STAPLETON! ... The referee's going to disallow it, I think. Once more, controversy surrounds Ireland in an important match. Now, what's the reason this time?'

Clearly, the whistle is blown *after* Stapleton dispatches the ball into the Belgian net. Raul Fernandes Nazaré asks to see it again. This time, it's clear the linesman doesn't signal at all and only raises his flag cautiously, almost apologetically, at least three seconds after the ball hits the rigging. Nazaré and Howard play and replay the incident. His recollection jolted, the retired official then claimed that he disallowed the goal because he'd signalled an indirect free kick and that no one had touched the ball after Liam Brady. More close inspection of the incident, now with the help of Nazaré's daughter and son-in-law, disabuses him of the notion. Another look and a final explanation – the ball, in fact, hit him, hence the necessity to disallow Frank Stapleton's goal.

Raul Fernandes Nazaré concedes that he's badly positioned for the set piece. In amongst the players, rather than on the edge of the penalty area and with a better vantage point. But the on-screen evidence still confounds his explanation. Raul Fernandes Nazaré suggests that he's buffeted by Stapleton as he tries to connect with Brady's cross and the ball flies into the net off his back. But the video says different. He's clearly several feet away from the ball as Stapleton finishes.

Seeing the doubts in Nazaré's family's eyes and with his efforts to explain taking on a desperate tone, Paul Howard decides not to press Nazaré any further. 'The sacred verities,' he writes, 'that give shape to his [Nazaré's] world are being challenged by a complete stranger and in front of the family he cherishes.'

Whatever the reason for Raul Fernandes Nazaré's decision on that apocryphal night at the Heysel Stadium – be it a question of competence or something more nefarious, as some, including Eoin Hand, still believe – the result was ultimately the same. Jan Ceulemans's late, late winner, which stemmed from yet more questionable refereeing, dealt a mortal blow to Eoin Hand's Republic of Ireland team and their Spanish dreams.

* * *

Despite my disappointment at the Republic of Ireland's failure to qualify for the 1982 World Cup in Spain, it'd be fair to say that the guts of a month of live football in a time when any live football was gold dust provided much in the way of compensation. The more so when I got to enjoy arguably the greatest World Cup of them all.

Perhaps everyone's first World Cup is the one they enjoy the most, the one they rate as the best? But having seen every World Cup since, for me 1982 has yet to be surpassed.

This, after all, was the World Cup where African nations finally made their mark. Where Cameroon put it up to the established European powers of Poland and Italy, where Lakhdar Belloumi and Rabah Madjer of Algeria, a nation playing in their first ever World Cup finals match, put the mighty European champions West Germany to the sword. And this was the World Cup where the Germans and the Austrians then colluded disgracefully to see the exciting North Africans eliminated. The 'Disgrace of Gijón', as the match was later dubbed, caused disgust and uproar in equal measure.

This was the World Cup where Kuwaiti sheikhs stormed a pitch in protest at a ghostly whistle and where tiny Northern Ireland beat hosts Spain and reached the second round. This was the World Cup where the 21-year-old Diego Maradona was hounded and kicked until he cracked, where Bryan Robson scored 28 seconds into England's first World Cup finals match since 1970 and where Zbigniew Boniek became a household name. This was the World Cup where the wonderful France of Platini, Tigana and Giresse laid down a marker and played gloriously. This was the World Cup where we witnessed the first ever penalty shoot-out, in the gut-wrenching semi-final where West Germany broke French hearts and Harald Schumacher broke Patrick Battiston's teeth and ribs.

And this was the World Cup of the greatest football team never to win a World Cup. The World Cup of Sócrates, Zico, Éder, Júnior, Falcão and Oscar, the most wonderful of Brazil teams, playing the most flamboyant and joyous football ever seen at any tournament. For me, they were the most enduring memory. Brazil were myth and legend. To see them play surpassed every expectation. To see them fail reduced me to tears.

And, ultimately, this was the World Cup of Paolo Rossi. The man who silenced the Samba drums, made me weep and created one of the game's greatest stories of redemption. And this was the World Cup of Italy, the Azzurri who came from seemingly nowhere to win it, and of Marco Tardelli, who's enraptured goal celebration in the final reverberated across the globe and resonated down through time.

It's hard to imagine, 40-odd years later, how my enjoyment of the 1982 World Cup could've been any greater had the Republic of Ireland qualified. But that still hasn't stopped me wondering through the years just how that fine Irish vintage might've fared had they made it. And no doubt it's something Eoin Hand must've pondered too, many times.

Hand recognises the personal and professional excitement that qualification would've engendered. He would've loved the opportunity and the challenge. And he's certain his players would've risen to the demands. But Eoin Hand finds it hard to talk about such things, to imagine such thrilling things, without his thoughts being clouded by memories of his difficult working relationship with the FAI. Even four decades on, Eoin Hand feels that the excitement of a World Cup qualification could well have been tempered radically by inevitable, frustrating dealings with the blazers in Merrion Square.

It's as if Eoin Hand is suffering from a form of post-traumatic stress disorder. And when he talks about his former employers, it's not too hard to understand why. 'It was a constant battle,' he says. 'The most enjoyable part of the whole thing was the football with your team and who you were playing against. But the horrible part was who you were dealing with, your bosses. They made it a battle. They made the games more difficult for everybody, for everybody.'

Even seemingly mundane, administrative issues like travel arrangements and other necessary pre-tournament preparations would've had the propensity to become nightmarish, the former Republic of Ireland manager believes. And Eoin Hand doesn't lack for examples to back up such fears. Take the fact that when he took the Ireland job, his employers in Merrion Square struggled to understand why he wanted to travel to England at weekends to run the rule over Irish players. And how, when he did convince them of the necessity, given the simple fact that this is where the majority of his players plied their trade, he often struggled to get his expenses back.

Or how on assuming the position of manager of the senior international side, his suggestion that he travel to the European Championship in Italy to scout the Belgians and the Dutch, who his team would face in World Cup qualification, was met with similar bewilderment and surprise. And then, having convinced the blazers that this was what an international manager should be doing, they sent him to a hotel in Rome that, shall we say, was more interested in its clientele paying by the hour than by the night!

Or how about Hand's constant battles with and failed attempts to convince the FAI of the benefits of selecting bigger squads for qualification matches to allow for better training sessions and preparation – rather than the 15 or 16 they'd insist on in their efforts to spare expense?

Or what about the time Eoin Hand took it on himself to negotiate a deal with the Green Isle Hotel on the outskirts of Dublin to get his players away from the substandard and unsuitable accommodation the FAI had regularly arranged for them in the city? The Green Isle Hotel was delighted to offer a favourable rate in exchange for the profile gained from hosting Eoin Hand's talented side. But the FAI wasn't especially impressed with the manager's solo run ... well, at least not until Hand told them that the deal he'd arranged would cost less than what they were currently paying. Unsurprisingly, the FAI jumped on it. Eoin Hand got a win here. And he was happy that his side were to get better digs. But Eoin Hand wasn't happy that, as manager of the international side, it was he who had to do the negotiating. It was he who had to show enterprise. It was he who was organising accommodation befitting professional footballers representing their country, when he should have been focusing on the football alone.

Eoin Hand well understood that the FAI was a small organisation that naturally had an amateurish outlook. He accepted that. But what he was never able to accept was that too many of those involved in the positions of power lacked vision and drive and saw the association as a vehicle for self-aggrandisement. And, so, Eoin Hand had good reason to believe that qualification for the World Cup wouldn't have changed the FAI's general tendency towards expediency, inertia and shambles, even if it would've altered the balance of power in his relationship with the association and put him in a much stronger position going forward.

Critically, if Eoin Hand's Republic of Ireland had qualified for the 1982 World Cup, the FAI would've had no option but to back him. The bigger squad would've been mandatory, for a start, as FIFA would've required a 22-man selection for the tournament. A proper training camp would've been key to preparations, a necessity. And with the eyes of the media trained upon them, the FAI would've found it difficult to squirm their way out of or around their responsibilities.

Nevertheless, Eoin Hand believes that it would still have been a battle. Eoin Hand believes that getting the training camp sorted would still largely have been down to him. Eoin Hand wouldn't have trusted the association to do it right anyway. So, Eoin Hand says that he would likely have worked with former Irish international team-mate Ray Treacy, then a travel agent, and Terry Conroy to get it sorted.

Ray Treacy was well versed in how those in Merrion Square functioned, or didn't function, as the case may be. But even with Ray Treacy's expertise, Eoin Hand believes that just getting the basic organisation in place, getting his training camp in place would've been hellish hard work for himself and Terry Conroy.

But such troubles and distractions aside, from a purely footballing perspective, a pre-tournament training camp would've been a massive boon for the Republic of Ireland. It would have been the first time ever that management and players would've got such a comparatively lengthy time to work together in concerted fashion. Crucial time over at least a month, both before and during the tournament, for developing and working on patterns of play, on ideas and tactics, on relationships and understanding.

Compare that to the short time Eoin Hand had with his players for even the biggest of European Championship or World Cup qualifiers, which were predominantly played on Wednesdays. With UK-based players figuring for their clubs on a Saturday, Eoin Hand would have his first training session the following Monday. But even then, he wouldn't see the likes of Liam Brady, Mick Walsh and Don Givens until late Monday night, as they'd have been in action on Sunday in Italy, Portugal and Switzerland. So, the first time Eoin Hand and Terry Conroy would work with their full complement would be on the Tuesday, on the eve of the game.

'I always thought that if we'd qualified and had a camp like that, we'd have been very strong at the 82 World Cup,' says Eoin Hand, 'because we did have very good players, both individually and collectively. Having them together wouldn't only have made a difference in the tournament itself but in later campaigns. It would've been invaluable.'

And the Republic of Ireland did have very fine players indeed. Back then and now, for the smaller countries like Ireland, having a core of players of high calibre in critical positions was and is the key to being competitive on the international stage. Ideally, if such players can form a spine in the team, from central defence through midfield and at least one in a forward position, then you can surround them with more workmanlike players and compete.

'The bones of your team has to be serious, respected, strong, experienced,' says Eoin Hand. And his team had such bones – Lawrenson, Moran, O'Leary, Daly, Grealish, Brady, Stapleton, Robinson – right up the middle of the park. For Eoin Hand, that team was the best ever assembled in the green of Ireland.

'Mark Lawrenson was one of the best footballers I ever worked with, both technically and in terms of consistency,' says Hand. 'His abilities were so good and he did the basic things so very well that he never dropped below a certain standard.'

It was no real surprise that Bob Paisley brought him to Liverpool at the height of the club's powers during that period and no surprise that he figured in the first team almost immediately. And had the Irish qualified for Spain, Mark Lawrenson would've been travelling to the World Cup with league title and League Cup winner's medals safely stowed in a drawer at home after a brilliant first season at Anfield, where he demonstrated his quality and versatility at left-back, in central midfield and at centre-half.

Eoin Hand loved that versatility. And he loved Mark Lawrenson's willingness to do a job wherever he was asked to play. 'If I asked him to play in goal, he'd just have said, "Okay." No fuss. He had a great brain and he was cool – cool as you like. He never got flustered and had a lovely mentality when it came to playing the game.' Mark Lawrenson was world class.

Eoin Hand and the Republic of Ireland had serious options at centre-back. Not just Lawrenson but Kevin Moran and David

O'Leary too. Moran had emerged during the qualification campaign, taking his opportunities to impress during O'Leary's unfortunate run with injury. The former Dublin Gaelic footballer learned quickly, both at Manchester United and with the Republic of Ireland, and, had the team qualified, would've had serious claims to a starting position.

'Kevin gave you that steel,' Eoin Hand recalls. 'He was as tough as nails. He tackled hard, was brilliant in the air and was afraid of nothing.' Kevin Moran epitomised the spirit Eoin Hand wanted in the team.

Meanwhile, David O'Leary was one of the most respected ball-playing centre-halves in the game. 'He was more of a thoroughbred,' says Hand. 'Very, very accomplished, very quick and a good reader of the game.' His calm and quality on the ball would've been invaluable in the heat of Spain, where building from the back and keeping possession would've been the order of the day.

And Eoin Hand's team had quality in midfield, where Liam Brady and Tony Grealish were crucial. 'Liam Brady was brilliant in the last third of the pitch. That's where you wanted him,' Eoin Hand recounts. John Giles had tended to play him deeper but Hand wanted him in possession higher up the field, going towards the opposition goal with the ball at his feet. For Eoin Hand, that's when Brady was most dangerous.

The Juventus midfielder was another player in the very top bracket, one of the best creative players in the game. Underlining that quality, he was picking up his second Serie A title on the bounce just before the 82 World Cup, scoring the penalty in the last game of the season that secured Juve the title. Had Eoin Hand's Republic of Ireland qualified, they'd have been travelling to the tournament with winners of Serie A and the English First Division in their ranks.

'Tony Grealish was a rock for me. Tony Grealish would give you everything, everything,' Hand recalls fondly. Grealish's energy levels and willingness to work, not to mention an eye for goal, made him the perfect midfield foil for the likes of Brady. Players like Tony Grealish allow players like Liam Brady to play.

Akin to Dave Langan at right full-back and Kevin Moran at centre-back, Grealish would die for the team, die for his country.

And if Eoin Hand's Republic of Ireland had quality, experience, grit and power in midfield and defence, then they had those qualities in spades up front too, in the shape of Frank Stapleton and Michael Robinson.

'Frank Stapleton was one of the best frontmen in the game at the time,' Eoin Hand observes. His ability to hold the ball with his back to goal was a good as that of any player, anywhere. Frank Stapleton wasn't particularly quick, but he was incredibly strong and his first touch, with either foot or off his chest, was top quality. When a ball was played to him, it stuck. 'Once he had it under his control,' recalls Hand, 'no one could push him off the ball.'

Frank Stapleton was crucial to how Eoin Hand wanted his team to play. He'd give you control. He'd give you an out ball. He'd give you a position higher up the pitch off of which you could build your play. But that wasn't all, because Frank Stapleton was also one of the best in the business when it came to heading a football. Frank Stapleton could head a ball as hard as many players could kick it. And Frank Stapleton had three other brilliant qualities: he was hard, he was brave and, crucially, he was clever.

And in young Michael Robinson, Frank Stapleton had an almost perfect partner – a strong powerful runner who could stretch teams in behind and out wide. 'Michael Robinson was a totally different type of player,' recalls Eoin Hand. 'With the ball in front of him,' he explains, 'and when he was running, he was extremely strong and very hard to stop.' And Michael Robinson was an excellent crosser of the ball and, to boot, was good in front of goal.

Lawrenson, Moran, O'Leary, Brady, Grealish, Stapleton and Robinson – had the Republic of Ireland qualified for Spain, they would've had the bones of a team, the core of a team that could've made a serious impact. But the quality in Eoin Hand's Republic of Ireland squad was not limited to those players alone.

Because Eoin Hand's Republic of Ireland also had cultured full-backs Chris Hughton and John Devine to call on, not to mention the fiery, aggressive, adventurous Dave Langan. And Eoin Hand's Republic of Ireland also had Ronnie Whelan, who, like Mark Lawrenson, would've arrived in Spain having won a league title and a League Cup with Liverpool in an extraordinary breakthrough season. The 21-year-old scored 14 league and cup goals – including two in the League Cup Final against Spurs – in 47 appearances for the Reds and had usurped the great Ray Kennedy in the Liverpool line-up.

Moreover, Eoin Hand's Republic of Ireland could also call upon the guile and midfield goal threat of Gerry Daly, the versatility and know-how of Mick Martin, the experience of Steve Heighway and Don Givens, the predatory instincts and European nous of Porto striker Mick Walsh, and the stylish and exciting wing play of Ipswich's Kevin O'Callaghan. And although he played no part in the qualification campaign, it was highly likely that had Ireland qualified, then Spurs' marauding FA Cup-winning wide man Tony Galvin would also have travelled to Spain, having declared for Ireland in late 1981. Indeed, Galvin's Irish declaration caused much consternation at the English FA at the time, as they feared that more quality English-born players with Irish heritage would go green ahead of the World Cup if England failed to qualify!

Whatever way you slice it, the Republic of Ireland had quality all over the pitch. And the Republic of Ireland could've made a splash at Espana 82. 'I always thought,' confesses Eoin Hand, 'that we would've done very well. We could've excelled. We certainly could've been better than Northern Ireland, simply because we had a better team and better players.' And with good preparation, and time with the players in a pre-tournament training camp, Eoin Hand believes his players would have responded. 'We would've done very well there, you know, we really would.'

Eoin Hand's approach to the game and his team's style of play – which favoured minding the ball and building from the back, albeit with a dose of pragmatism – may also have boosted their tournament prospects. There's no doubt that Jack Charlton's direct, *put 'em under pressure* football yielded results. But there's long been an argument that greater respect for possession and progressive play could well have yielded even more success in that period, especially when you consider the quality players the Englishman had at his disposal.

Put simply, the further the Irish went into a tournament playing a brand of football where possession was often sacrificed for position, tournaments always played in baking heat and humidity, the more difficult it became to play as Jack Charlton required. Chasing, pressing and harrying the more proficient sides in 100 degree heat in the condensed, intense and energy-sapping tournament format eventually took its toll. Think Gelsenkirchen against the Dutch in 1988. Think Rome in 1990 against Italy. Think the Dutch again in Orlando in 1994.

Under such conditions, Eoin Hand's approach may have proven more effective. Hand wasn't against playing long balls in behind full-backs, turning them around and squeezing up on them as an option, just not as *the only option*. Eoin Hand recognised the importance of simple messaging and clear communication around a tactical approach when it came to international management, given the limited time available to work with players. But his approach, while relatively straightforward, was more nuanced than that of Jack Charlton.

Eoin Hand believed that the ball over the top offered limited possibilities, given the standard of the international game. Eoin Hand didn't believe in ceding possession in such a fashion. He preferred to play out from the back and encouraged passes into the feet of his frontmen. Good hold-up play was crucial and, in Frank Stapleton, Eoin Hand had the one of the best in the business. Balls into Stapleton stuck like glue and the Dubliner would bring the Irish midfield into play as Hand required, allowing Brady, Grealish, Whelan and their colleagues to receive passes facing the right way – towards the opposition goal.

But if the passing channel to Stapleton wasn't an option, then Eoin Hand wanted his defenders to go diagonally to the wide men. Again, if such options weren't available, they should go square or, as a last resort, backwards, even to the keeper, and then start again. It was a simple approach; one that players could follow easily, one that required less energy than the Charlton method, one that made good use of the ball players he had available – and one that may well have paid dividends in the heat of Spain.

\* \* \*

Given how closely matched Eoin Hand's Republic of Ireland were with the Belgians and French in qualification, it wouldn't be unfair to suggest that the Irish could've performed equally as well as both ultimately did in the 1982 World Cup. But given it was the Belgians the Irish would've replaced had Frank Stapleton's goal stood, it makes most sense to picture Eoin Hand's men in Belgian boots.

Tantalisingly, on that basis, had the Republic of Ireland qualified, they'd have kicked off the tournament against the holders, Argentina, at the iconic Camp Nou in Barcelona, with the whole world watching. And there'd have been an interesting subtext to the game – the Falklands War – which began with the Argentine invasion of the disputed islands on 2 April that year. Eoin Hand worried about how the FAI might've made preparations for Spain difficult, so one can only imagine how the conflict might further have muddied the waters and potentially upset his preparations. Just his luck!

In the run-up to the tournament (in the real world), Margaret Thatcher's government considered pulling England, Scotland and Northern Ireland from the competition because of Argentina's involvement. Indeed, it wasn't just the government who were reluctant for the teams to be involved. Reportedly, players from each of the home nations were said to feel uncomfortable about featuring in the same tournament as the Argentinians, given the loss of life amongst the British forces in the conflict.

There had been initial hopes that FIFA would bar Argentina. However, when it became clear that this wouldn't be the case, the UK government decided that withdrawing their teams would hand the Argentinian military junta a propaganda opportunity. It was believed that no other competing nations would follow their lead and, hence, it would be the UK sides, rather than Argentina, that would be set apart.

As events transpired, by the time the tournament kicked off on 13 June, the invading Argentine forces were on the point of surrender. Indeed, they did so in the Falklands capital of Port Stanley the following day.

Perhaps in a *what if* world in which Eoin Hand's men qualified, by dint of a Stapleton goal in Brussels, rather than the Belgians, the subsequent altered timelines and butterfly effects might somehow have seen the generalissimos in Buenos Aires thinking again on their ill-conceived plans. More likely, however, the invasion would've proceeded. And its highly likely that the UK-born contingent of the Republic of Ireland squad would've had some serious soul-searching to do before their Camp Nou World Cup debut. There's no question this would've been a diplomatically sensitive and emotionally charged time for those players and for their colleagues employed by UK clubs. And a potential nightmare for Eoin Hand and Terry Conroy to navigate in the run-up to the tournament.

But for the purposes of our parallel universe, the game at the Camp Nou goes ahead, with more than the usual interest and tensions. Perhaps pressure is brought to bear from the UK press on the Irish players to pull out. Perhaps the FAI and FIFA insist that sport and politics mustn't mix and the game must proceed. Perhaps the FAI realise that they simply can't afford to opt out, for financial reasons. And perhaps, as a show of defiance, some of the Republic of Ireland team refuse to shake hands with the opponents before or after the game. I'll leave the ponderables and imponderables to your imagination. Suffice to say, for the purposes of this book, the game goes ahead.

Intriguingly, Argentina were also Eoin Hand's first opponents when he took the reins as caretaker manager after John Giles's exit. That May evening back in 1980, his weakened side struggled to contain the touring Argentines, yet produced a creditable performance in losing by a single goal. But in Barcelona, in this new timeline, things would hopefully have been very different. Eoin Hand's Republic of Ireland squad would've been together for a couple of weeks prior to the game. And, with luck, they'd have faced César Luis Menotti's men with their first-choice XI on the back of a positive training-camp experience.

When the nations met in Dublin two years previously, there was no Liam Brady, there was no Frank Stapleton, there was no Mark Lawrenson. Michael Robinson had yet to receive his international clearance. Ronnie Whelan was just a kid in the Liverpool reserves and Kevin Moran was only making his second appearance in green. But all going well, the Republic of Ireland side that would face Argentina in Barcelona before the eyes of the world would be a significantly different prospect to the one Menotti's side faced at Lansdowne Road.

And it wouldn't be stretching credulity to suggest that this Republic of Ireland team would've had the wherewithal to do what the Belgians did in the real world – beat the world champions in the tournament's opening fixture. So, let's imagine that Eoin Hand's men do just that.

Belgium went on to top Group Two, narrowly beating El Salvador in Elche before picking up the point they needed to progress in first place in their last game with Hungary at the same venue. Again, given the quality in the Republic of Ireland ranks and given how convincingly they'd competed with Guy Thys's men in qualification, Eoin Hand's players certainly had it within them to produce similar results against both of those opponents and move through to the second phase. And let's say that's what transpires and the Irish march on!

The 1982 World Cup featured, uniquely, a second-round stage of four three-nation groups, made up of the winners and runners-up from the six first-round groups, and then semi-finals featuring the winners of these second-round groups. Belgium featured in Group A, where they faced the winners of Group One, Poland, and the runners-up from Group Six, the Soviet Union. And Belgium struggled, which might suggest, if we are being fair, that this is where any Irish adventure may well have come to a halt.

Jan Ceulemans and his team-mates were soundly thumped, 3-0, by Poland on 28 June. Widzew Łódź forward Zbigniew Boniek, ably abetted by the inspired performances of wingers Grzegorz Lato and Włodzimierz Smolarek, scored a scintillating hat-trick and was more or less unplayable on the night. Three days later, a 1-0 defeat to the USSR saw Belgium exit the tournament. A tense 0-0 draw between the Poles and the Soviets, two more states whose relations were strained, saw Poland qualify for the semi-finals. Two goals from Paolo Rossi ultimately broke Polish hearts and ended their dreams of making the final. But a 3-2 win over France saw them at least match their best ever performance at a World Cup finals, their third-place finish in 1974.

Now, who is to say what might have happened had the Poles and the Soviets faced off against the Irish? But given how Poland dismantled Belgium – and how they had easily beaten the touring Irish party in Bydgoszcz a year previously – a similar fate may have befallen the Republic of Ireland in the Camp Nou. They may have fared better against Oleg Blokhin and his comrades in the same venue three days later, given the Soviets hadn't exactly set the tournament alight. But the upward trajectory of the Polish through the tournament suggests it might be too much of a stretch to believe the Irish could've progressed to the last four.

And, so, in our alternative timeline, the road ends where it started for the Republic of Ireland, in Barcelona and at the Camp Nou.

*\*\**

Just imagine …

*On Tuesday afternoon, 6 July 1982, Eoin Hand's Republic of Ireland squad travel from Dublin Airport to a public homecoming on College Green amidst unprecedented scenes. Estimates put the crowds thronging the route down through Santry, Whitehall, Drumcondra,*

*Dorset Street, O'Connell Street and across the River Liffey to College Green at over half a million. Such was the excitement and the crowds that came to greet their returning heroes that the journey itself took almost three hours …*

\* \* \*

Those of a certain vintage will well recall the crowds that turned out to welcome home Jack Charlton's squad after their Euro 88 and World Cup 90 exploits. They might also remember the massive crowds that welcomed Stephen Roche after his extraordinary victories in the 1987 Tour de France, Giro d'Italia and World Championship road race. The huge outpourings of pride at the success and impact of our sportspeople on the international stage spoke much for a populace desperate for inspiration and exploding with delight on finding it. Such high-profile feats showed us the possible, showed us just what we were capable of and, perhaps, bred a new and much-needed self-confidence that spread across and through the fabric of society.

Doubtless those who witnessed the scenes of unbridled joy across the country after Jack Charlton's men beat Romania in the 1990 last-16 penalty shoot-out will never forget it. They were unprecedented – as were the almost entirely empty streets, such was the level of rapt interest whenever the team took to the field in those major tournaments. And, so, it wouldn't be unfair to imagine similar scenes across Ireland in the summer of 1982 had Eoin Hand's men lined up on the playing fields of Spain and then surely returned home to a heroes' welcome.

The positive vibes and goodwill around the game in Ireland would've presented the FAI with wonderful opportunities to develop the game here six years before the breakthrough to the international stage eventually came. However, given how the association ultimately mishandled such opportunities when they did come and given the parlous state of the FAI now, it's difficult to imagine that things would've turned out much differently for the game in general. Despite the many good people in the Irish game over the years and the many good people who've worked in the association, it appears to have a genetic predisposition that leaves it depressingly open to factional fighting, folly and failure.

But if the evidence suggests that the outcome for the wider game in Ireland might've been no less gloomy, then perhaps things might've turned out very differently for Eoin Hand and his players. On the playing side, qualification could've been huge in terms of confidence and togetherness, which may have had a positive impact on later qualification campaigns. We saw that in the Charlton era, with his side qualifying for two of the next three major tournaments after the initial breakthrough. And they should also have qualified for the 1992 European Championship. Indeed, given that tournament was won by the Danes, who had replaced war-torn Yugoslavia very late in the day and with very little preparation, there are some who feel that the Irish could well have gone far in Sweden and that a historic opportunity was missed.

But a confidence boost wouldn't have been the only positive. Qualification would also have improved the Republic of Ireland's seeding, thereby easing their passage to future tournaments. And more players with Irish heritage may have decided to declare allegiance, broadening and deepening Eoin Hand's options, as the Republic of Ireland copper-fastened its new-found *serious football nation* status. Indeed, those that might've been swayed would've been coming into a seasoned set-up with players who rightfully believed they should be competing at the major tournaments, rather than believing that the world and every official had it in for them.

Sadly, of course, that wasn't the reality and Eoin Hand is convinced that the manner in which his side were denied participation in the 1982 World Cup had a crippling impact on the psyche of his side. The loss of belief, the loss of confidence, the sense that no matter how well they performed insurmountable obstacles would be placed in their way went some way to derailing their efforts to qualify for the 1984 European Championship in France. Indeed, Eoin Hand feels that his players' spirit had been crushed and they simply weren't the same team from then on.

For Eoin Hand himself, qualification for Spain would at the very least have shifted the balance of power in his relationship with his employers. 'You know, it would've opened up all sorts of different avenues,' he says, 'but the most important one was you would then be the boss and you would have the luxury of choosing which avenue you wanted to go down.'

So, if Eoin Hand wanted to select bigger squads for qualifiers, his stance would've been harder for the FAI blazers to ignore. If Eoin Hand wanted his players to have separate rooms on away trips, rather than two and even three to a room, his request would've been harder to fob off. If Eoin Hand wanted to travel to scout players or opponents, he'd no longer have to plead and justify. And if Eoin Hand wanted to bring the chef from the Burlington Hotel, often used by Liverpool on their European trips, to Moscow for a World Cup qualifier to avoid *Moscow tummy*, then the FAI blazers would've found it harder to resist. Amazingly, the FAI did refuse Hand's suggestion in relation to bringing a professional chef to Russia for the World Cup qualifier in the Soviet capital in 1984. And when Hand, in an effort to embarrass his employers, suggested he bring his wife as an alternative to cook the travelling party's meals, bizarrely the association accepted! The FAI in those days were not so easily embarrassed.

'The hardest part of my job was dealing with the FAI,' Eoin Hand says, 'not dealing with the players, not dealing with the clubs in England and not dealing with anybody else.

'If we qualified, I'd have had a completely different power base. And I knew that the level of respect I would get from everybody, the clubs in England, other countries would change. Everything would change. As far as I was concerned, it would lead to unbelievable change for the better, given where we were coming from, in every conceivable way.'

Qualification could also have had a massive impact on Eoin Hand's career. Taking the unheralded Republic of Ireland to their first tournament would've been a stunning achievement. Doing so as a 36-year-old whose only managerial experience was in the League of Ireland would've been extraordinary. Imagine if someone was to emulate such achievements today – they would be the blue-eyed boy of football. Doors would open. Job offers would abound.

But then, as Eoin Hand points out, the football landscape was very different in the 1980s to what we see now. Opportunities for English-speaking managers in Europe were even more limited and, according to Hand, there was a certain reticence amongst English clubs when it came to hiring Irish managers, an unfortunate by-product of the tensions of the time. That said, World Cup qualification at such a tender age with such an unfashionable football outpost would most certainly have raised his profile and strengthened his appeal. Where such success could have taken him and what opportunities might have presented themselves is difficult to discern. But there's little doubt that his career path would've been elevated, with respect, above and beyond St Patrick's Athletic and Huddersfield Town or the footballing backwaters of Al-Taawoun of Saudi Arabia and AmaZulu in South Africa.

It could've been a very different world for Eoin Hand and his family. But does the former Ireland manager harbour any regrets? Does he still wonder about what might have been? Or is Eoin Hand, now senior, seasoned and wizened, sanguine and philosophical?

'Well, I mean, I look back and I think what might've been and then the thing is you've got to be realistic about it and say, "Well, okay, it wasn't." No, I mean, as far as I was concerned, I did a good job. Like I did it to the best of my ability. I couldn't have done it any better. I couldn't have done any more to try and improve the whole situation. I worked very hard at it, even to the detriment of my family.

'So, what I say to people is: "Listen, maybe I've got to look at it this way. Maybe if I was the first one to qualify, I would've been a hero. I would've been this. I would've been that. And who knows then, I might've then become very wealthy. And who knows, maybe I might've bought a helicopter. And who knows, maybe I might've crashed my helicopter. And who knows, I might be dead now because of it all!"

'So that's my attitude about it. And to me, it's the right attitude.

'You know, I have gotten on with life. I have. I'm very happy now. I'm 78 years of age. I can look back and say that I gave it everything I had. There's no way I could say to myself, "If only I'd worked a bit harder doing that." I can't. I don't. I don't say that. I can't because I know it's not true. I know I worked as hard as I possibly could.'

For those who witnessed that campaign, who experienced the injustices and misfortune, it's hard not to look back with regret. To look back and wonder. But maybe, maybe, we should instead take a leaf from Eoin Hand's book. Maybe we should just accept it for what it was, refocus on the positives of that campaign and celebrate those who brought us a few steps closer to international football's wondrous promised lands. Celebrate what was one of the finest qualifying campaigns produced by a Republic of Ireland football team and the finest to that point in our long football history. Reflect on how wonderfully they played at times and how thrillingly they competed with stellar opposition. Recognise the professionalism of Eoin Hand and John Giles, who worked so hard to change the culture of the international set-up – and did so in the face of often ridiculous and farcical obstacles placed in their way by the supposed guardians of the Irish game. Guardians too often devoid of vision, who consistently missed opportunities to promote and develop football and who took for granted for so long the development of talent in this country, leaving the international side in the depressed state we see today.

And let's be glad that many of those who strived under Eoin Hand and John Giles did make it to the biggest of international tournaments and got the recognition they deserved. And let's spare a thought for those who didn't but who helped mightily along the way. And who, had a door slid in their favour, might also have achieved their international dreams. And, mostly, let's celebrate a Republic of Ireland side who offered a glimpse of the possible in the troubled, dog days of the early 1980s and who fired the dreams of a ten-year-old boy and many others besides.

# Acknowledgements

HEARTFELT THANKS to Eoin Hand for his patience, insight and the hours spent talking to me on the phone. My inner ten-year-old continues to pinch himself. Many thanks also to Gary Hand, old school friend from too long ago. Thanks, Gary, for so kindly putting me in touch with your dad.

I must also express my gratitude to Paul Howard for sending me on his wonderful piece for the *Sunday Tribune* in which he tracked down and confronted the infamous Raul Fernandes Nazaré. A superb piece of sports journalism that stuck with me since its publication 20-odd years ago. Something I simply had to work into the book.

Thanks must also go to the great football commentator George Hamilton for his corroborating phone conversation.

And last, but not least, thanks to my family. Trish – your patience and understanding will be rewarded by my return to the couch in the evenings. How quickly will you wish that I might go and write something else?

Emily, Kate, Noah and Joe – my children, my special friends – always make time for your passions, pastimes and hobbies. They can open a door to your dreams.

And lastly, a special thanks to the youngest of them, Joe, whose web-wizardry allowed me to watch the key matches in Ireland's World Cup qualifiers of 1980 and 1981 in full. Well played.

# Bibliography

**Newspapers and Online Sources**

*Cork Examiner*
*Evening Herald*
*Evening Press*
Footballia.eu
*Irish Independent*
Irish Newspaper Archives
*The Irish Press*
*The Irish Times*
*Sunday Independent*
*Sunday Press*
*Sunday Tribune*

**Books and References**

Hand, E., and Browne, J., *First Hand: My Life and Irish Football,*
The Collins Press, October 2017
O'Brien, J., *EURO SUMMITS, The Story of the UEFA European Championship, 1960 – 2016*, Pitch Publishing 2021